Chronoi – Topoi

CHRONOI

Zeit, Zeitempfinden, Zeitordnungen
Time, Time Awareness, Time Management

Edited by
Eva Cancik-Kirschbaum, Christoph Markschies and
Hermann Parzinger

on behalf of the Einstein Center Chronoi

Volume 24

Chronoi – Topoi

Concepts of Time and Space as Literary Devices in Second Temple Judaism

Edited by
Alexandra Grund-Wittenberg and Martina Kepper

DE GRUYTER

ISSN 2701-1453
ISBN 978-3-11-22403 5-9
ISBN 978-3-11-224036-6 (PDF)
ISBN 978-3-11-224037-3 (EPUB)
DOI https://doi.org/10.1515/9783112240366

Library of Congress Control Number: 2026937913

Bibliographic information published by the Deutsche Nationalbibliothek
The Deutsche Nationalbibliothek lists this publication in the Deutsche Nationalbibliografie; detailed bibliographic data are available on the internet at http://dnb.dnb.de.

De Gruyter and Walter de Gruyter GmbH are part of De Gruyter Brill.
www.degruyterbrill.com

Questions about General Product Safety Regulation:
productsafety@degruyterbrill.com

Preface

The present volume derives from the international conference *"Chronoi – Topoi. Time Politics and the Interrelation of Time and Space in Second Temple Judaism,"* organized at Philipps University of Marburg and held online from October 29 to 31, 2024. The conference was conducted in collaboration with the Einstein Center Chronoi, Berlin, and we remain deeply appreciative of the opportunity to engage in scholarly exchange on the interrelation of time and space within this institutional framework. Our particular thanks are due to the Board of the Einstein Center Chronoi, especially Prof. Dr. Dr. h.c. mult. Christoph Markschies and Prof. Dr. Eva Cancik-Kirschbaum, for endorsing the project and for agreeing to integrate both the conference and the present volume into the Einstein Center Chronoi research program and publication series. We also gratefully acknowledge the financial support provided by the German Research Foundation (DFG).

We were honored that Prof. Dr. Menahem Ben Sasson, longtime Professor of the History of the Jewish Nation at the Hebrew University of Jerusalem and former President of the Hebrew University, conveyed words of greeting on behalf of the Einstein Center Chronoi. We are likewise grateful to Prof. Dr. Angela Standhartinger, who delivered a welcome address on behalf of the Dean's Office of the Department of Protestant Theology at Philipps University of Marburg. We thank both speakers for granting permission to reproduce their greetings in the present volume. As the concept of the chronotope was unfamiliar to many participants, the conference assumed a pronounced workshop character, fostering collective exploration of the applicability of Bakhtin's theoretical framework, notwithstanding the constraints of the online format.

We wish to acknowledge the valuable assistance of *cand. theol.* Alexandra Bruckmann and *stud. theol.* Alena Stellmach, whose committed support before, during, and after the conference was indispensable to its success. We gratefully acknowledge the invaluable assistance of *stud. theol.* David Tibken in meticulous proofreading and in the compilation of the index. Finally, we express our sincere gratitude, in particular, to *mag. theol.* Stefanie Rabe and *M.A.* Franziska Küster of the Einstein Center Chronoi for their dedicated involvement in the organization of the conference and their careful support in the preparation and final editing of this volume. It is our hope that the present collection will stimulate further scholarly inquiry into the reciprocal relationship between time and space — understood as chronotopes — within the literature of antiquity.

Marburg, January 2026
Alexandra Grund-Wittenberg and Martina Kepper

Menahem Ben-Sasson

Welcome Address

I am honored to open this conference from Jerusalem. Welcome to the “Chronoi – Topoi” conference on “Time Politics and the Interrelation of Time and Space in Second Temple Judaism.”

It is indeed no coincidence that the opening remarks for a conference that deals with time and space during the Second Temple period are being delivered from the city of Jerusalem:

a. How could Jerusalem, the city of the Temple in its construction and destruction, not be a suitable place to open the conference?
b. How could the Hebrew University of Jerusalem, the public sphere of activity of the relativity theorist Albert Einstein, not be a suitable place to open the conference?
c. How could the Berlin-Jerusalem partnership with the Einstein Foundation, within which the Einstein Center Chronoi in Berlin operates, not be a suitable place to open the conference?
d. How could the campus of the Hebrew University of Jerusalem, which houses the archive in which Albert Einstein deposited more than eighty thousand documents, including materials relating to his theory of relativity, or its second campus on Mount Scopus, where the tombs of the Nicanor family, donors of the gates to the Second Temple, are located, not be a suitable place to open the conference?

We could multiply the justifications for opening in Jerusalem. Still, above all, the refreshing cooperation between Berlin and Marburg has brought participants from all over the world to this unique conference that operates beyond place and time in the literal sense. Thank you very much to the diligent, learned organizers, Alexandra Grund-Wittenberg and Martina Kepper of Philipps-Universität Marburg, and their efficient team, as well as to our home in Berlin, the Einstein Center Chronoi.

But the conference has another crucial pillar, and that is Bakhtin’s concept of “chronotope.” This concept deals with the multiplicity of times and places in sources of different genres and periods. The lecturers and participants in the conference are going to point out the way in which people of the Second Temple period, in various and diverse connections, combine their conceptions of time, which came to offer temporal alternatives to the holy place and temporal interpretations of the crises that befell them. As the organizers say in the introduction:

https://doi.org/10.1515/9783112240366-203

> "the colonial time policy of the Hellenistic rulers challenged the subjugated people by forcing to assimilate to their guidelines. Those, however, often responded by developing their own new concepts of time and history in a counter reaction. Hellenistic Judaism, for example, contrasted the Empire's chronotope with their own specific narrative of the past and the future" (p. 2). "The traumatic experience of losing sacred space and place such as Jerusalem and the Temple was obviously dealt with by an even more intensive focus on time structures, dates and calendars. This is evident in the increasing importance of the Shabbat [. . .], in the dominating dating system in the Book of Ezekiel [. . .] and seems to continue in the competing calendar systems between the Persian and Roman periods." (p. 1)

The research questions and the goals were described in the invitation to the conference:

What is the significance of the connection between space and time in terms of the concept of history, calendar, festivals, and end-time expectations? This conference aims to examine the meaning of time and space, particularly with regard to their fluidity and socio-political implications.

The conference is a valuable opportunity for researchers from around the globe to come together and collaborate in this innovative field of research.

Our best wishes from Jerusalem are for great success.

Angela Standhartinger

Welcome Address

As the academic vice dean, it's my pleasure and honor to welcome you to this international conference: "Chronoi – Topoi. Time Politics and the Interrelation of Time and Space in Second Temple Judaism".

In recent years, space theories have been fruitfully applied to the Bible and ancient Jewish texts. Bakhtin's ideas on intertextuality and less so also on carnival are well-known among biblical scholars. Yet, to my knowledge, few biblical scholars have approached ancient Jewish and Early Christian texts and artefacts with Bakhtin's observations on *chronotopos*. As this conference impressively proves, this is a research gap that urgently needs to be filled. Therefore, I'm thankful to my three colleagues, Alexandra Grund-Wittenberg, Martina Kepper, and Maike Schult, who engaged in this project with the Einstein Center Chronoi in Berlin. This research center focuses on temporality from an interdisciplinary and transdisciplinary perspective.

Bakhtin defined chronotopos (literally, 'time-space') as the intrinsic connectedness of temporal and spatial relationships that are artistically expressed in literature, especially in narratives like novels. The few New Testament scholars who have applied Bakhtin's concept of the chronotope have observed how the space and time of the Gospel of Luke intersect with the chronotopes of the Old Testament, or how Luke rewrites and transcends the chronotope of the Gospel of Mark (Fischer 2006; Becker 2016). Some used the theory to describe time and space in the relationship between Jesus and John the Baptist in the Gospel of John (Rakotoharintsifa 2000). As visionary literature that simultaneously refers to an extensive imagery repertoire and its allegorical interpretation by transcendent figures to contemporary readers — and which transcends this and other worlds, earth and heaven, as well as present, past, and future — the apocalyptic genre also proves fruitful for chronotopical analysis. Therefore, it seems no accident that the first application of Bakhtin's chronotope centers on this genre (Vines 2007). More recently, others have observed the constant replacing of the reader in the Shepherd of Hermas visionary experience and its explanation (Maier 2019). Some argue that the apocalyptic author Paul does not link salvation to a linear narrative but insists on the abrogation of time, the *kairos* of the current end time, and presents his own experience as the medium for salvation history (Beaude 2008).

This conference does not restrict itself to straightforward-moving narratives but also discusses archaeological artifacts and documents from Elephantine, wisdom literature, prophets, cultic rules, and many forms of apocalyptic writing.

 | https://doi.org/10.1515/9783112240366-204

For Bakhtin, chronotopos expresses the inseparability of space and time. This conference, however, seems to prove exactly this, as it brings together, at least in the virtual space, participants from Würzburg, Halle, Utrecht in the Netherlands, University Park in Pennsylvania (USA), Oxford in England, and — especially in these difficult times — we are particularly grateful to welcome participants from Jerusalem in Israel.

I would like to thank the German Research Foundation (DFG) and the Einstein Center for helping to finance this conference and all of you for your participation in this exciting project. We hope that the shared time made possible in this virtual space will foster new friendships and perspectives on collaborative research.

Bibliography

Beaude, Pierre Marie. 2008. "Paul et le chronotope de l'empire." *Studies in Religion/Sciences Religieuses* 37/3–4:467–479. https://doi.org/10.1177/000842980803700306.

Becker, Eve-Marie. 2016. "Konzepte von Raum in frühchristlichen Geschichtserzählungen: Vom markinischen Chronotop zur spatial history des Lukas." In *Geschichte und Gott: XV. Europäischer Kongress für Theologie (14.—18. September 2014 in Berlin)*, Veröffentlichungen der Wissenschaftlichen Gesellschaft für Theologie 44, edited by Michael Meyer-Blanck, 381–394. Leipzig: Evangelische Verlagsanstalt.

Fischer, Bettina. 2006. "The Chronotope and Its Discursive Function in the Gospel of Luke." In *The New Testament Interpreted: Essays in Honour of Bernard C. Lategan*. NTSuppl 124, edited by Cilliers Breytenbach, 325–337. Leiden: Brill. https://doi.org/10.1163/9789047410591_018.

Maier, Harry O. 2019. "Making History with the Shepherd of Hermas." *Early Christianity* 10/4: 501–520. https://doi.org/10.1628/ec-2019-0031.

Rakotoharintsifa, Andrianjatovo. 2000. "Les séjours de Jésus à Béthanie au-delà du Jourdain selon le chronotope de l'Évangile de Jean." In *La narrativité dans la Bible et les textes apparentés*, BEThL 149, edited by George J. Brooke and Jean-Daniel Kaestli, 119–130. Leuven: Leuven University Press.

Vines, Michael E. 2007. "The Apocalyptic Chronotope." In *Bakhtin and Genre Theory in Biblical Studies*, SBLSS 63, edited by Roland Boer, 109–118. Atlanta: Society of Biblical Literature.

Contents

Authors

Moritz F. Adam, Dr. theol., born 1997, is the Ernest S. Frerichs Professor at the W.F. Albright Institute for Archaeological Research, 26 Salah ed-Din St, Jerusalem, Israel, moritzfranz.adam@uzh.ch.

Bob Becking, Dr. theol., born 1951, is retired senior research professor for Bible, Religion and Identity at the Faculty of Humanities of Utrecht University, de Hunze 8, NL-3448 XH Woerden, the Netherlands, b.e.j.h.becking@uu.nl.

Jonathan Ben-Dov, Ph.D., born 1971, is Professor of Biblical Studies at Tel Aviv University, Department of Bible, The Lester and Sally Entin Faculty of Humanities, Tel Aviv University, Rosenberg – Jewish Studies, Room 118, Tel Aviv 6997801, Israel, jonbendov@tauex.tau.ac.il.

Lucas Brum Teixeira, Dr. of Sacred Scripture, born 1974, is Research Assistant at the Faculty of Catholic Theology of Julius-Maximilians-University, Bibrastr. 14, 97070 Würzburg, lucas.brum@uni-wuerzburg.de.

Daniel K. Falk, Ph.D., born 1965, is Chaiken Family Chair of Jewish Studies and Professor of Classics and Ancient Mediterranean Studies at The Pennsylvania State University, The College of the Liberal Arts, University Park, PA, 16802, USA, dkf16@psu.edu.

Alexandra Grund-Wittenberg, Dr. theol., born 1971, is Professor of Old Testament at the Faculty of Protestant Theology of Philipps University Marburg, Lahntor 3, 35032 Marburg, Germany, alexandra.grund@staff.uni-marburg.de.

Martina Kepper, Dr. theol., born 1966, is Lecturer of Biblical Hebrew and Old Testament Studies at the Faculty of Protestant Theology of Philipps University Marburg, Lahntor 3, 35037 Marburg, Germany, kepper@staff.uni-marburg.de.

Barbara Schmitz, Dr. theol., born 1975, is Professor of Old Testament at the Faculty of Catholic Theology of Julius-Maximilians-University, Bibrastr. 14, 97070 Würzburg, barbara.schmitz@uni-wuerzburg.de.

Frank Ueberschaer, Dr. theol., born 1972, is Professor of Hebrew Bible at the Faculty of Theology of Martin-Luther-University Halle-Wittenberg, Franckeplatz 1, 06110 Halle, Germany, frank.ueberschaer@theologie.uni-halle.de.

Sarah Wisialowski, DPhil, born 1995, is a Postdoctoral Fellow at the Einstein Center Chronoi funded by the Einstein Foundation Berlin, Otto-von-Simson-Straße 7, 14195, Berlin, Germany, sarah.wisialowski@theology.ox.ac.uk.

Alexandra Grund-Wittenberg and Martina Kepper

Introduction

This volume explores the fundamental insight that concepts of time and space are interconnected, which can be observed particularly well in the texts of Second Temple Judaism. In general, time and space are closely connected: Spatial concepts are often metaphorically transferred to the temporal domain in order to be able to talk about time. However, sometimes the reverse can happen: Temporal notions can be transformed into spatial concepts.[1] Beyond that, metaphors such as 'the way' or 'the journey' encompass both temporal and spatial dimensions. Metaphors that connect time and space shape both literature and the story world of a narrative. In the run-up to this project, the editors of this volume independently made specific observations in different textual areas, which nevertheless converged in principle: The traumatic experience of losing sacred space and place, such as Jerusalem and the Temple, was addressed through an intensified focus on time structures, dates, and calendars. This is evident in the increasing importance of the Shabbat (see, for example, Grund 2011, 273–287 and passim), in the dominating dating system in the Book of Ezekiel (see still Kutsch 1985 among others), and seems to continue in the competing calendar systems between the Persian and Roman periods. This led the editors of this volume to ask how concepts of time are interconnected with concepts of space in religious writings from Second Temple Judaism.

For decades, questions regarding concepts of time and space were largely absent from the history of research; space and time appeared as given and readily available.[2]

Interest in concepts of time increased in the twentieth century, followed — especially with the spatial turn — by growing attention to conceptions of space. Although much research has already been done on space in the Hebrew Bible, on the one hand (Janowski and Ego 2004; Berquist and Camp 2008; Geiger 2010; see the publications of the Excellence Cluster Topoi, Berlin) and time on the other (Kratz and Spieckermann 2009; Hedwig-Jahnow-Forschungsprojekt 2010; Kotjatko-Reeb, Ziemer, and Schorch 2014; Staszak and Leroy 2018; Schröter and Witte 2020; Beyerle and Goff 2022; see the publications of the Einstein Center Chronoi in general), their relationship and interconnectedness have only rarely been examined in depth. It

1 This was obviously the case with the lemma עולם which had an only temporal meaning in Biblical Hebrew 'long duration, most distant time, eternity', but adapted also a spacial, cosmic meaning in Middle Hebrew 'world', 'universe', 'cosmos'. In detail, see the contribution of Frank Ueberschaer in this volume.

2 Moritz Adam rightly points out in the introduction to his article in this volume.

https://doi.org/10.1515/9783112240366-001

seems particularly fitting for a project of the Einstein Center Chronoi, which bears the name of the developer of the theory of relativity, to address the connection and interactions between concepts of space and time.

It is obvious that concepts of time and space never emerge 'out of thin air' but come into being in a particular political situation and in a specific cultural environment. According to Paul Kosmin's monograph, "Time and Its Adversaries in the Seleucid Empire" (Kosmin 2018), the influence of changing political hegemonies on new concepts of time can be seen as a stimulus for new developments. In particular, the colonial time policy of the Hellenistic rulers challenged the subjugated people by forcing them to assimilate to imperial guidelines. Those subject to the Seleucid Empire, however, often responded by developing their own new concepts of time and history in a counter reaction. Hellenistic Judaism, for example, contrasted the Empire's chronotope with their own specific narrative of the past and the future; this can be seen in the visions of the Book of Daniel.[3] Beyond that, Hellenistic Judaism had to cope with the diaspora situation. When translating Hebrew expressions of time or space into Aramaic or Greek language and culture, the concepts often proved incompatible or even incommensurable with the target language. This made conceptual innovations necessary. Texts from the diaspora needed to mediate between traditional ideas and the requirements of the country and culture of residence. Some Hellenistic texts, for instance, connected places in the diaspora to the Jerusalem temple via temporal hints.[4]

The texts from Second Temple Judaism originate from very different genres and contexts and thus offer varying answers to issues regarding the relationship between time and space. This requires considering the difference between everyday texts, such as most of the sources from Elephantine, texts with implicit and explicit norms (such as the community rules in Qumran) that are intended to influence the behavior of people in a particular group, and genuinely 'narrative' texts.

We understand 'narrative texts' in a broad sense, referring to both fictional and historiographical texts. The latter mostly claim to represent events that 'actually happened' but still use a wide range of narratological tools (White 1978 among others). Therefore, applying literary concepts such as Bakhtin's concept of chronotope to historiographical texts, as Felix Maier did, can be judged plausible (Maier 2016). On the other hand, even purely fictional texts depict a world that is in some

---

3 On Dan 9, see Sarah Wisialowski's article in this volume. Similarly, the apostle Paul according to Beaude largely ignores the political-historical chronotope of the Roman Empire; in doing so, he creates a new space-time structure in which the *kairós* of Christ interrupts the Chronos of the world (Beaude 2008).

4 For instance, Daniel's prayer in Dan 9 in Babylon is set explicitly at the time of the evening sacrifice in Jerusalem (on Dan 9, see again the article of Sarah Wisialowski in this volume).

respect comparable to the world familiar to the readers (otherwise, they would be incomprehensible to the recipients), but also differs from it in at least some way (otherwise, they would be uninteresting or not worth reading to the recipients). Thus, they frequently paint a world as it could or should be, thereby influencing, transforming, or stretching the reader's understanding of the world they live in.

Since we often do not know enough about the context and intention of ancient texts, it is not always clear to us in terms of how far the world described in the text corresponds to the world assumed to be 'real' by the recipients, i.e., whether it was assumed that something could actually happen or could have happened and to what extent they are fictional. This makes them difficult to decipher, but at the same time also appealing. However, in a broader sense, literary texts outline a concept of time and space and it is their interconnectedness which can be examined.

Normative texts, in comparison to everyday texts, focus more on explicit ideas about correct practices. However, they also contain an implicit or explicit ontology, including a concept of time and space. They often assume their ontology corresponds to the 'real' world of the recipients, or that the recipients should even adapt their practices and belief systems to the ontology of the text. Although these texts are not fictional narrative texts, they often use a wide range of literary devices, narrative tools, or at least imaginative motifs to develop their ontology — and thus also use their understanding of the relationship between space and time. In this respect, Bakhtin's literary concepts can also be helpful for these texts (see convincingly Daniel Falk in his article in this volume). Obviously, references to space and time can be concrete, but also metaphorical, or even sometimes both, which makes them difficult to explore but at the same time more enigmatic and interesting.

Texts from everyday life as well presuppose implicit ontologies and conceptions of space and time which are taken for granted. However, they mostly remain implicit in such texts and are not explicitly stated. One can examine these texts for implicit ontologies, or for conceptions of space, time, and their relationship (see Bob Becking in his contribution in this volume), but sometimes the textual basis is simply insufficient to answer such questions since they lie far beyond the text's purpose.

Since the interrelationship between time and space is mainly represented in literature, particularly in narratives, it seemed appropriate to apply tools of literary analysis such as the concept of the 'chronotope' coined by Mikhail Bakhtin in the 1930s. While Bakhtin's theories on intertextuality and carnival have already been widely received in biblical studies, the heuristic potential of his chronotope concept has so far been sparsely researched. However, we assume that it is also of heuristic value if applied to religious-normative Jewish texts from Persian to Roman times.

How do we understand Bakhtin's concept of the chronotope? Bakhtin himself gave a definition of chronotope in his essay "Forms of Time and of the Chronotope in the Novel":

> We will give the name chronotope (literally, 'time space') to the intrinsic connectedness of temporal and spatial relationships that are artistically expressed in literature. [. . .] What counts for us is the fact that it expresses the inseparability of space and time (time as the fourth dimension of space). [. . .] In the literary artistic chronotope, spatial and temporal indicators are fused into one carefully thought-out, concrete whole. Time, as it were, thickens, takes on flesh, becomes artistically visible; likewise, space becomes charged and responsive to the movements of time, plot, and history. This intersection of axes and fusion of indicators characterizes the artistic chronotope. [...] (Bakhtin 1981, 84)

The basic insight of the chronotope theory is that narrative texts not only consist of a sequence of narrated events and speech acts, but also primarily consist of the construction of a specific fictional world or chronotope. In order to better understand Bakhtin's concept of the chronotope, it might also be helpful to approach it from the perspective of general narratology, namely from the more familiar concept of the text world / story world (see Barbara Schmitz's and Lucas Brum Teixeiras essay in this volume). Actions in the narrative cannot be separated from their references to time and space, and time and space are always related to one another. Thus, to inquire about the chronotope means to ask: How are time and space, in their interconnectedness, established in the world of the narrative? The intrinsic interconnectedness of time and space meant by the expression chronotope "is tantamount to the world construction that is at the base of every narrative text, comprising a coherent combination of spatial and temporal indicators." (Bemong and Borghart 2010, 3).

However, a certain degree of ambiguity has remained in the interpretation of Bakhtin's chronotope and in the operationalization of the theory to this day (see Steinby 2013, 105). This might be due to the fact that Bakhtin does not offer a precise determination of the concept apart from the initial definition mentioned above. "Bakhtin starts off with the formulation of some initial remarks, and proceeds to alternate between concrete examples and further generalizations, as a result [sic] the concept seems to acquire ever new related meanings" (Bemong and Borghart 2010, 3). We will not delve into the resulting ramifications and discussions here, nor is it necessary to mention all the more recent applications of the theory (see Bemong et al. 2010). At this point, we can only state that even though the scope of Bakhtin's chronotope concept is widely praised (see Wegner 1989), its conceptual innovation is still far from being fully explored in literary studies,[5] (see Bemong and Borghart 2010).

For our purposes, only a few basic points are important. It is crucial to note that the chronotope theory was originally conceived as an analytical tool for establishing genre classifications in the history of the Western novel. According to Bakhtin, chronotope and genre are intertwined: "The chronotopes we have discussed provide the basis for distinguishing generic types; they lie at the heart of specific varieties of the novel genre, formed and developed over the course of many centuries" (Bakhtin 1981, 250–251). The genre entails a world-design, an ideological framework that structures the world, produces typical characters, and determines the meaning of their actions (Vines 2007, 110–112). With the words of Morris: "[s]pecific chronotopes correspond to particular genres, which themselves represent particular world-views. To this extent, chronotope is a cognitive concept as much as a narrative feature of texts" (Morris 1994, 246). Therefore, each genre creates a specific spatio-temporal horizon (chronotope) within which human action is evaluated. Thus, a specific chronotope also implies anthropological implications, as Bakhtin already underlined: "The chronotope as a formally constitutive category determines to a significant degree the image of man in literature as well. The image of man is always intrinsically chronotopic" (Bakhtin 1981, 84).

The concept of the chronotope is clearly relevant not only to novels: "Lately, a number of scholars have hypothesized that some chronotopic configuration underlies every kind of narrative, however minimal, including jokes, strip cartoons, fairy tales, animal stories, narrative poetry and the like" (Bemong and Borghart 2010, 9; see, for example, Schmidt 2010). This underscores that not only 'narrative texts' in the wider sense explained above can be examined with this theory but also normative texts or letters. The fact that the chronotope theory was developed from the Hellenistic novel by Bakhtin certainly makes ancient narratives including narrative biblical texts an appropriate subject.

Thus, the chronotope concept has been discussed and applied already in New Testament studies.[6] Bettina Fischer (2006), for example, applied Bakhtin's chrono-

---

5 See esp. Wegner 1989, 1357–1358; Frank and Mahlke 2008; Bemong et al. 2010. In Germany, the chronotope theory was applied, for example, by Christoph Grube (2006) to the temporal structure of Joseph Eichendorff's 1862 novel "Aus dem Leben eines Taugenichts" (From the Life of a Good-for-Nothing), which, to a remarkable degree, represents a revitalization of the Hellenistic novel with its departure into an age of adventure and the vast world of foreign lands, culminating in a return to the familiar, stable, domestic microcosm. According to Uwe Spörl (2006), the classic detective novel, in a different way, aims at restoring the "idyll destroyed" by the crime.

6 See also the contribution of Angela Standhartinger in this volume. Eve-Marie Becker (2016) clarifies the narratological significance of space and time: "So wie die geschichtliche Zeit voranschreitet, muss sie vom Erzähler auch räumlich gefüllt werden."(As historical time progresses, it

tope concept to the Gospel of Luke, distinguishing it from Burridge's interpretation of the Gospels as ancient biographies. She considers it highly valuable for determining the genre and the world concept, which in the case of Luke's Gospel is characterized by the conflict between the Kingdom of God and the kingdom of Satan. Bakhtin's concept highlights the differences between the Gospel of Luke and ancient biographies, as well as its radical nature, which challenges the old discourse with its supernatural dimensions. However, the concept of the chronotope has also been applied to literature that is not genuinely narrative or novelistic. Beaude (2008) explored the chronotope of Paul's letters, which is decisively shaped by his Damascus experience and closely intertwined with the cosmic-apocalyptic expectation of the end.

Particularly relevant to our volume is Michael E. Vines's study contribution on the Apocalyptic Chronotope (Vines 2007). Using Bakhtin's theory, he seeks to define the genre of apocalypse primarily through its distinctive chronotope and thus its formative ideology. In the apocalypse, time and space transcend the boundaries of the everyday world and human lifespan. Historical events can thereby be examined and evaluated across vast, boundless timescales, and future events of world-historical significance can be revealed. The boundless chronotope is a necessary vehicle for conveying the moral or ethical judgment, the ultimate truth about the order and meaning of history, from a divine perspective.

For the question of this volume about transformations of the chronotope, Vines's approach is of great interest, because assumptions prevalent in earlier literature from the Second Temple period no longer seem to hold true in the Hellenistic period. The conviction of the Torah or Deuteronomistic historiography that God's covenantal faithfulness ensures the success and well-being of his people is deeply called into question by the political situation which resulted in new genres and chronotopes. According to Vines, the role of the human protagonists here is a new one. The hero in the apocalypses is typically a righteous figure from Israel's past, such as Enoch, Abraham, Baruch, or Daniel. They embody the values that once sustained God's people and guaranteed their blessing. That is why they are capable of receiving such important truths. However, their time as active agents is over. Their role is now merely that of messengers, affirming God's sovereignty while simultaneously acknowledging the hopelessness of the human condition. This distinguishes them also from the role of the 'classical prophets', who mostly had to prove themselves in their time within a society that was often hostile to them, but whose present was generally still considered capable of reform.

must also be filled spatially by the narrator; Becker 2016, 381). She hereby also refers to Bakhtin's definition of the chronotope, for historiography in the present and antiquity, as well as for the Gospels, although Bakhtin's concept does not play a special role in its overall context for her approach.

The heuristic and hermeneutic significance of Bakhtin's concept of the chronotope in its application to writings from the Second Temple period proved helpful for the analysis of some texts under focus. However, for the authors of our volume, there was no need to apply Bakhtin's concept, as is indicated by choosing the title Chronoi – Topoi with a hyphen.

Alexandra Grund-Wittenberg examines the interplay of time and space in the Priestly Writings, one of the fundamental literary conceptions of the Pentateuch and an elementary starting point for exploring the interrelationship of time and space in Second Temple Judaism. Here, time structures dominate the story and give the narrated world its foundation. Space serves as an area for living but often remains undefined, without a particular center. References to political history are lacking, concrete places in the known world are rarely mentioned. Placeless divine speeches prevail over deeds; the temporal orientation dominates the spatial orientation. Even where a center of the textual world emerges, it is not Jerusalem, but a mobile sanctuary led by the presence of God. Unlike the temple in Jerusalem, the sanctuary in the desert is indestructible. The same applies to the Shabbat as a sanctuary in time. Beyond that, the narration as such creates a textual sanctuary which is indestructible and can serve as a kind of safe space or, with words from Heinrich Heine, as a portable fatherland. While P focused on a stable past, the visions in the Book of Daniel from the Hellenistic period replace the mythical past with the knowledge of the end of history through divine revelation, incorporating heavenly realms into historical events. Despite these changes, the structures of time and the significance of festivals and calendars remain central, with the concept of 'year weeks' extending P's structure of weeks and years to reinforce world order.

The heuristic value of the chronotope concept is demonstrated by Barbara Schmitz and Lucas Brum Teixeira in the Book of Judith. In their outline of the research history on the significance of space and time in narrative theory, they demonstrate that the category of space was only discovered in narrative analysis with the spatial turn. Embedded within narratological research, they offer a careful introduction to Bakhtin's theory of the chronotope and its significance. They illustrate that, according to Bakhtin, a narrated world can contain various chronotopes, which become all the more complex when one considers the chronotopes in the exchange process between narrator and recipient. This can be shown in the Book of Judith which constructs its narrative world through a deliberate blend of historical periods and geographical references. The Neo-Babylonian king Nebuchadnezzar is portrayed as an Assyrian king, and Jerusalem is situated both in the period after the Babylonian exile and after the Macedonian desecration of the Temple. This creates a fictional collage that does not depict a specific historical period but rather intertwines various Jewish crises in a literary way. At least two chronotopes can be identified in the text: (1) The chronotope of the Temple threat, characterized by year-related references and repeated emphasis on the endangerment of the Temple in Jerusalem. It connects the destruction of the First Temple (587 BCE) with its desecration under Antiochus IV. (2) The chronotope of an implicit calendar, derived from month references and agricultural allusions. This reconstructs a narrative timeframe from Kislev to Kislev, precisely the month in which Hanukkah is celebrated. In the end, the two chronotopes coincide: Israel and the Temple are saved from the Assyrian King Nebuchadnezzar by the "Jewish woman Judith", at approximately the same time that Jerusalem and the Temple are destroyed by the Babylonian King Nebuchadnezzar. This allows the attentive reader to connect Judith's story with the Hanukkah festival, which takes place in the month of Kislev. In the history of its reception — especially since the Middle Ages — this implicit annual arc has led to Judith's increasing association with the festival of Hanukkah. Hebrew retellings, liturgical poems, and medieval rabbinic commentaries explicitly portray Judith as a Hanukkah heroine. The authors thus demonstrate how the book's two chronotopes open an interpretive window through which Judith's story acquires a new, festive significance within Jewish traditions.

Bob Becking examines the different configurations of time and space in the Aramaic documents from Elephantine by searching for traces of chronotopes in the context of expressions for time in their various text types — letters, lawsuits, memoranda, and other literary compositions. Time references associated with day, month, and year exist, while expressions equivalent to minute, hour, week, decade or century are missing in these documents. It is noteworthy that both the Egyptian and Babylonian calendars were used, and that in most cases equations were established between the two systems. Furthermore, texts from the administrative elite were related to the ruling Persian king. Even in documents from everyday life, an awareness of the past, of the lifetime of the individual, or, in the case of the making of a will, an awareness of one's own transience and the limited lifetime, is evident. Becking concludes that while the Elephantine texts do not possess a fully developed philosophy of time, they certainly reveal an awareness of the interconnectedness of time, space, and social action. The texts convey a picture of everyday time organization in a Persian provincial society. The interweaving of space and time in the Aramaic Achiqar narrative is interesting: it points to a distant, exemplary past (the Neo-Assyrian Empire), which rather serves as a paradigmatic framework. The central setting is the royal court, a place of power, intrigue, and, above all, of testing for Achiqar. The collection of sayings, on the other hand, appears timeless: The advice and wisdom convey an 'eternal' validity. At the same time, they span a cross-cultural, almost limitless space, similar to the Book of Ecclesiastes (see also Moritz Adam's contribution in this volume).

While spatial concepts are often used metaphorically to articulate temporal facts, a reverse tendency can be discerned in the expression עולם which in the course of its conceptual history has undergone a remarkable change in meaning from a temporal meaning 'long duration, most distant time, eternity' in Biblical Hebrew to a spatial sense 'world, universe, cosmos' in Middle Hebrew. Jesus Sirach was assessed as a document of transition with both aspects of meaning by Horst Dietrich Preuß in 1986, as Frank Ueberschaer shows in his careful study of all עולם evidence available in the textual history of Sirach including ancient and medieval translations. Besides temporal or spatial meanings, a (third) qualitative or intensive use is particularly noteworthy.

This usage occurs especially in the position of the nomen rectum in constructus compounds, for example in expressions such as חרפת עולם ("immeasurable shame"). Spatial connotations of עולם in the sense of 'world' or 'world order' are rarely found in early manuscripts, but primarily in later scripts and translations. In the earliest documents, עולם plays a large role in its temporal meaning, with a striking frequency in the sections Praise of the Fathers (Sir 44–50) and the final chapter, especially because, not believing in a 'life after death' by himself, the good reputation in the collective memory of Israel is the only and therefore most important form of continuation and long duration or even eternity.

Moritz F. Adam examines concepts of time and space in the book of Ecclesiastes in the context of Second Temple Judaism. After preliminary considerations of time and space as hermeneutical constituents in discussion with, among others, Pierre Nora's concept of memory, he demonstrates the extent to which Ecclesiastes detaches itself from the way other texts in the Hebrew Bible use places, people, or events as „spaces of memory." In detail, he shows, using Ecclesiastes 8:10–14; 4:17–5:2; 2:4–6, that the few spatial references ('holy place', 'house of God', 'the city') are exemplary and ambiguous, and thus serve as a foil for abstract and timeless reflections that are themselves open rather than propositional. Starting with Eccl 1:4–11, he develops a shift from temporal thinking as a succession of generations to a new understanding of overall history and a more abstract underlying time, which allows for timeless and more abstract reflections. While Biblical Hebrew has no concept (and, incidentally, no aspectual forms) for past and future in the modern sense, Eccl 1:9, with the expressions מה־שהיה, literally 'that which was,' and הוא שיהיה, literally 'that will be,' contains the earliest evidence in the Hebrew language for temporal categories that have no object as a reference point, thus paving the way to concepts of overall history. The differences from most contemporary apocalyptic literature, whose construction of meaning is more closely tied to concrete spaces of memory in the sense of Pierre Nora, become clearly apparent. Yet it is precisely this abstraction and openness that gives Ecclesiastes relevance as an independent, unusual interlocutor within the world of Jewish thought.

Martina Kepper focuses on the interrelation of, so to speak, traditional methodological approaches within the fields of Septuagint and Old Testament / Hebrew Bible studies and Bakhtin's concept of the chronotope. The potential of this approach is tested through three deliberately selected case studies: the Book of Ezekiel in its Hebrew and Greek textual forms, the Book of Baruch, and the Wisdom of Solomon. These texts represent different periods of origin, linguistic contexts, and stages in textual history. The analysis demonstrates that chronological and spatial references in these writings rarely serve the purpose of historical precision; instead, they are employed in a literary and theological manner. Dates, locations, and temporal sequences structure the texts, qualify events as salvifically significant, and situate judgment, hope, and restoration within specific configurations of time and space.

It becomes particularly evident that different textual versions — the Masoretic Text of Ezek and its Greek versions — develop distinct theological emphases by shaping chronology and space in divergent ways. So, the riddle of the meticulous datings that confuse scholars up to the present day, surely cannot be solved by the findings alone, but shed new light on the manifold old problems: whereas the older idea that God's salvific acting already starts with the destruction of Jerusalem by the Babylonians, the younger Masoretic version dates the turning point later, in connection to the victory over the utmost enemies, by aligning these dates verbally to those already given in the Torah. In Baruch, on the other side, the chronotope "days of the heaven upon the earth" functions as a theological statement, probably even with political implications. The Wisdom of Solomon, though, adopts the contemporary concept of 'world-time', but highlights the idea that this is not a philosophical construct, but merely a self-evident idea within the framework of the biblical creation paradigm. Contemplating about time and space thus emerges not merely as an auxiliary tool of historiographical reconstruction, but as a genuinely theological discourse. Applying the concept of the chronotope opens new perspectives on exegetical strategies and theological conceptions in the writings of the Second Temple period, while also highlighting the potential of literary methodologies for biblical studies.

Daniel K. Falk examines the motif of 'wilderness' or 'way of the wilderness' in two text complexes of the Dead Sea Scrolls: the Community Rule (1QS and parallel texts), and the Words of the Luminaries (4Q504/506). While earlier scholarship interpreted the wilderness motif in the Community Rule as indicating an actual stay in a concrete wilderness-like place, more recent analyses read it more symbolically. According to Falk, 'the way of the wilderness' refers rather to a liminal situation, which should be dominated by communal study of scripture and an appropriate conduct including prayer. For Falk, the chronotope of the 'wilderness' in 1QS can be compared to Bakhtin's more static chronotope called 'adventure novel of ordeal', a period of trial, but without transformation, since the fate of humans is predetermined. The Words of the Luminaries (4Q504/506), a predominantly non-community-related collection of daily prayers, call to remembrance the biblical story from creation to the post-exilic period but are focused on Sinai and the wilderness. Unlike in the Community Rule, the wilderness is a chronotope of transformation: the community atones for the sins of the fathers and the present through liturgy. This corresponds rather to Bakhtin's chronotope called 'adventure novel of everyday life' in which characters are changed by their journey. Even if both text complexes are assigned to genres other than the novel, Bakhtin's concept of the chronotope proves heuristically valuable.

Sarah Wisialowski examines the significance of time and the construction of history in the Book of Daniel, while focusing on the supplication in Dan 9. She demonstrates that, like Neh 9 in the context of Neh 8–10, Dan 9 should not be read in isolation, but rather in the context of the visions in Dan 7–12. By reinterpreting Jeremiah's unfulfilled prophecy about 70 years of exile in prayer, prayer becomes an act of revelation in which history is transformed: past, present, and future are connected into a new whole of meaning. By transforming history in the mode of remembering and forgetting, traumatic experiences of the Diaspora can be processed. Following on from Dan 9, in 4Ezra, past, present, and future are interwoven in prayer through historical reinterpretation in order to create hope and orientation in times of crisis and loss. Wisialowski advocates a reading of the Book of Daniel beyond narrow genre boundaries: apocalypticism, prayer, and revelation intertwine to make time tangible and theologically interpretable. Wisialowski emphasizes the performative dimension of prayer: the 'time of prayer' at the time of the evening sacrifice is considered equal to the sacrificial cult, even without the temple. Daniel describes how the mediator of revelation, Gbriel, approaches him during prayer, precisely: "at the time of the evening sacrifice" (Dan 9,21). It is remarkable how this brief reference to a particular time establishes a spatial connection between the Diaspora and the Jerusalem Temple cult.

Based on the discovery of a small sundial from late Second Temple Period Jerusalem, Jonathan Ben-Dov analyzes the scientific, historical, and cultural significance of sundials, particularly regarding the role of timekeeping in ancient Judaism and its connection to the Temple cult. Among twelve other sundials from Jerusalem from that period, this one is unique for its incised menorah on the back. By providing an instructive context for the cultural history of timekeeping with sundials, he demonstrates that in the Hellenistic-Roman world, they became widespread symbols of education, urbanity, social status, and public order. Hourly indications gained importance for daily routines, administration, law, and, not least, religious practice. This is also evident in Hellenistic and Rabbinic Judaism, and especially in its use of religious timekeeping. While other large and precise sundials from the same region exhibit high mathematical accuracy, the sundial in question is more of a status symbol than a precise instrument for measuring time. The incised menorah is not yet to be understood as a general Jewish symbol, but rather as an astral one; it was a sacred object of the Temple, symbolizing cosmic order. While for the Hellenistic-Roman period — particularly based on apocalyptic texts — the religious and astronomical significance of calendars is the central focus of research, this analysis starting with a material artifact draws attention to a far less considered area: the cultural and religious dimension of the increasingly differentiated measurement of time.

The potential of Bakhtin's concept of the chronotope has not been exhausted in biblical scholarship, not even from this volume. The research on the interconnectedness of time and space can of course bear more fruit also in the future. The aim of this volume is to draw more attention to these topics in future research.

Bibliography

Bakhtin, Mikhail. 1981. "Forms of Time and of the Chronotope in the Novel." In *The Dialogic Imagination: Four Essays*, 84–258. Austin: University of Texas Press.

Beaude, Pierre-Marie. 2008. "Paul et le chronotope de l'empire." *Studies in Religion/Sciences Religieuses* 37/3–4:467–479. https://doi.org/10.1177/000842980803700306.

Becker, Eve-Marie. 2016. "Konzepte von Raum in frühchristlichen Geschichtserzählungen: Vom Markinischen Chronotop zur Spatial History des Lukas." In *Der früheste Evangelist*, WUNT 380, 103–116. Tübingen: Mohr Siebeck. https://doi.org/10.1628/978-3-16-155424-7.

Bemong, Nele, and Pieter Borghart. 2010. "Bakhtin's Theory of the Literary Chronotope: Reflections, Applications, Perspectives." In *Bakhtin's Theory of the Literary Chronotope: Reflections, Applications, Perspectives*, edited by Nele Bemong, Pieter Borghart, Michel De Dobbeleer, Kristoffel Demoen, Koen De Temmerman, and Bart Keunen, 3–16. Ghent: Academia Press.

Bemong, Nele, Pieter Borghart, Michel De Dobbeleer, Kristoffel Demoen, Koen De Temmerman, and Bart Keunen, eds. 2010. *Bakhtin's Theory of the Literary Chronotope: Reflections, Applications, Perspectives*. Ghent: Academia Press. https://doi.org/10.26530/OAPEN_377572.

Berquist, Jon L., and Claudia V. Camp, eds. 2008. *Constructions of Space*. Vol. II. *The Biblical City and Other Imagined Spaces*. LHBOTS 491. New York: T&T Clark.

Beyerle, Stefan, and Matthew Goff, eds. 2022. *Notions of Time in Deuterocanonical and Cognate Literature*. Berlin: De Gruyter. https://doi.org/10.1515/9783110705454.

Fischer, Bettina. 2006. "The Chronotope and Its Discursive Function in the Gospel of Luke." In *The New Testament Interpreted: Essays in Honour of Bernard C. Lategan*, NT.S 124, edited by Cilliers Breytenbach, 325–337. Leiden: Brill. https://doi.org/10.1163/9789047410591_018.

Frank, Michael C., and Kirsten Mahlke. 2008. Afterword to *Chronotopos*, by Mikhail Bakhtin, 201–242. Translated by Michael Dewey. Frankfurt a. M.: Suhrkamp.

Geiger, Michaela. 2010. *Gottesräume: Die literarische und theologische Konzeption von Raum im Deuteronomium*. BWANT 183. Stuttgart: Kohlhammer.

Grube, Christoph. 2006. "Chronotopos und intertextuelle Struktur: Zur Zeitgestaltung in Eichendorffs 'Aus dem Leben eines Taugenichts' unter Rekurs auf das Volksbuch 'Die schöne Magelona'." In *Bachtin im Dialog: Festschrift für Jürgen Lehmann*, edited by Markus May and Tanja Rudtke, 315–333. Heidelberg: Winter.

Grund, Alexandra. 2011. *Die Entstehung des Sabbats: Seine Bedeutung für Israels Zeitkonzept und Erinnerungskultur*. FAT 75. Tübingen: Mohr Siebeck. https://doi.org/10.1628/978-3-16-157808-3.

Hedwig-Jahnow-Forschungsprojekt, ed. 2010. *Zeit wahrnehmen: Feministisch-theologische Perspektiven auf das Erste Testament*. SBS 222. Stuttgart: Katholisches Bibelwerk.

Janowski, Bernd, and Beate Ego, eds. 2004. *Das biblische Weltbild und seine altorientalischen Kontexte*. FAT 32. 2nd ed. Tübingen: Mohr Siebeck.

Kosmin, Paul J. 2018. *Time and Its Adversaries in the Seleucid Empire*. Cambridge, MA: Harvard University Press.

Kotjatko-Reeb, Jens, Benjamin Ziemer, and Stefan Schorch, eds. 2014. *Nichts Neues unter der Sonne? Zeitvorstellungen im Alten Testament*. BZAW 450. Berlin: De Gruyter. https://doi.org/10.1515/9783110297935.

Kratz, Reinhard G., and Hermann Spieckermann, eds. 2009. *Zeit und Ewigkeit als Raum göttlichen Handelns: Religionsgeschichtliche, theologische und philosophische Perspektiven*. BZAW 390. Berlin: De Gruyter.
https://doi.org/10.1515/9783110211030.

Kutsch, Ernst. 1985. *Die chronologischen Daten des Ezechielbuches*. OBO 62. Göttingen: Vandenhoeck & Ruprecht.

Leroy, Marc, and Martin Staszak, eds. 2018. *Perceptions du temps dans la Bible*. Études bibliques, nouvelle série 77. Leuven: Peeters.

Maier, Felix. 2016. "Chronotopos: Erzählung, Zeit und Raum im Hellenismus." *Klio* 98/2:465–494. https://doi.org/10.1515/klio-2016-0040.

Schmidt, Oliver. 2010. "Zwischen Raumzeit und Spielraum: Anmerkungen zu Bachtins Chronotopos als Kategorie filmischer Analyse." In *Medien – Texte – Kontexte*, edited by Stephanie Großmann and Peter Klimczak, 127–140. Marburg: Schüren. https://doi.org/10.25969/mediarep/14540.

Schröter, Jens, and Markus Witte, eds. 2020. *Gott und Zeit: Religiöse und philosophische Zeitvorstellungen von der Antike bis zur Gegenwart*. BThZ 37. Berlin: De Gruyter.

Spörl, Uwe. 2006. "Die Chronotopoi des Kriminalromans." In *Bachtin im Dialog: Festschrift für Jürgen Lehmann*, edited by Markus May and Tanja Rudtke, 335–363. Heidelberg: Winter.

Steinby, Liisa. 2013. "Bakhtin's Concept of the Chronotope: The Viewpoint of an Acting Subject." In *Bakhtin and His Others: (Inter)Subjectivity, Chronotope, Dialogism*, edited by Liisa Steinby and Tintti Klapuri, 105–126. London: Anthem Press. https://doi.org/10.7135/9780857283108.009.

Vines, Michael E. 2007. "The Apocalyptic Chronotope." In *Bakhtin and Genre Theory in Biblical Studies*, SBL Semeia Studies 63, edited by Roland Boer, 109–118. Leiden: Brill.

Wegner, Michael. 1989. "Die Zeit im Raum: Zur Chronotopostheorie Michail Bachtins." *Weimarer Beiträge* 35/8:1357–1367.

White, Hayden. 1978. *Tropics of Discourse: Essays in Cultural Criticism*. Baltimore: Johns Hopkins University Press.

Alexandra Grund-Wittenberg

From the Mythification of History to the Transcending of Empires

Transformations of Space–Time Relations from the Priestly Composition to Hellenistic Writings

Abstract: The article explores how time and space interact in the Priestly writings (P) and how this shifts in later Hellenistic literature. In P, temporal structures such as genealogies, Sabbath rhythms, and covenantal acts dominate. Space, however, is rarely defined in political or geographical terms and seems to be depoliticized. A centered yet mobile sacred space emerges only with the Sinai tabernacle. This "mythification of history" creates a universal narrative shaped by divine speech, anchoring history in a sacred past. In contrast, Hellenistic Judaism integrates concrete empires and apocalyptic visions, relocating history's fulfillment beyond earthly powers. The study thus traces the transformation from the mythic chronotope of P to a transcendent construction of world history.

1 Bakhtin's Chronotope and the Hebrew Bible

When examining the interrelation of time and space in religious writings from Second Temple Judaism, Mikhail Bakhtin's concept of the chronotope offers a particularly fruitful point of departure. Developed in the context of ancient narrative literature, the chronotope provides a heuristic framework for analyzing how temporal and spatial relations are intrinsically intertwined in literary texts. In applying Bakhtin's concept to the following analysis, I draw primarily on his own definition from the essay "Forms of Time and of the Chronotope in the Novel":

> We will give the name *chronotope* (literally, 'time space') to the intrinsic connectedness of temporal and spatial relationships that are artistically expressed in literature. [. . .] What counts for us is the fact that it expresses the inseparability of space and time (time as the fourth dimension of space). [. . .] In the literary artistic chronotope, spatial and temporal indicators are fused into one carefully thought-out, concrete whole. Time, as it were, thickens, takes on flesh, becomes artistically visible; likewise, space becomes charged and responsive to the movements of time, plot, and history. This intersection of axes and fusion of indicators characterizes the artistic chronotope.[. . .] . (Bakhtin 1981, 84)

 | https://doi.org/10.1515/9783112240366-002

This definition highlights the chronotope not merely as a descriptive category, but as a constitutive principle through which narrative worlds are organized and made intelligible.

In the first part of his essay, Bakhtin distinguishes three chronotopic configurations in ancient narrative literature. These include: (1) the chronotope of adventure time in the Greek "adventure novel of ordeal," in which the protagonist remains essentially unchanged despite extensive travel; (2) the chronotope of the life path in the "adventure novel of every day life," characterized by moral and existential transformation; and (3) the chronotope of the biographical novel, structured by the life course of an individual.

Despite its analytical appeal, the concept of the chronotope remains disputed. As Liisa Steinby has observed, "The chronotope has proved to be a valuable tool of literary analysis, despite the fact that it is far from clear what Bakhtin actually meant by the concept" (Steinby 2013, 105). Precisely because of this openness, the chronotope possesses significant heuristic value. After all, Bakhtin developed the concept with reference to the ancient novel and the historian Felix Maier applied it to Greek historiography in a beneficial way (Maier, 2016). Thus, it can also be valuable for the analysis of other ancient narrative texts. Even if the application to texts of the Hebrew Bible is still somewhat experimental at this point, I will apply it to the Priestly writings (P) of the Pentateuch in the following. While describing the chronotope of P, I will focus on the relationship between space and time in the P narrative, one of the fundamental literary conceptions of the Pentateuch and, therefore, an elementary starting point for exploring the interrelationship of time and space in Second Temple Judaism.

2 What do I mean by "Priestly Writings"?

According to the classic list by Theodor Nöldeke,[1] the following texts belong to the Priestly writings (Tab. 1).

1 Nöldeke 1869. For an overview of the current state of research and the relevant literature, see Weimar 2010; Shectman and Baden 2009; Boorer 2016, 2–130. It is determined by literary historical questions such as the thesis of a Holiness School advocated by Knohl 2007; Milgrom 1991–2001; Nihan 2007, 395–401; for a recent research overview on H, see Rhyder 2019, 25–30. Combined with this, there is a growing tendency of differentiations within the Priestly writings beyond the more traditional discriminations between narrative and legal materials. In view of this increasing pluralization of literary-historical models on the priestly text area, there is no literary-historical consensus on the basis of which conceptual and narrative aspects of the Priestly writings can be worked out. Therefore, in the following, I will base my considerations on the still accepted con-

Tab. 1: The content of the Priestly Writings according to Theodor Nöldeke.

Period	Subject	Texts
Primeval History	Creation	Gen 1:1–2:4a
	Genealogy from Adam to Noah	Gen 5:1–32*
	Flood with Noah's Covenant	Gen 6:9–9:17*
	Table of Nations	Gen 10:1–7*,20.22–23,31–32
	Genealogy	Gen 11:10–27,31–32*
Ancestors' History	History of Abraham	Gen 12:4b,5; 13:6,11b,12abα
	Abraham Covenant	Gen 17*
	Burial of Sarah	Gen 23*
	Intercultural marriages of Esau and weddings of Jacob	Gen 26:34–35; 27:46–28:9; 29:24,28b,29
	Appearance of El Shaddai to Jacob in Bethel	Gen 35:9–13a,15
	Joseph and Jacob in Egypt	Gen 41:46a; 46:6–7
Israel's History as a People	Oppression of Israel in Egypt	Exod 1:1–7*,13–14; 2:23–25
	Calling of Moses	Exod 6:2–12
	Five plagues	Exod 7:8–12,19–22*; 8:1–3.11*,12–15; 9:8–12; 12:1–20*,28,40–41
	Sea miracle	Exod 14*
	Manna + Sabbath	Exod 16*
	Construction of the tent sanctuary	Exod 24:15–29:46*; 39:32,43; 40:17,33–35*
	Beginning of the cult	Lev 8–9*
	Spies	Num 13–14*
	Unbelief of Moses and Aaron	Num 20:1–13
	Death of Aaron	Num 20:22–29*
	Announcement of the death of Moses	Deut 32:48–52*
	Death of Moses	Deut 34:1*,7–9*

Since the texts are relatively easy to identify, there is some consensus about which texts belong to the Priestly writings, and consensus is rather unusual in Pentateuch research. Even though pre-exilic dates for P are currently proposed by some

sensus formulated by Nöldeke. On this consensus regarding Nöldeke's demarcation of P, see Blum 2015, 32; Gertz 2015, 65. For this study, it is not necessary — and would be impossible — to provide an exhaustive discussion of research, but instead, reference is made to relevant, exemplary works.

scholars,[2] I presume an early post-exilic dating, in line with the bulk of research. At the same time, I assume, like most scholars, that the texts assigned to the Priestly tradition are not homogeneous but consist of several editorial layers in addition to included material.

> The debate as to whether P is either a source or a redactional layer is still vehemently conducted, at least in German-speaking research (see the volume by Hartenstein and Schmid 2015). Probably, this is a false alternative, given the equally established third option that P is neither a source nor a redactional layer but rather a composition that linked its own material to existing non-Priestly traditions and imposed its own interpretive framework on them, in a similar sense to how the Chronicles or the Gospels are neither a source nor a redaction.[3]

I would not need to pay so much attention to the literary peculiarity of P if it did not also shape its chronotope. In Nöldeke's overview, as well as in corresponding lists, it becomes clear from the outset that the narrative texts are only connected by lists and genealogies and that they are dominated by speeches from God — and thus hardly contain actions beyond divine speech acts. This skeleton-like structure also led to the problematization of the existence of a source called "P" as an independent narrative.

Despite the presumed heterogeneity, P represents a complex and meaningful overall narrative that can be analyzed using literary-scientific concepts such as Bakhtin's. P is characterized by succinct theological terminology and constructive intentions.[4] According to more recent theories of Pentateuchal research, P first introduced the overarching narrative thread from primeval history to Sinai and thus provided a universal framework for the history of the world, the patriarchs, and Israel.

---

2 For an overview of the increasing number of scholars who assume a pre-exilic dating, see Faust 2019, 174–176. In a recent article that assumes a pre-exilic dating of P, Joel Baden makes it clear that the trauma caused by the destruction of Jerusalem simultaneously destroys all elementary certainties of the Priestly texts (Baden 2025, 81–94). The predominant early post-exilic dating of P, however, offers a reading of P as a document of hope after the trauma of exile, which can be seen as a testimony to a post-traumatic growth process.

3 See Blum 2015, 33. The problems raised by the thesis of P as either a source or a revision are, in my opinion, most convincingly solved in the composition model presented by Blum (see also, apart from the article cited above, esp. Blum 1990, 229–285).

4 Holzinger 1893, 335, already classically described P in 1893 as a legislative text in historical form and with historical substructure.

3 The Chronotope in P

3.1 A Chronotope in the Making: The Priestly Creation Story in Gen 1:1–2:3

Certainly, the Priestly creation story has a key position in the chronotope of the Priestly narrative and is presumably one of the best-known P texts.

Which chronotope does the P creation story present as a framework for the further narrative, and what is the relationship between space and time in this story?

I	1:1	Beginning of Creation		
		רֵאשִׁית / הָאָרֶץ / הַשָּׁמַיִם		
	1:2	Before Creation		
	1:3–5	*Time*: Initial Rhythmization		I–IV
II	1:6–8	*Space*: – Heaven (/ Air)		Areas of life
III	1:9–13	*Space*: – Earth, Sea		
		– Plant Bearing Earth		
IV	1:14–19	*Time*: Continuing Order		
Dominion on Time				
V	1:20–23	Aquatic Animals / Animals of the sky	Blessing	
VI	1:24–31	Land Animals		V–VI
		Humankind	Blessing	Creatures
Dominion on Creatures (“*dominium terrae*”)				
VII	2:1–3	Completion of Creation	Blessing	VII
		/ הָאָרֶץ / כלה pi.	Sanctification	

Fig. 1: The structure of Gen 1:1–2:3.

The overview of its structure (Fig. 1)[5] already provides a basic description of the relationship between space and time in this text. The sequence of the works of creation is arranged in a genuine temporal order. It includes the order of time (days I and IV), space (days II and III), and the related living beings (days V and VI).

According to the hypotactic interpretation of Gen 1:1–5, which I find rather convincing, this is not yet a *creatio ex nihilo*. Thus, a pre-worldly, life-hostile “something”, in which there is a תְהוֹם (primeval ocean), water, and a moving רוּח אֱלֹהִים (mighty storm or spirit of God), is transformed into a life-serving world and struc-

5 For the discussion of the structure of Gen 1:1–2:3(/4a), as well as the following, see in detail Grund(-Wittenberg) 2011, 193–237.

tured time and space. Creation means structuring time and space through God's creative speech acts.

The first thing that is created is the light itself — the light of the luminaries is created only on Day 4. The change of day and night is obviously more fundamental than the division of time by a calendar. Nevertheless, the calendar and the festivals are so important that an entire day of creation is dedicated to them — Day 4, with the creation of the luminaries.

The creation of spaces for living beings is inserted between the order of time on Day 1 and Day 4. As Thomas Wagner has rightly observed, the exclusion of the waters of chaos by the רָקִיעַ (firmament, vault of heaven) leads to the biosphere being understood as a closed space inhabited only by the creatures created by God.[6] This space of creation is only demarcated upwards, not explicitly downwards. The biosphere is depicted as a space between the celestial firmament and the dry land surrounded by waters of chaos.[7] The areas for living beings are separated in order to exclude competition for food; the space does not yet have a center, even if the space for humans is ultimately the focus. In any case, this is the space in which the plot will continue.

Can we say something about the question of where God is? God appears here as being beyond space, "trans-spatial". There is no mention of God dwelling, for example, beyond the firmament of heaven, רָקִיעַ, nor of a particular spatial center on earth. Gen 1:1–2:3 also remains silent on questions that are predetermined by the spatial-physical frameworks of later theological tradition, for example, whether God can only be found outside of creation, meaning God is radically transcendent, whether creation is in him as in panentheism, or whether God is everywhere, and thus ubiquitous. There is only one indication in the text of where God is present. God makes himself present in creation through a statue that represents him, namely humankind. Humanity, as the Imago Dei, embodies God in his creation.[8]

---

6 Wagner 2023, 127. "Die Ausgrenzung der Chaoswasser durch den *raqia* [sic] führt dazu, dass die Biosphäre als abgeschlossener Raum verstanden wird, der allein von den von Gott geschaffenen Lebewesen bewohnt wird."

7 Wagner, 2023, 127: "Vielmehr wird die Biosphäre als zwischen der Himmelsfeste und dem Trockenen [. . .] vom Chaoswasser umgebener Raum gezeichnet."

8 The discussion on the Imago Dei of the last decades cannot be summarized here in brief. It should be emphasized that the creation of man for the permanent purpose of being the Imago Dei is not linked to a special human quality such as reason, or the like, or of partnership in the covenant but is closely linked to the task of the *dominium terrae* and *regnum animalium*. Of course, against the background of the Egyptian royal ideology in particular, the royalization of humankind should not be underestimated, nor should the connection between Gen 1:26–28 and Gen 9:5–6, which places the life of every human being under God's protection under threat of death. See, among others, Neumann-Gorsolke 2004, 136–315; Janowski 2004,183–214; Schellenberg 2011, 29–142.

The creation of humankind as Imago Dei is certainly a climax of creation and the Hexaemeron. Bakhtin already underlined that the category of the chronotope has anthropological implications: "The chronotope as a formally constitutive category determines to a significant degree the image of man in literature as well. The image of man is always intrinsically chronotopic (Bakhtin 1981, 85)." Explicit statements about the significance of humanity correspond to the universal claim of the genre "creation narrative".

However, the ultimate climax of the Priestly creation story is not the creation of humankind. The climax is only reached on the seventh day. The seventh day lacks all the formulas familiar from the other days, for example, the speech introduction, the naming formula (1st–3rd work), the approval formula, and the day formula. This underlines its special status. Only the blessing already bestowed on aquatic and air creatures and humans applies to the seventh day, yet in a different way. God's cessation of work refers to the practice, first named "Shabbat" in Exod 16, according to which Israel will live in the rhythm of six days of work and one day of rest, as God had shown it at the very beginning (Grund[-Wittenberg] 2011, 193–202, 224–237). In the beginning, God sets the example for a rhythm according to which everyone in Israel should have an equal share of work and rest. Here, above all, it is neither a space nor something material but a time set apart for God, sanctified, before a spatial sanctuary or temple is even conceived. In a later Priestly layer, in Exod 31:14 and 35:2, the Sabbath can even be referred to as קֹדֶשׁ , a sacred place or a sanctuary (Grund[-Wittenberg] 2011, 273–287), which is reminiscent of A. J. Heschel's influential interpretation of the Sabbath as a palace in time. In my opinion, however, this metaphor of Heschel is not entirely accurate here since a palace itself is merely a profane space, whereas קֹדֶשׁ, "sanctuary" in time, is the expression chosen by the Hebrew Bible.

The intercultural comparison is also instructive for the temporal structure of the story. There are indeed some stories from the surrounding cultures — especially Mesopotamia and Greece — in which we can find the motif "six days/the seventh day", albeit not in such a formative way for the overall structure. In fact, not a single cosmogonic myth that has the form of "six days/the seventh day" is known in the history of culture. Presumably, this compositional idea, with the seventh day as a climax, is even the reason why the division into days became the comprehensive ordering category of the work of creation. Time, in the form of the basic rhythm of day and night, must be created first so that it can become the basic structure of the creation story. The spatial order of the works of creation is encompassed by the temporal order of the days of creation — spaces are put in a temporal order.

The chronotope, the 'time space', of the Priestly narrative emerges before our eyes in Genesis 1 as ordered time and ordered space for life, universal but still unfilled. The spaces for life are to be filled by the animals and humans assigned to them. With regard to humans, this is immediately realized in the next Priestly text following Gen 2:4a, the *Toledot Adam* in Gen 5:1–32.

3.2 The *Toledot Adam* in Gen 5

Gen 5 shows the manifestation of the blessing of creation and the genetically transmitted succession of the image of God throughout humanity. אָדָם / human being shiftsfrom a generic term to a personal name in v. 3 when a male person called Adam fathers a son called Seth.

The genealogy offers a highly repetitive structure with only minor deviations over 10 generations

1 This is the document of the genealogy of אָדָם (human being)
On the day that God created אָדָם,
He made him in the likeness of God,
2 Male and female He created them.
And He blessed them,
and called their name אָדָם
on the day they were created.
3 And אָדָם (Human Being) lived 130 years
and fathered a likeness of himself, like his image,[9]
and named him Seth.
4 And אָדָם (Human Being) lived 800 years after he fathered Seth,
and he fathered other sons and daughters.
5 And all days of אָדָם (Human Being) that he lived were 930 years; then he died.

Gen 5 continues the numerical symbolic structuring of time already laid out in Gen 1. I do not want to add any further assumptions about the meaning of the numbers in detail.[10] As Claus Westermann aptly formulated, these are symbolic numbers that, in their excess, point to the realm of mythical events beyond history. In a prehistoric form of representing the extension of time, it is expressed that the history of humanity extends into a great expanse of the past that cannot be measured by the dimensions of present history.[11]

9 The reversal of the wording of Gen 1:26 also implies that Seth only functions in his meaning as a likeness like a statue of his father Adam, cf. Schellenberg 2011, 73–84.

10 See in detail Jacob 1934, 158–160; Ziemer 2009, 1–18; Gertz 2015, 81–91.

11 Westermann 1974, 479: "mythische Zahlen, die in ihrem Übermaß auf den der Geschichte jenseitigen Bereich mythischen Geschehens weisen. [. . .] In einer vorgeschichtlichen Darstellungs-

> And PN1 lived xy years, and begat PN2
> And PN1 lived after he begat PN2 yz years,
> and begat sons and daughters.
> And all the days of PN1 were zx years, and he died.

The genealogy seems to be a kind of time lapse between the creation and the flood story.[12] It condenses time into an abstract continuum[13] in which no action takes place apart[14] from conception and death. Of course, temporal extension, or linearity, predominates; the frequent assignment of genealogies to a purely linear concept of time (Breitmaier 2009, 91–92 and passim), however, overlooks that this line consists of cyclical structures.

It is a concept of time that is both cyclical and linear, extending far into time like a chain stitch; thus, it is linearized cyclicity. However, Gen 5 is not only linear. At each stage, nameless sons and daughters are born. The image that emerges is that of a family tree with side branches on ten levels and a branching crown (Shem, Ham, and Japheth),[15] even if all those who are not "sons and heirs"[16] are released from history namelessly.

The blessing of creation is realized here. Life spans are enormous but are already considerably reduced compared to the Sumerian king list and tend to decrease.[17] The *Toledot Adam* have a certain emphasis on finitude (Breitmaier 2009, 90; Hieke 2003, 70). They illustrate dying and being born that could, in principle,

---

form von Zeiterstreckung wird hier zum Ausdruck gebracht, daß sich die Menschheitsgeschichte in eine große Weite der Vergangenheit erstreckt, die mit den Maßen der gegenwärtigen Geschichte nicht zu messen sind."

12 Breitmaier, 2009, 73: "eine Art Zeitraffer zwischen zwei Erzählsträngen".

13 It is possible that what appears to us today as only abstract numbers was new and timely in the early Persian period, as is suggested in Joachim Schaper's monograph (Schaper 2019, esp. 211–223), according to which the emergence of money, alphabetic writing, and monotheism at the same time is a symptom of a new way of abstract thinking, which may also be manifested in the priestly preference for a calendar based on month numbers rather than month names or even peasant harvest times.

14 Here, I don't agree with Breitmaier, 2009, 90, according to which the concept of time that characterizes the individual sections is concrete time. On the contrary, nothing is said about the concrete lives and the peculiarities of the people and their actions; rather, more than 1600 years have passed in fast motion.

15 Breitmaier, 2009, 73: "Es entsteht das Bild eines Stammbaums mit Seitenästen auf 10 Stockwerken und einer sich verzweigenden Krone (Sem, Ham und Jafet)".

16 It may be surprising that after the creation of humans as male and female, the procreation is narrated purely patrilineally, but this is probably due to inheritance law; cf. Fischer 2000, 18–21.

17 See for example Hieke, 2003, 71.

continue indefinitely. At least, it is open to the future. It is only disturbed when God intervenes and takes away Enoch, who does not die.[18]

But what is also of interest to the chronotope is what is *not* said,[19] and that is *where* this multiple procreation and birth takes place. The space remains unspecific and without a center. This line of cycles takes place in a "somewhere" that is still as placeless as the creation of humankind in Gen 1.

The cycles of birth and death of Gen 5 are interrupted at the onset of the *Toledot Noah* (P: Gen 6:9–13), when God declares: קֵץ כָּל־בָּשָׂר בָּא לְפָנַי "The end of all flesh has come before me":

9 This is the genealogy of Noah:
Noah was a righteous man, blameless among his contemporaries;
Noah walked with God.
10 And Noah fathered three sons: Shem, Ham, and Japheth.
11 Now the earth was corrupt in God's sight, and the earth was filled with wickedness.
12 God saw how corrupt the earth was,
for every creature had corrupted its way on the earth.
13 And God said to Noah:
The end of all flesh has come before me (קֵץ כָּל־בָּשָׂר בָּא לְפָנַי)
for the earth is filled with wickedness because of them;
therefore, I am going to destroy them along with the earth.

Again, it remains unclear *where* God speaks to Noah and *from where* the ark sets sail. In the flood narrative, the human space of living is restricted to the interior of the ark, while the wider space "under the sky" is filled with water again. The water runs off again at the end of the flood narrative.[20] Mount Ararat is mentioned as the place of arrival of the ark, finally citing a place that belongs to the world known after the flood. However, otherwise, specific locations are left out.

---

18 Aptly Breitmaier 2009, 90.

19 After the conception of the firstborn and the explicit mention of the father's age, further sons and daughters are named. What they did, how they lived, whether they developed into ethnic groups or lived in cities or villages — all of this is of no interest; they are dismissed from history without a word. Ultimately, they and their cultures later drowned in the waters of the flood.

20 Wagner 2023, 152: In the flood narrative "wird der menschliche Lebensraum eingeengt, indem die Biosphäre auf den Innenraum der Arche beschränkt wird, während der weitere Raum [. . .] (‚unter dem Himmel') wieder von Wasser gefüllt wird. Dieses läuft am Ende der Fluterzählung wieder ab".

At the same time, Noah's age plays a central role in the flood story, as Isa Breitmaier sums up: At 500 years of age, Noah begot Shem, Ham, and Japheth (Gen 5:32), the flood came when he was 600 years old (Gen 7:6), the waters dried up when he was 601 (Gen 8:13), and he lived for another 350 years after the flood (Gen 9:28).[21] Only in Gen 9:29 is Noah's lifetime after the flood added to his entire lifetime. Thus, the genealogy of Gen 5 ends in 9:28,[22] so the *Toledot Noah* bridges the whole flood story: Years of life and calendar dates, and, in sum, time continues to dominate the largely undefined space.

The primeval history that concerns the entire humanity remains focused on one family alone. The experiences of Adam's other children and grandchildren who perished in the flood are not part of the plot. The story of a catastrophe for all flesh somehow does not focus on the history of "others" that is happening in the meantime. This makes the universality of the table of nations of post-flood humanity in Gen 10 all the more remarkable, even if P in Genesis largely remains true to the focus on one ancestor and his family at a specific time.

3.3 The Table of Nations in the Priestly passages of Gen 10

The blessing of creation from Gen 1:28 was realized in time in Gen 5. The renewed blessing of creation in Gen 9:1 is realized in space, spatially, in the P passages from Gen 10.[23] The formulation וּמִלְאוּ אֶת־הָאָרֶץ "fill the earth" (1:28) is only now realized. Despite several parallels in antiquity, Gen 10 is quite special, as it emphasizes the unity of the human race despite its differences, in contrast to the more common differentiation into "we" and "the strangers".[24]

In contrast to Gen 5, the Priestly passages of Gen 10 contain neither dates of birth and death nor chronologies,[25] but only the basic note אַחַר הַמַּבּוּל "after the flood" (10:1,32). With only a few narrative forms such as in v. 1 ("and unto them were children born"; וַיִּוָּלְדוּ לָהֶם בָּנִים), it contains even less narrative action than

21 Breitmaier 2009, 71: "Er zeugt mit 500 Jahren Sem, Ham und Jafet (Gen 5,32), die Flut kommt, als er 600 Jahre alt ist (Gen 7,6); getrocknet sind die Wasser, als Noach 601 ist (Gen 8,13) und er lebt nach der Flut noch 350 Jahre (Gen 9,28)".

22 Breitmaier 2009, 92: "Erst 9,29 wird die Lebenszeit Noachs nach der Sintflut und seine gesamte Lebenszeit nachgetragen. So beendet P die Genealogie von Gen 5 erst in 9,28."

23 For a recent overview of research on Gen 10, see Carr 2024, 343–348.

24 Hieke 2014, 32. See already Westermann 1974, 705.

25 Lux 1995, 256: "Die Toledot Noach sind der einzige Abschnitt der priesterschriftlich bearbeiteten Urgeschichte, in dem horizontale, multilineare Genealogien ins Spiel [kommen]. Diese sind nicht mit der Chronologie verknüpft (alles Zahlenmaterial entfällt), sondern mit dem Raum."

Gen 5. Instead, it mainly offers the lists of the sons of Noah under headings in Gen 10:2,6,22 and a subscription in v. 32:

1 And these are the תּוֹלְדֹת of the sons of Noah:
Shem, Ham, and Japheth: and unto them were children born after the flood.
2 The sons of Japheth are: [. . .]
6 The sons of Ham are: [. . .]
22 The sons of Shem are: [. . .]
32 These are the families of the sons of Noah, according to their תּוֹלְדֹת in their nations;
and of these were the nations divided in the earth after the flood.

The Priestly passages of Gen 10 P are, as Markus Witte rightly points out, a static representation of the relationships between nations.[26] Mankind differentiates itself from the family of Noah into various groups with their own clans, languages, countries, and peoples, as the captions of the subsections in 10:5,22,31 underline (cf. Köckert 1995, 150). Japheth obviously stands for peoples in the north and west, Ham for peoples in the south (except for Canaan), and Shem for peoples in the east (Witte 2011). Research ever since has attempted to explain the geographical references of the Table of Nations, as well as its receptions in the Book of Jubilees, Josephus, the War Scroll of Qumran, and others.

The Priestly Table of Nations has also been compared with the concept of peoples in the Achaemenid Empire, as documented in ancient Iranian royal inscriptions such as the Behistun inscription or the reliefs in Persepolis or Naqsh-i-Rustam (Köckert 1995, 150 fn. 15). However, the Priestly Table of Nations only gains a deeper political dimension through the Non-Priestly pieces, as Markus Witte has rightly emphasized (Witte 2011). The center of this mental map remains Israel / Palestine (Wagner 2023, 152). Apart from this general perspective, no cultic, political, or national center is mentioned (Witte 2011). Through the Table of Nations, the known peoples are conceptualized as a family tree.

26 Witte 2011: “statische Darstellung der Völkerverhältnisse”; vgl. Westermann 1974, 672: “die Völkertafel von P ist nicht mehr Genealogie der Verteilung der Völker über die Erde, sondern listenmäßige Zusammenstellung der Völker der Erde.”

3.4 Finally, a Centered World: YHWH's Indwelling in Israel at Sinai

After the "time of beginning" as the chronotope of primeval history, the chronotope "time of journey", which is also "revelation time" from time to time, begins with Abraham. In the patriarchal narratives, it is a journey through the land given to Abraham and his family while still strangers in their own land, whereas in the book of Exodus, it is mainly the way of the people out of Egypt and through the desert. The ancestors' history is, again, dominated by notes on their age, travel notes, and divine speeches to Abraham and Jacob. I can keep it brief with regard to the following speeches of God because these, too, as with Noah in Gen 6:9–13, usually take place in a spatial somewhere. In Abraham's case, the context only shows that he must have been in Canaan after his separation from Lot, and instead of spatially, it is again located temporally in the lifetime of Abraham. However, it is precisely this placelessness of God's speeches that gives them an "unconditional" validity, which seems appropriate for statements such as the eternal (!) covenant with Noah and Abraham.

As is usual in Priestly texts, the narrative moments are used very sparingly, and there are no dialogic structures, quite unlike in Non-Priestly texts on Abraham. Since there are almost no interventions in God's speeches by the narrator, who summarizes actions, the narrative time and the narrated time are almost identical, in clear contrast to the genealogies. There is almost no action, or rather, the action consists, similarly to Gen 1, of God's speech acts. But there is certainly an irrefutable Before and After: God's covenants and announcements are irreversible.[27]

Can something be said about the question of *where* God is here? In Gen 17:1, YHWH appears to Abraham and introduces himself as El Shaddai, but it is not clear from where YHWH appears. He expects Abraham to walk "before El Shaddai" (17:1). That means wherever Abraham walks, El Shaddai alias YHWH is present in a certain way, whereby this walking before him is obviously not just a spatial category but aims at an ethical way of life and an awareness of living under the assessment and in the company of God.

With the promise of the land in Gen 17, suspense is built up: There is now a spatial destination — a place where Abraham finds himself already, but where he is still a "stranger in his own land"[28]. This introduces a tension between what is

27 Beth-El is explicitly mentioned as a place, but this assumingly has a polemical point against the Non-Priestly cult etiology in Gen 28:11–19 by emphasizing (against Gen 28:26–27) that this is merely the place where God spoke with Jacob and from which God then ascended again, cf. Blum 2015, 48; Schmid 2018, 99.

28 Cf. the title of the monograph by Wöhrle "Fremdlinge im eigenen Land" 2012, esp. 189–202.

already and what is not yet. Israel's stay in Egypt and on Mount Sinai even removes them further from their destination. This suspense is not resolved until the end of P — it is never told in P that Israel reaches its destination, and P lacks a happy ending in the land.[29]

God repeatedly encounters the wandering patriarchs on their journey in different places and promises them that he will be *with* them. However, we cannot speak of a migrating God in the true sense of the word. What is missing is that God's constant perceptible presence at their side is narrated.

This only changes in the Sinai narrative[30] when the כְּבוֹד יְהוָה (glory of YHWH) appears to Israel.[31] The כְּבוֹד יְהוָה apparently had not dwelt permanently at Sinai since it had to take up residence at Sinai in Exod 24:16. Still, it is not told where exactly it came from.

Exod 24:15b–18a

15 b	And the cloud covered the mountain.
16	The כְּבוֹד יְהוָה settled on Mount Sinai, and the cloud covered it six days. The seventh day he called to Moses out of the midst of the cloud.
17	The appearance of the כְּבוֹד יְהוָה was like devouring fire on the top of the mountain in the eyes of the children of Israel.
18 a	Moses entered into the midst of the cloud, and went up on the mountain.

In Exod 40:34, the cloud covers the tent of meeting, and the כְּבוֹד יְהוָה fills the tabernacle.

Exod 40:34–37

34	Then the cloud covered the tent of meeting, and the כְּבוֹד יְהוָה filled the tent.
35	Moses wasn't able to enter into the tent of meeting, because the cloud stayed on it, and the כְּבוֹד יְהוָה filled the tent.

---

29 The problem of the promised land that is never reached in the P narrative remains a vividly disputed topic; see, for example, Schmitt 2014, 137–155; Frevel 2000, 6–387; Noort 2008, 99–119; Röhrig 2023, 384–401; Ska 2008, 631–653; Boorer 2016, 22–34.109–140.

30 For a more detailed discussion of the Priestly Sinai narrative, see Grund(-Wittenberg) 2011, 257–273; Grund(-Wittenberg) 2016, 302–321; Grund(-Wittenberg) 2023, 165–177.

31 See for the discussion of the כְּבוֹד יְהוָה in the Priestly writings Struppe 1988, passim; Owczarek 1998, passim; Wagner 2012, 52–122; Boorer 2016, 352–375.

36 When the cloud was taken up from over the tent, the children of Israel went onward, throughout all their journeys;
37 but if the cloud wasn't taken up, then they didn't travel until the day that it was taken up.

In the indwelling of the כְּבוֹד יְהוָה in the tent of meeting, a clearly centered space is now created. However, this center is not locally bound since the sanctuary is not connected to a single place but is mobile. Wherever the אֹהֶל מוֹעֵד (tent of meeting) is set up, the center is located (Wagner 2023, 163). The camp, which is still centered in itself through various levels of holiness,[32] becomes a moving center with the departure from Sinai toward the promised land (Wagner 2023, 152).

As the story continues, Israel sets out as soon as the cloud rises (Exod 40:36). Thus, YHWH is now continuously present amongst Israel (cf. Boorer 2016, 365–375). However, here, YHWH is not a God who goes with his people wherever the people go — rather, Israel follows YHWH.

How the relationship between the כְּבוֹד יְהוָה and YHWH is meant cannot be said with entire clarity.[33] After all, it is YHWH "personally" who, according to Lev 1:1, speaks to Moses from the tent of meeting and not the כְּבוֹד יְהוָה. Obviously, the כְּבוֹד יְהוָה appears at particular places but does not speak.

Thus, here, the chronotope is characterized by the motif of the "path" of the wandering people of God, who align themselves with the presence of God, set out with him or stay with him, and gather around him on the way to the promised land, which, however, is never reached in P.

4 Conclusion

4.1 Mythification of History – Historicization of Myth

The characteristics of the Priestly chronotope are evident: space often remains undefined, without a particular center for a long time. Time structures, which are sometimes meticulously reproduced, dominate the story and give the narrated world its genuine foundation. References to political history are lacking, and concrete places in the known world are rarely mentioned. Placeless divine speeches

32 See esp. Jenson 1992, 89–219.

33 Cf. Boorer 2016, 364: "Although the כְּבוֹד יְהוָה in Pg clearly signifies the visible presence of YHWH on earth, it is difficult to determine the exact relationship between the כְּבוֹד יְהוָה and YHWH himself"; for more discussion, see Boorer 2016, 364–366.

prevail over deeds, and the temporal orientation dominates the spatial orientation. All this creates a rather mythical space-time.

The phenomenon of mythification in P has already been discussed in former research but under different auspices.[34] In a lecture to the IOSOT in Göttingen in 1977, Norbert Lohfink emphasized that the Priestly writings did not ask how things really happened — "wie es eigentlich gewesen ist" — nor did they aim to communicate what really happened (Lohfink [1977] 1988, 227). Rather, the selection of material and the technique of presentation made the story transparent to the intended readers and their situation. Lohfink assessed that the Priestly writings reject a dynamic world, erase references to the future, and transform history back into myth (Lohfink 1988, 241). Lohfink's pointed opinion was rejected — at least in part, and certainly rightly so — by Volkmar Fritz (Fritz 1987, 434–439) and Bernd Janowski (Janowski 1993, 240–245), who took a more moderate position. Recently, Konrad Schmid and Thomas Wagner have again stressed the peculiar "depoliticization"[35] in the Priestly writings. It does not come as a surprise that literature that is part of a cultural memory composed before the beginnings of historiography with Herodotus is not critically oriented toward how things "actually" were and what "actually" happened. It is in keeping with its function that essential elements of the way of life of the narrating community are anchored in a foundational past. The Priestly narrative is less aimed at the events of the past *per se* than at how God's relationship with the world and Israel was organized by Elohim, or El Shaddai, or Adonaj, in a pre-historic past. It is about how things really were, but in the sense of the "core meaning" of what happened (Tab. 2)[36].

Tab. 2: The structure of the Priestly narrative.

	Period	**God's name**	**Theological keywords**
Primeval History	Creation (1st act)	Elohim (God)	Elohim blesses (ברך) humankind and gives them the earth
	Flood Creation (2nd act)	Elohim (God)	Elohim blesses (ברך) humankind and establishes/ gives his covenant (בְּרִית) and gives them the earth

34 For a detailed history of research, especially see Boorer 2016, 175–215.

35 Wagner 2023, 165: "Mit der Konzentration auf den Kult weist PG eine von machtpolitischen Interessen losgelöste Gemeindestruktur auf. Diese orientiert sich allein an der Kultfähigkeit des Menschen. Diese Entpolitisierung scheint mit den Machtverhältnissen der persischen Zeit im Einklang zu stehen".

36 The table is a translated version of the instructive figure from Zenger / Frevel [9]2015, 199–200.

Table 2: (continued)

	Period	God's name	Theological keywords
Ancestors' History	Abraham	El Shaddai (the Almighty)	El Shaddai gives/establishes his covenant (בְּרִית) and blesses Abraham and his seed (Gen 17:7–8: Content of the בְּרִית: Promise of God's presence and the gift of land)
	Jacob	El Shaddai (the Almighty)	El Shaddai blesses Jacob and his seed (Gen 35:12: Renewal of the promise of land)
Israel's History as a People	Exodus	YHWH	YHWH remembers his covenant and creates glory (כָּבוֹד) before the gods of Egypt (Exod 6:2–8: repetition of the בְּרִית -promise of Gen 17:7–8)
	Sinai	YHWH	YHWH's glory (כְּבוֹד יְהוָה) appears and settles in the midst of his people (Exod 29:43–46; 40:34–35, Lev 9:23: fulfilment of the presence of God in Israel)

P recognizes a periodization of history from creation to Sinai not through historiography focused on political history, but through various revelations of the same God under different names and delivered to different addressees. The fact that structures of this story often repeat themselves emphasizes the similarity and reliability of God's actions across the different phases of history. To stress the mythical ambience of P texts is certainly still correct. Especially compared to Non-Priestly texts, P is more comparable to mythical texts from the Ancient Near Eastern environment, particularly with regard to the plot "From creation to the indwelling of God(s) in the sanctuary." However, if one starts from the expectations of ANE mythical texts, one would rather expect the historical, existing urban temple in Jerusalem to be explicitly connected to the creation of the world in primordial times. *Enuma Elish*, like other Mesopotamian myths that were assumed to be known at the time, explicitly links the creation of the world with the Marduk sanctuary Esagila in the city of Babylon, the center of its mental map. In P, the mythical plot "From cosmogony to sanctuary" was transformed into the early history of Israel. In this respect, the Priestly narrative has not transformed history into myth, but rather myth into a universal and Israel-centered story. It certainly has a mythical coloring.

Lohfink's evaluation that P is an archetypal sequence, a myth, an event that is always and everywhere and for everyone[37] will, however, have to be modified. Yes,

37 Lohfink 1977, 199: "urbildlicher Ablauf, Mythos, Ereignis, das immer und überall und für jeden gilt".

God's speeches to Noah, Abraham, Jacob, and Moses take place in an unspecific somewhere, but they are nevertheless irreversible statements by God in a fundamental past.[38]

Despite the transparency of the desert sanctuary for the temple and the cult of the post-exilic period, it is remarkable that the Priestly narrative evidently did not attempt to provide an explicit legitimation of the post-exilic Jerusalem Temple.[39] Jerusalem is never mentioned. The difference between the time of the desert sanctuary and the authors' own historical time is obvious. The center of the Priestly world is not Jerusalem, unlike in so many other texts of the Hebrew Bible that display a strong symbolism of the center.[40] With the desert sanctuary, an inaccessible "U-topos" is placed at the beginning of all further history of cult, sacrifice, and sanctuary in Israel. The desert sanctuary, unlike the temple in Jerusalem, is also indestructible, especially since it lies beyond the politically relevant world. Here, everything is centered around the mobile presence of God, which is on the move with his people toward the promised land.

Beyond that, the textual sanctuary is indestructible, and so a kind of safe space is created. The textual sanctuary is particularly safe from the threats of political history. Through textuality, it detaches itself from time and can, again and again, be concretized in time because, with each new reading, YHWH comes down to Sinai, enters the *tent of meeting*, and sets off with the people of Israel into the promised land. It is precisely these characteristics of the text that made the Pentateuch, the Torah, as Heinrich Heine put it, a portable fatherland.

Just as indestructible as this textual sanctuary is the Shabbat as a sanctuary in time. It is accessible from any place and comes to Israel with every sunset of the sixth day, without the need for a temple to which one would have to make a pilgrimage.

---

38 It is interesting that Boorer, without taking into consideration the Mesopotamian parallels in detail, comes to a similar conclusion (Boorer 2016, 500: "Pg's picture, [. . .] has been shown here to be both historiographical and paradigmatic at every point and as a whole. It is historiographical in that it comprises a trajectory of contingent elements extending from the original cosmic creation through its reversal and the emergence of the new creation whose stability is guaranteed and within which the story of the nation Israel and its ancestors unfolds along its trajectory of the forward movement of the Abrahamic covenant promises. It is historiographical in that at every point, earlier traditions are echoed, albeit in reshaped form, inseparable from its historiographical nature is its paradigmatic nature at every point and as a whole." Cf. Boorer 2016, 455–502.

39 See for a more detailed justification Grund(-Wittenberg) 2016, 314–320.

40 In his dissertation, Friedhelm Hartenstein used the model of the symbolism of the center as a basis for further studies on Old Testament spatial concepts (Hartenstein 1997, 18–23); Bernd Janowski developed it further and illustrated it in a useful graphic representation, see Janowski 2003, 35–36.

4.2 From the Priestly Writings to the Literature of Hellenistic Judaism

What changes between the Priestly writings and Jewish literature of the Hellenistic period concerning the relationship between time and space? I would like to briefly look at this, taking as an example the visions in Dan 7–12.

According to Konrad Schmid, for P, the end of history was reached with the Achaemenid Empire: "For P, the Persian period is — to use an anachronistic saying — the end of history: God's political will has become clear with the Achaemenid rule over the world (Schmid 2011, 4–5; cf. Schmid 2018, 106)." Due to the force of the political events of the Hellenistic period, especially under Seleucid rule, Hellenistic Judaism obviously found itself challenged to cope with the changing empires and integrated them into a construction of world history. For Daniel, the end of history can only be reached beyond the increasingly threatening political empires. The empires can only be transcended by the knowledge that the "Ancient of Days" will judge the empires that the animals symbolize.

Whereas the mobile sanctuary in the desert could not be easily destroyed or desecrated in P, now the temple was again under concrete threat during the reign of Antiochus IV Epiphanes. P has a periodization of the past, but this in no way refers to concrete political history, as is the case in the animal visions in Dan 7. The succession of cruel empires up to Antiochus IV challenges the concept of the kingdom of God. This challenge is dealt with in special revelations to figures such as Daniel, who long ago foresaw future history — the "Future of the Past" time structure, which is also known from Mesopotamian Literary Predictive Texts.

The knowledge of the future achieved through revelation takes the place of a stable mythical past, as it was represented in P. The heavenly spheres, which did not yet play a recognizable role in P, are now involved in historical events. In the heavenly spheres, the course of events is decided.

In sum, a lot has obviously changed compared to the Priestly writings. The weeks and the years, so popular in P, are exceeded by the more comprehensive concept of "year weeks". What has persisted, however, is the stabilization of the world order through temporal structures and the importance of festivals and calendars.

Bibliography

Baden, Joel. 2025. "Trauma and the Fragmentation of Theology in Lamentations." In *Readings of Trauma: Hermeneutical Perspectives on Biblical and Modern Trauma Narratives*, Studies in Cultural Contexts of the Bible, edited by Alexandra Grund-Wittenberg and Maike Schult, 81–94. Leiden: Brill.

Bakhtin, Mikhail. [1937] 1981. "Forms of Time and of the Chronotope in the Novel." In *The Dialogic Imagination*, 84–258. Austin: University of Texas Press.

Becker, Eve-Marie. 2017. "Konzepte von Raum in frühchristlichen Geschichtserzählungen: Vom Markinischen Chronotop zur Spatial History des Lukas." In *Der Früheste Evangelist*, WUNT 380, 103–116. Tübingen: Mohr Siebeck. https://doi.org/10.1628/978-3-16-155424-7.

Blum, Erhard. 1990. *Studien zur Komposition des Pentateuch*. BZAW 189. Berlin: De Gruyter. https://doi.org/10.1515/9783110879506.

Blum, Erhard. 2015. "Noch einmal: Das literargeschichtliche Profil der P-Überlieferung." In *Abschied von der Priesterschrift?: Zum Stand der Pentateuchdebatte*, edited by Friedhelm Hartenstein and Konrad Schmid, 32–64. Leipzig: Evangelische Verlagsanstalt.

Boorer, Suzanne. 2016. *The Vision of the Priestly Narrative: Its Genre and Hermeneutics of Time*. Ancient Israel and Its Literature 27. Atlanta: SBL Press. https://doi.org/10.2307/j.ctt1gxxq00.

Breitmaier, Isa. 2010. "Angestaunte Gegenwart. Zur Zeitkonstruktion in Genealogien (Gen 5)." In *Zeit Wahrnehmen*, edited by Hedwig-Jahnow-Forschungsprojekt, 66–99. Stuttgart: KBW-Verlag.

Carr, David M. 2024. *Genesis 1–11*. Internationaler exegetischer Kommentar. Stuttgart: W. Kohlhammer GmbH. https://doi.org/10.17433/978-3-17-040871-5.

Emmendörffer, Michael. 2019. *Gottesnähe: Zur Rede von der Präsenz JHWHs in der Priesterschrift und verwandten Texten*. WMANT 155. Göttingen: Vandenhoeck & Ruprecht. https://doi.org/10.13109/9783788733407.

Faust, Avi. 2019. "The World of P: The Material Realm of Priestly Writings." *VT* 69(2):173–218. https://doi.org/10.1163/15685330-12341352.

Fischer, Irmtraud. 2000. "Die Ausnahme von der Regel. Israels weibliche Generationenfolge." *Schlangenbrut* 70:18–21. https://doi.org/10.15496/publikation-52910.

Frevel, Christian. 2000. *Mit Blick auf das Land die Schöpfung erinnern: Zum Ende der Priestergrundschrift*. HBS 23. Freiburg i. Br.: Herder.

Fritz, Volkmar. 1987. "Das Geschichtsverständnis der Priesterschrift." *ZThK* 84:426–439.

Gertz, Jan-Christian. 2018. *Das erste Buch Mose, Genesis: die Urgeschichte Gen 1–11, translated and explained by Jan-Christian Gertz*. Vol. 1, *Das Alte Testament deutsch: Neues Göttinger Bibelwerk, Neubearbeitungen*. Göttingen: Vandenhoeck & Ruprecht. https://doi.org/10.13109/9783666570551.

Gertz, Jan-Christian. 2015. "Genesis 5. Priesterliche Redaktion, Komposition oder Quellenschrift?" In *Abschied von der Priesterschrift?: Zum Stand der Pentateuchdebatte*, edited by Friedhelm Hartenstein and Konrad Schmid, 65–93. Leipzig: Evangelische Verlagsanstalt.

Grund(-Wittenberg), Alexandra. 2011. *Die Entstehung des Sabbats: Seine Bedeutung für Israels Zeitkonzept und Erinnerungskultur*. FAT 75. Tübingen: Mohr Siebeck. https://doi.org/10.1628/978-3-16-157808-3.

Grund(-Wittenberg), Alexandra. 2016. "Geschichte und Kult: Die Einsetzung des Heiligtums in der priesterlichen Geschichtserzählung." In *Geschichte und Gott: XV. Europäischer Kongress für Theologie (14.–18. September 2014 in Berlin)*, VGWTh 44, edited by Michael Meyer-Blanck, 302–21. Leipzig: Evangelische Verlagsanstalt.

Grund(-Wittenberg), Alexandra. 2023. "'Ich werde in Israels Mitte Wohnung nehmen' (Ex 29,45). JHWHs Gegenwart in Israel und der Gottesdienst coram Deo." In *Präsenz als Schlüsselthema Praktischer Theologie: Festschrift für Thomas Kabel*, edited by Simone Ziermann and Konrad Müller, 165–177. Leipzig: Evangelische Verlagsanstalt. https://doi.org/10.5771/9783374073993.

Hartenstein, Friedhelm. 1997. *Die Unzugänglichkeit Gottes im Heiligtum. Jesaja 6 und der Wohnort JHWHs in der Jerusalemer Kulttradition.* WMANT 75. Neukirchen-Vluyn: Neukirchener Verlag.

Hartenstein, Friedhelm, and Konrad Schmid, eds. 2015. *Abschied von der Priesterschrift?: Zum Stand der Pentateuchdebatte.* VWGTh 40. Leipzig: Evangelische Verlagsanstalt.

Hieke, Thomas. 2003. *Die Genealogien der Genesis*. Herders Biblische Studien 39. Freiburg i. Br.: Herder.

Hieke, Thomas. 2014. "Die Völkertafel von Genesis 10 als genealogische Raumordnung: Form, Funktion, Geographie." In *Genealogie und Migrationsmythen im antiken Mittelmeerraum und auf der arabischen Halbinsel*. Berlin studies of the ancient world 29, edited by Almut-Barbara Renger and Isabel Toral-Niehoff, 23–40. Berlin: Edition Topoi. https://doi.org/10.17171/3-29-2.

Holzinger, Heinrich. 1893. *Einleitung in den Hexateuch*. Freiburg i. Br.: Mohr.

Hutzli, Jürg. 2023. *The Origins of P: Literary Profiles and Strata of the Priestly Texts in Genesis 1.* FAT 164. Tübingen: Mohr Siebeck. https://doi.org/10.1628/978-3-16-161641-9.

Jacob, Benno. 1934. *Das erste Buch der Tora. Genesis*. Berlin: Calwer.

Janowski, Bernd. 1993. "Tempel und Schöpfung. Schöpfungstheologische Aspekte der priesterschriftlichen Heiligtumskonzeption." In *Gottes Gegenwart in Israel*, Beiträge zur Theologie des Alten Testaments 1, edited by Bernd Janowski, 214–245. Neukirchen-Vluyn: Neukirchener Verlag.

Janowski, Bernd. 2003. *Der Gott des Lebens*. Beiträge zur Theologie des Alten Testaments 3. Göttingen: Vandenhoeck & Ruprecht.

Janowski, Bernd. 2004. "Die lebendige Statue Gottes. Zur Anthropologie der priesterlichen Urgeschichte." In *Gott und Mensch im Dialog: Festschrift für Otto Kaiser zum 80. Geburtstag*, vol. 1, BZAW 345, edited by Markus Witte, 183–214. Berlin: De Gruyter. https://doi.org/10.1515/9783110910001.181.

Jenson, Philip Peter. 1992. *Graded Holiness: A Key to the Priestly Conception of the World*. Journal for the Study of the Old Testament. Supplement Series 106. Sheffield: JSOT Press.

Knohl, Israel. 2007. *The Sanctuary of Silence: The Priestly Torah and the Holiness School*. Winona Lake: Eisenbrauns.

Köckert, Matthias. 1995. "Das Land in der priesterlichen Komposition des Pentateuch." In *Von Gott Reden. Beiträge zur Theologie und Exegese des Alten Testaments. Festschrift für Siegfried Wagner zum 65. Geburtstag*, edited by Dieter Vieweger and Ernst Joachim Waschke, 147–162. Neukirchen-Vluyn: Neukirchener Verlag.

Lohfink, Norbert. 1988. "Die Priesterschrift und die Geschichte." In *Studien zum Pentateuch.* SBAB 4, edited by Norbert Lohfink, 213–253. Stuttgart: Katholisches Bibelwerk. (Originally published in: Zimmerli, Walther, ed. 1978. Congress Volume Göttingen 1977, 189–225. Leiden: Brill. https://doi.org/10.1163/9789004275522_012).

Lohfink, Norbert. 1977. *Unsere großen Wörter. Das Alte Testament zu Themen dieser Jahre*. Freiburg: Herder.

Lux, Rüdiger. 1995. "Die Genealogie als Strukturprinzip des Pluralismus im Alten Testament." In *Pluralismus und Identität*, VWGTh 8, edited by Joachim Mehlhausen, 242–258. Gütersloh: Kaiser / Gütersloher Verlagshaus.

Maier, Felix. 2016. "Chronotopos. Erzählung, Zeit und Raum im Hellenismus." *Klio* 98(2):465–494. https://doi.org/10.1515/klio-2016-0040.

Milgrom, Jacob. 1991–2001. *Leviticus*. Vols. 1–3. The Anchor Bible 3. New York: Doubleday.

Neumann-Gorsolke, Ute. 2004. *Herrschen in den Grenzen der Schöpfung: Ein Beitrag zur alttestamentlichen Anthropologie am Beispiel von Psalm 8, Genesis 1 und verwandten Texten*. Neukirchen-Vluyn: Neukirchener Verlag.

Nihan, Christophe. 2007. *From Priestly Torah to Pentateuch: A Study in the Composition of the Book of Leviticus*. FAT II 25. Tübingen: Mohr Siebeck. https://doi.org/10.1628/978-3-16-151123-3.

Nöldeke, Theodor. 1869. "Die sog. Grundschrift des Pentateuchs." In *Untersuchungen zur Kritik des Alten Testaments*, edited by Theodor Nöldeke, 1–144. Kiel: Schwers.

Noort, Edward. 2008. "Bis zur Grenze des Landes? Num 27,12–23 und das Ende der Priesterschrift." In *The Books of Leviticus and Numbers*, EThL 215, edited by Thomas Römer, 99–119. Leuven: Leuven University Press.

Owczarek, Susanne. 1998. *Die Vorstellungen vom Wohnen Gottes inmitten seines Volkes in der Priesterschrift. Zur Heiligtumstheologie der Priestergrundschrift*. EHS.T 625. Frankfurt (Main): Lang.

Rhyder, Julia. 2019. *Centralizing the Cult: The Holiness Legislation in Leviticus 17–26*. FAT 134. Tübingen: Mohr Siebeck. https://doi.org/10.1628/978-3-16-157686-7.

Röhrig, Meike. 2023. "Das mehrfache Ende der Priesterschrift." *ZAW* 135:384–401. https://doi.org/10.1515/zaw-2023-3005.

Schaper, Joachim. 2019. *Media and Monotheism: Presence, Representation, and Abstraction in Ancient Judah*. Orientalische Religionen in der Antike 33. Tübingen: Mohr Siebeck. https://doi.org/10.1628/978-3-16-157511-2.

Schellenberg, Annette. 2011. *Der Mensch, das Bild Gottes? Zum Gedanken einer Sonderstellung des Menschen im Alten Testament und in weiteren altorientalischen Quellen*. Zürich: Theologischer Verlag Zürich.

Schmid, Konrad. 2011. "Judean Identity and Ecumenicity: The Political Theology of the Priestly Document." In *Judah and Judeans in the Achaemenid Period: Negotiating Identity in an International Context*, edited by Oded Lipschits, Gary Knoppers, and Manfred Oeming, 3–26. Winona Lake: Eisenbrauns. https://doi.org/10.1515/9781575066493-003.

Schmid, Konrad. 2018. "Die Priesterschrift als antike Historiographie: Quellen und Darstellungsweise der politischen und religiösen Geschichte der Levante in den priesterschriftlichen Erzelternerzählungen." In *The Politics of the Ancestor: Exegetical and Historical Perspectives on Genesis 12–36*, edited by Mark Brett and Jakob Wöhrle, 93–111. Tübingen: Mohr Siebeck. https://doi.org/10.5167/uzh-158459.

Schmitt, Hans-Christoph. 2014. "Die Jahwenamenoffenbarung in Ex 6,2–9 und die zwei Zeiten der Landgabe. Zum Ende der Priesterschrift und zu ihrem Zeitverständnis." In *Nichts Neues unter der Sonne? Zeitvorstellungen im Alten Testament. Festschrift für Ernst-Joachim Waschke zum 65. Geburtstag*, BZAW 450, edited by Jens Kotjatko-Reeb, Stefan Schorch, Johannes Thon, and Benjamin Ziemer, 137–155. Berlin: De Gruyter. https://doi.org/10.1515/9783110724448-009.

Schüle, Andreas. 2020. *Die Urgeschichte (Gen 1–11)*. Zürich: Theologischer Verlag Zürich.

Shectman, Sarah, and Joel S. Baden, eds. 2009. *The Strata of the Priestly Writings: Contemporary Debate and Future Directions*. AThANT 95. Zürich: Theologischer Verlag Zürich.

Ska, Jean-Louis. 2008. "Le récit sacerdotal: Une «histoire sans fin»?" In *The Books of Leviticus and Numbers*, EThL 215, edited by Thomas Römer, 631–653. Leuven: Leuven University Press.

Steinby, Liisa. 2013. "Bakhtin's Concept of the Chronotope: The Viewpoint of an Acting Subject." In *Bakhtin and His Others: (Inter)Subjectivity, Chronotope, Dialogism*, edited by Liisa Steinby and Tintti Klapuri, 105–126. London: Anthem Press. https://doi.org/10.7135/9780857283108.009.

Struppe, Ursula. 1988. *Die Herrlichkeit Jahwes in der Priesterschrift: Eine semantische Studie zu kəbôd YHWH*. ÖBS 9. Klosterneuburg: Österreichisches Katholisches Bibelwerk.

Wagner, Thomas. 2012. *Gottes Herrlichkeit: Bedeutung und Verwendung des Begriffs kābôd im Alten Testament.* VT.S 151. Leiden: Brill.

Wagner, Thomas. 2023. *Raumdeutung: Transformationen der Vorstellung vom Raum in den hebräischen Schriften der persischen Zeit.* Mundus Orientis 4. Göttingen: Vandenhoeck & Ruprecht.

Weimar, Peter. 2010. "Priesterschrift." *Das wissenschaftliche Bibellexikon im Internet.* https://bibelwissenschaft.de/stichwort/31252. March 7, 2025.

Westermann, Claus. 1974. Genesis 1-11 BK I/1. Neukirchen-Vluyn: Neukirchener Verlag.

Witte, Markus. 2011. "Völkertafel." *Das Wissenschaftliche Bibellexikon im Internet.* https://bibelwissenschaft.de/stichwort/34251. March 7, 2025.

Wöhrle, Jakob. 2012. *Fremdlinge im eigenen Land: Zur Entstehung und Intention der priesterlichen Passagen der Vätergeschichte.* FRLANT 246. Göttingen: Vandenhoeck & Ruprecht.

Zenger, Erich, and Christian Frevel, ed. 2015. *Einleitung in das Alte Testament.* Kohlhammer-Studienbücher Theologie 1.1. 9th. ed. Stuttgart: Kohlhammer. https://doi.org/10.17433/978-3-17-030352-2.

Ziemer, Benjamin. 2009. "Erklärung der Zahlen von Gen 5 aus ihrem kompositionellen Zusammenhang." *ZAW* 121:1–18.

Lucas Brum Teixeira and Barbara Schmitz

Chronotopoi and the Making of a Calendar in the Book of Judith

How References to Time and Space Can Reshape the Meaning of an Ancient Jewish Story

Abstract: The Book of Judith tells the story of the victory of the Israelites over the foreign "Assyrian" general and confidant of King Nebuchadnezzar / Nabouchodonosor, Holofernes, at the hands of the beautiful widow Judith. The account of this victory is told in a deeply coded narrative with multiple references to time and space. Using key categories from Mikhail Bakhtin's seminal essay "Forms of Time and the Chronotope in the Novel", particularly his idea of the "chronotope", we locate the coexistence of two chronotopes in Judith. Analyzing these chronotopes in their two-sided dimension of production and reception, we revisit the suggestions of Jan van Goudoever and Pierre-Maurice Bogaert regarding a Judith linked to Hanukkah through its calendar. At least since the early Middle Ages, Judith, rediscovered and intensively reworked, has been linked to the Maccabees and, through them, to the feast of Hanukkah. The fusion of the two chronotopes of Judith in the act of reading seems to have played a fundamental role in this connection.

The Book of Judith tells the story of the threat posed by the unleashed power of the "Assyrian" king, Nabouchodonosor ("Nebuchadnezzar"), who wants to conquer the whole world and be worshiped as a god. The king's blatant desire for power is expressed in his speech in Jdt 2, which leads to extensive conquests and the submission of many peoples (Jdt 1–3). Beginning in Chapter 4, the perspective shifts from global to Israel, and the following chapters tell the story of the imperial threat posed by the Assyrian leader Holofernes and his army from Israel's point of view. Israel is said to have just returned from exile and rededicated the temple in Jerusalem (Jdt 4). The reader witnesses the interrogation of the military leaders of Israel's neighboring nations (Jdt 5–6), the siege of the city of Bethulia, and the starvation of its people (Jdt 7). At this point, Judith enters the story, delivers a pivotal speech, prays to God (Jdt 8–9), and leaves for the Assyrian camp (Jdt 10). The plan Judith devised is successfully implemented, and the killing of Holofernes brings about the salvation of Israel and the whole world (Jdt 11–14). The Assyrian troops are driven out, and a great celebration is held for the salvation and the deliverance of Israel (Jdt 15–16). The Book of Judith, which was probably written in Greek around 100

 | https://doi.org/10.1515/9783112240366-003

BC, thus tells an exciting and gripping story that, like a blockbuster, depicts the dramatic events and actions of the protagonists in space and time in a broad and opulent manner.

In this paper, we revisit the references to time and space in Judith, using Bakhtin's idea of chronotope (and therefore from a "chronotopic" perspective). In the book of Judith, as we see it, two chronotopes are woven through its various references to time and space. After showing the process of their making, these chronotopes are considered in terms of production and reception and in their merging in the act of reading. Through this analysis, we wish to reconsider the suggestion of earlier commentators that a yearly calendar is constructed in the background as the story of Judith unfolds and how this dimension of the text reshapes the meaning of the book of Judith on the reception side. We begin our discussion with a summary of developments in recent narrative theory regarding time and space and Michael Bakhtin's original contribution to them (Part 1). We then consider Bakhtin's central concept of the chronotope in relation to Judith (Part 2). Based on these considerations, we then present the creation of the two chronotopes identifiable in Judith (Part 3) and finally discuss how the merging of Judith's chronotopes in the act of reading opens a window for the reader to invent new and creative meanings for the Judith story.

1 Time and Space in Narrative Theory

In narrative theory, space and time are the fundamental narrative categories through which the "text world" or the "story world" is established. The "storyworld" can be defined as "the world evoked implicitly as well as explicitly by a narrative. [...] Storyworlds are global representations enabling interpreters to frame inferences about the situations, characters, and occurrences either explicitly mentioned or implied by a narrative text or discourse (Herman 2009, 106)."[1] Space and time therefore provide the framework within which characters act and the plot unfolds. Early narrative theory and method described space and time as central parameters of narrative texts. In this respect, it is not surprising that space and time have had different "careers" in narratological theory-building: while the category of time was considered important early on, and a very differentiated methodology and tools were developed for it, the category of space only later moved to the center of narrative theory-building.

1 For storyworld, see Herman 2009, 105–136; Herman 2004, 9–24.

With regard to time, the difference between *fabula* and *sujet* in Russian formalism and between *histoire* and *discourse* in French structuralism was addressed by Gérard Genette in his seminal study *Figures I–III* (Genette 1966–1972, passim), representing a pivotal moment in the development of narratological theory. Genette developed a precise terminology and an elaborate system for narratological analysis,[2] with a particular emphasis on the analysis of time. As a result of his influence on all subsequent narratological studies, space was neglected as a "stepchild" in narratological theory for a notably long time (de Jong 2014, 129; Herman 2009, 131; Dennerlein 2009, 3–5; Nünning 2009, 33–52). In the field of literary theory, Jurij Lotman is credited with being one of the first scholars to introduce the concept of space, spatial oppositions, and their liminal areas as a significant area of inquiry for narrative texts (cf. Lotman 1977, passim). In recent decades, following the spatial turn, narratological theory has increasingly focused on the role of space in narrative texts, leading to the development of new theoretical approaches, including the theory of possible worlds, deictic shift theory, and others (Zoran 1984, 309–335; Ronen 1986, 421–438; Bal 1997, passim; Ryan 1991, passim; Herman 2004, passim; Döring and Thielemann 2008, 7–45). However, despite this shift in focus, narratology has not yet established a widely accepted terminology or a systematic view of space in comparison to the analytic tools for time.

Since time and space are the basic categories for establishing textual worlds, it makes sense to consider time and space separately, on the one hand, because some narratives tend to be more space-oriented and others more time-oriented, and this can set different accents in the course of the story; on the other hand, however, space and time belong together as two basic categories and cannot be separated from each other. The insight that actions cannot be separated from their setting in time and space was introduced by Mikhail Bakhtin in his essay "Forms of Time and of the Chronotope in the Novel" published in 1937/1938 (Bakhtin 1981, 84–258).[3] In his essay, Bakhtin reflected not only conceptually but also theoretically on the relationship between space and time (Riffaterre 1996, 244–256; Scholz 2003, 145–172).

His point is that time and space are fundamentally related: Time and space are "the intrinsic connectedness of temporal and spatial relationships that are artistically expressed in literature. [. . .] What counts for us is the fact that it expresses the inseparability of space and time (Bakhtin 1981, 84)." The peculiarity of the concept of "chronotope" is the intersection of χρόνος ("time") and τόπος ("space"). Bakhtin assumes that all determinations of time and space are inseparable. Moreover,

2 Genette distinguishes between *ordre*, *durée*, and *fréquence* on the one hand and between narration (*qui parle?*) and focalization (*qui voit?*) on the other hand.

3 With "Concluding Remarks", written in 1973.

according to him, the interconnection of time and space is represented in narrative events through processes of “thickening” or “materialising”: “In the literary artistic chronotope, spatial and temporal indicators are fused into one carefully thought-out, concrete whole. Time, as it were, thickens, takes on flesh, becomes artistically visible; likewise, space becomes charged and responsive to the movements of time, plot and history. This intersection of axes and fusion of indicators characterizes the artistic chronotope (Bakhtin 1981, 84).” Bakhtin himself applied his considerations, which John Pier describes as “a multifaceted concept that escapes sharp definition” (Pier 2005, 64), primarily to questions of genre and their classification, as Bakhtin thinks that specific chronotopes correspond to particular genres.

In his “Concluding Remarks”, however, an addition to his essay forty years later (1973), Bakhtin discusses the chronotope on a more theoretical level. In these remarks, he reflects on various issues, two of which have been notably valuable for our analysis of Judith. The first is that there can be not only one chronotope in the storyworld but that each chronotope can contain an unlimited number of minor chronotopes. In Bakhtin’s words, “We have been speaking so far only of the major chronotopes, those that are most fundamental and wide-ranging. But each such chronotope can include within it an unlimited number of minor chronotopes (Bakhtin 1981, 252).” This idea is central to Bakhtin’s theory because space and time and their interrelationship do not span one storyworld; rather, one storyworld can contain different chronotopes. These different chronotopes may overlap or coexist in the text. The second is that the multiplication of chronotope(s) in a storyworld as a phenomenon of the text itself constitutes only one dimension of the concept, i.e., that of its production. According to Bakhtin, yet another dimension of the text is chronotopic, i.e., the reception side: the reception of a text takes place in chronotope(s) as the world of the author and the world of readers are structured chronotopically. “We find the author outside the work as a human being living his own biographical life. But we also meet him as the creator of the work itself, although he is located outside the chronotopes represented in his work, he is as it were tangential to them (Bakhtin 1981, 254).”

Therefore, Bakhtin reflects on the different chronotopes as a dialogical process between text, author, and reader and thereby develops a polyphonic concept of chronotopes in terms of the production and reception of texts (Bakhtin 1981, 252–254). Central to Bakhtin’s work is the idea that the interweaving of time and space is not only a phenomenon of the text but must be considered in terms of production and reception. Space and time are interrelated categories that are formed by the producer and recognized and renewed by the reader in the process of reading. This exchange between author and reader is itself chronotopic, as it unfolds in time and space: at a particular time, in a particular world, in a particular place, and in response to particular situations. For Bakhtin, the chronotopic organization of a narrative bridges the gap between production and reception. Thus, the chronotopic framework established by the author of the narrative world extends into the world of the reader, through which a merging of the horizons of the author, the text, and the reader takes place. For our study, these elements of Bakhtin's theory have proven particularly productive, as the reader will begin to see more concretely as we now apply them to Judith.

2 The Chronotope in the Book of Judith

The Book of Judith has a very specific chronotope as it narrates an amalgamation of historical epochs, events, and persons. The first verse of the book is emblematic in this regard: "It was the twelfth year of Nabouchodonosor, who reigned over the Assyrians in the great city of Nineveh. In those days, Arphaxad was reigning over the Medes in Ecbatana" (Jdt 1:1).[4] Nabouchodonosor, the Greek name for the Babylonian king Nebuchadnezzar, is presented as the Assyrian king residing in Nineveh fighting against the Median King Arphaxad. From its very first sentence, therefore, the narrative develops through a blending of time and space. This narrative strategy is continued throughout the story, for example, when the Assyrian-Babylonian-Persian king Nabouchodonosor conquers the whole world to the same extent as Alexander the Great. Nabouchodonosor wants to be worshipped as a god, a characteristic of the Hellenistic ruler cult. Thereby, the Nabouchodonosor of the Book of Judith is portrayed as an Assyrian-Babylonian-Persian-Hellenistic king.

In this Assyrian-Babylonian-Persian-Hellenistic setting, Israel is presented as having just returned from exile, which clearly refers to the Babylonian exile in the 6th century BC. At the same time, Israel is presented as having just rededicated the temple in Jerusalem (Jdt 4:3), which clearly refers to the events of the Maccabean revolt and the rededication of the temple and the Hanukkah festival in the 2nd century BC (1Macc 4:36–61; 2Macc 10:1–9) (Schmitz and Engel 2014, 140–142). This merging of different times into one story is also true in terms of space. In the book of Judith, there are about 90 names for various cities, regions, villages, etc., including well-known cities such as Nineveh, Damascus, Jerusalem, and Scythopolis, but one-third of the names cannot be associated with any known place. It is very likely that they are indeed fictitious (Schmitz and Engel 2014, 56–59). One of these fictitious cities is Bethulia, the city where Judith comes from. In terms of space, therefore, we have a blending of well-known and fictitious locations.[5]

4 See in this regard the interesting contribution of Martina Korytiaková 2023a, 85–98.

5 The geography of the book Judith has been studied by Friedrich Stummer (Stummer 1947, passim) , the construction of space by Barbara Schmitz (Schmitz 2021, 290–307) and Martina Korytiaková (Korytiaková 2023b, 151–186; 2024a, 37–58; 2024b, passim).

The specific chronotope, which the Book of Judith enrolls, constructs a storyworld that has never existed in this way. Erich Zenger calls the Book of Judith a “Geschichtskonstrukt” (Zenger 1981, 434), Deborah Gera speaks of “the overall fictionality of the book (Gera 2014, 177)”, Schmitz and Engel refer to the “ausdrücklich fiktionale[n] Charakter der Erzählung (Schmitz and Engel 2014, 50–51)”, and Jennifer Koosed and Paul Seesengood even speak of “a general soup of Jewish conquest and survival narrative (Koosed and Seesengood 2022, xliv)”. In other words, the narrative does not want to locate its story in a specific historical framework that could be assigned to a specific time. In this respect, the Judith narrative differs significantly from the Book of Ruth, for example. As a narrative that presumably originated in Persian times, the Book of Ruth places itself clearly in the time of the Judges (Ruth 1:1) and tells its story as if it took place at that time. The Book of Judith, on the contrary, by avoiding any connection to a specific time and space, tells the story in an imaginary chronotope, a collage, a time-space that spans epochs and spaces.

3 Chronotopoi and the Building of a Calendar in Judith: The Production Side

When we consider Judith in terms of chronotope, we realize that at least two different chronotopes are discernible in the book: the first is linked to years on the temporal axis and to the temple of Jerusalem on the spatial axis; the second is linked to monthly or agricultural dates on the temporal axis and to festivals that are both spatial and temporal in character.

Concerning the first chronotope: Judith begins with “the twelfth year of the reign of Nebuchadnezzar”, which corresponds historically to the year 593 BC (Schmitz and Engel 2014, 79–82; Candido 2020, 58–61).

This is a blurry and ironic blend of references, especially in connection with the king’s name. At first glance, this time reference may not seem relevant, given the articulation of the verse and our ignorance of any significant event that took place in that particular year of the paradigmatic Babylonian king. However, when read in connection with the next temporal reference (Jdt 1:13), this year acquires an interesting meaning. In Jdt 1:13, we read that only in the seventeenth year of his reign (that is, 588 BC), after a five-year rally gathering allies, Nebuchadnezzar is able to win over Arphaxad of Media. Regarding the number five that results from this initial calculation, one may ask whether it could not indicate an intentional time-play on the production side (i.e. the author’s). In Judith, the number five is mentioned only a second time in connection with crucial temporal information in the story: the five days that the population presses the city elders, after which they would surrender to the Assyrians. More significantly, on the night of the fourth of those five days, Judith alone will defeat Nebuchadnezzar's general, Holofernes, and consequently his army. Five years are needed by the powerful "Nabouchodonosor" to defeat Arphaxad with a large army; in less than five days, the Assyrians are shamefully defeated through the hand of Judith.

Jdt 2:1 then gives a precise date: the twenty-second of the first month of the eighteenth year. This complete calendar information is given as the beginning of Nebuchadnezzar's military campaign against all the peoples of the West who had refused to join him against Arphaxad despite his authoritative appeal (Jdt 1:6–12). This eighteenth year corresponds historically to 587 BC, the well-known year of the destruction of the temple in Jerusalem and the exile of the Judeans. Although implicit, the link with the Babylonian exile, and in particular the destruction of the temple, is strategically emphasized from this point onwards. Through this articulation of time and space, a first chronotope in Judith is composed. The First Temple and its historical destruction are the barycenter, which is why we will refer to it hereafter on as the "threat to the temple in Jerusalem". This motif is, in fact, taken up several times throughout the narrative, beginning with the next sequence. Indeed, as the Assyrian army advances westwards, the narrator immediately highlights that the Assyrian army is destroying all the national shrines with their gods so that all the nations worship Nebuchadnezzar alone, calling him a god in their own tongues and dialects (Jdt 3:8). This is the second time that the theme of the Hellenistic cult of rulers is evoked in the text. From this, the reader realizes that Holofernes' military campaign in Judith has more than a purely political dimension; it has a clearly ideological-religious one. The theme of the imposition of foreign worship by a foreign king is, in fact, a key idea in the book of Judith.

In Jdt 4, then, the chronotope "threat to the temple in Jerusalem" is continued by pointing out that the "Israelites living in Judea" (4:1), hearing of the Assyrians' plundering and destruction of the national shrines, were "greatly terrified and alarmed for Jerusalem and the temple of the Lord their God" (4:2), for they had just returned from exile (a clearly ironic anachronism) and had rededicated the sacred vessels, the altar, and the temple after their desecration (4:3). It is worth noting that the sole information that the Israelites received regarding the Assyrian campaign at this point regards the temple. Moreover, in the last sentence, all the terms appear carefully chosen, especially those of "rededication" and "profanation." These terms allude not only to the Babylonian destruction of the temple in Jerusalem but also, by explicitly mentioning the altar, to their profanation by Antiochus IV Epiphanes and rededication after the Maccabean resistance (Schmitz and Engel 2014, 138–142). The diction of Jdt 4:3 thus creates a fusion of the two main events concerning the temple and its altar, the destruction of the temple by the Babylonians in 587 BC (Jdt 2:1), and its rededication in Persian times; the desecration by the Seleucids and the rededication by the Maccabees in 164 BC (Jdt 4:3) are evoked in it. This central idea of Judith's first chronotope continues especially in Judith's speeches in Chapters 8 and 9, which emphasize that the main purpose of Judith's "awesome act" is to defend the temple in Jerusalem and its altar from desecration and defilement (see Jdt 8:21,24; 9:8,13; 16:20).

Parallel to this chronotope, a second one is woven. This chronotope is created by explicit and implicit references to months and festivals as the story unfolds. This chronotope has its central concept in the deliverance of Israel from a foreign threat, and that is how we will refer to it. The novelty of this chronotope is that through its references to months and festivals, a peculiar calendar in filigree is composed in the book. Due to the coexistence of different calendars during the Second Temple period, it is difficult to give absolute dates, although some eventually appear in the narrative. Nevertheless, Judith's calendar can be reconstructed with remarkable accuracy.

Its starting point is the exact date of Jdt 2:1: the twenty-second day of the first month. According to the Jewish calendar, this would be the 22nd of Nisan. We are in the eighteenth year of Nebuchadnezzar's reign — or 587 BC. With respect to this date, the first observation regards the event recounted at the end of Jdt 1 (Nebuchadnezzar's 120-day feast of victory over Arphaxad, indeed, a typical Hellenistic motif). Counting backward, this victory feast would have begun, according to the Jewish calendar, on the 22nd of Kislev in the previous year (i.e. 588 BC). Up to now, the key elements to keep in mind are the ideas of "victory feast" and the month, the ninth in the Jewish calendar, i.e. Kislev.

Nebuchadnezzar's general in charge of the western campaign, Holofernes, is then said to have arrived in the plains of Damascus during the wheat harvest (Jdt 2:27). Since the offering of the first fruits of the wheat took place in the third month, this information places the story in the month of Sivan, the third on the Jewish calendar. Holofernes and his army remain camped in the plains of Damascus for a whole month to gather supplies (Jdt 3:10). At this point, the reader comes to the beginning of Jdt 4, where the Israelites, though already mentioned in passing in Jdt 1:8–9.12, come to the fore as characters. In the next three chapters, Jdt 4–6, a series of events occur simultaneously both in the Assyrian camp and for the Israelites of Bethulia (with occasional narrative shifts involving Jerusalem). While the Assyrian army rests and gathers supplies, Israel fortifies and secures its cities (Jdt 4). This leads to the scene of Holofernes and Achior in the Assyrian camp (Jdt 5:1–6:9). Holofernes hears that the Israelites of Bethulia are preparing to engage in war against him, becomes angry, and asks the Ammonites and Edomites' commanders about them. Achior, the chief commander of the Ammonites, takes the floor and gives a long reply in the form of a discourse about the history of Israel and the power of their God (Jdt 5:5–21). Because of his answer, Achior is banished to Bethulia and interrogated again (Jdt 6:10–21). This month's stay in Damascus adds still another month to the Judith calendar, moving the story to the fourth month, Tammuz, in the Jewish calendar.

In Jdt 7:1, we hear of a "next day" (ἐπαύριον) which refers to the day after the liberation of Achior in Bethulia, and from the context and flow of the narrative, the reader understands that it is the day after the thirty days just mentioned (see Jdt 3:10). On this day, Holofernes orders his army to break camp and march on Bethulia. A second day then comes (τῇ δὲ ἡμέρᾳ τῇ δευτέρᾳ), in which Holofernes parades his cavalry before the Israelites (Jdt 7:6) and visits their water supplies, seizes them, and sets up guards over them (Jdt 7:7). When he returns to camp, the Edomite and Moabite commanders who have joined his army advise Holofernes to take a special approach to the Israelites: to stay in camp and take possession of the water springs at the foot of the mount where Bethulia lies and thus kill its inhabitants by thirst (Jdt 7:9–15). Holofernes then carries out the plan exactly as the commanders suggested (Jdt 7:16–18). At this point, the focus shifts to Bethulia, where the people begin to suffer from thirst. In 7:20, the reader is proleptically told that the siege of Bethulia lasted 34 days. Two days plus 34 days gives us the second half of the fifth month, which is Av.

Jdt 7:23–31 tells of the gathering of the people of Bethulia around the elders of the city and their demand to surrender to the Assyrians. The elders ask for five more days: if God does not deliver them within these days, they will surrender. At this point, on the 34th day of the siege, Judith enters the story. Judith talks to the elders (Jdt 8), prays to God during the evening sacrifice in the Jerusalem temple (Jdt 9), embellishes herself, and leaves Bethulia towards the Assyrian camp (Jdt 10). Judith's arrival in the Assyrian camp, therefore, takes place on the night of the first of these five difficult days. She remains in the camp for three full days (Jdt 12:7). On the evening of the last day (i.e. the fourth), Holofernes holds a private banquet to seduce Judith and lie with her (Jdt 12:10). It is in this context that Judith kills Holofernes by beheading him (Jdt 13:8–10). The killing of Holofernes, which signifies the victory of the Israelites over the Assyrians, is made to take place, according to the Jewish calendar, somewhere at the end of Av.[6]

It is particularly interesting that, according to Judith's calendar, the deliverance of Israel and the whole world from the Assyrian threat takes place at about the same time that Israel remembers the destruction of the temple in Jerusalem by Nebuchadnezzar. The two chronotopes now line up: Israel and the temple are saved from the Assyrian king Nabouchodonosor by the "Jewess Judith" at about the same time that Jerusalem and the temple are destroyed by the Babylonian king

6 It is worth noting that when Judith enters the stage, she has been a widow for three years and four months. Judith's husband, Manasseh, is said to have died "during the barley harvest" (8:2), which normally took place at the end of Nisan. This temporal reference makes Judith's entrance in the story at the end of Av, the exact time our calculations gave us.

Nebuchadnezzar. The book of Judith thus becomes a counter-story. The calculation then continues with the narrator referring to the people in Jerusalem celebrating their deliverance at the hand of Judith for three months, ninety days (Jdt 16:20). These later ninety days bring the story up to the month of Kislev. Thus, the Israelite feast ends exactly when Nebuchadnezzar's feast in Jdt 1 began. This means that the underlying calendar in the Book of Judith, which surfaces in the second chronotope, is made to run from Kislev to Kislev.

4 Chronotopoi and the Building of a Liturgical Calendar in Judith? The Reception Side

As we have just shown, the attentive reader can decipher an underlying calendar created by the second chronotope of Judith that does not run from the first month, i.e. Nisan, to Nisan, but curiously from the ninth month to the ninth month, i.e. from Kislev to Kislev. In the course of its reception history, this peculiarity has become a window through which later readers have peered and invented even sharper meanings in Judith. In this final part, we will therefore take a brief look at the argument for Judith's calendar from the reception side.

From at least the early Middle Ages, Judith was rediscovered in Jewish circles and her story was repeatedly translated into Hebrew in long and short forms (we now count at least four complete forms of the story in Hebrew, plus 13 midrashim and several piyyutim).[7] In this context it seems particularly significant that at least two of the long Hebrew versions are based on the Vulgate of Judith, a unique version of Judith. As we shall see, a unique Latin reading received in the medieval Hebrew texts becomes a central motif that even reshapes the way in which Jews in some circles still celebrate Hanukkah. From at least the early Middle Ages, Judith became associated with Hanukkah.

In recent times, Jan Van Goudoever (1959) was apparently the first scholar to propose a reconstruction of the Judith calendar, suggesting that Judith's main storyline does not merely end in Kislev but "may have ended with the Hanukkah festival, which came into existence in Maccabean times (Van Goudoever 1959, 91)." Van Goudoever's prudent suggestion is then embraced by Pierre-Maurice Bogaert (1984), who affirmed that "on peut être plus catégorique que ne l'est Van Goudoever (Bogaert 1984, 67)." Realizing the beginning of the one hundred twenty days

7 See, in this regard, Gera 2010, 23–39. A list of the main Medieval Hebrew Judith texts so far identified, with their sources and fundamental literature, is found on pages 37–39.

count to fall exactly on the 22nd of Kislev (according to him, an approximate date of the feast of the Dedication), Bogaert categorically sustains: “On ne peut mettre en doute que l’auteur ait voulu distribuer les événements sur douze mois, de Hanukka à Hanukka” (Bogaert 1984, 72). Bogaert goes even further to propose that Judith’s author has indeed inscribed the feast of Hanukkah “comme en filigrane”[8] and concludes that the link between Judith and Hanukkah is at least as old as the book itself. But is this so? And if so, why did Judith’s author not explicitly link his story with the feast of Dedication, as Esther’s did with the festival of Purim?

In a subsequent study four years later (1988), Bogaert brought into the discussion of Judith’s calendar some interesting extra-biblical information. Relying on the so-called “Scroll of Fasting” (*Megillat Ta’anit*), an Aramaic text from between the second BC and the first AD,[9] we find the mention of a festival, no longer celebrated in modern Judaism, for the 24th of the fifth month, i.e. Av. Of this festival, the document says, “On the 24th [*NDR: of Av*] we returned to our law” (בעשרים וארבעה ביה תבנא לדיננא), which is interpreted as referring to a celebration of regained independence. Van Goudoever pointed out that the author’s mention of Judith’s various fasting right at the beginning of her presentation (see Jdt 8:6) could be evocative of one of the fast days still kept in Judaism in the month of Av in remembrance of the fall of Jerusalem (See Van Goudoever 1959, 89). Bogaert sees the mention of the festivals during which fasting was not permitted in Jdt 8:6, information which is not found in the Torah but mentioned in the *Megillat Ta’anit*, as its main link with the *Ta’anit* (Bogaert 1988, 165). From this he goes on to suggest that Judith could have originally been a festive scroll for the celebration of that late but no longer celebrated Independence Festival of 24th Av and indirectly of Hanukkah at the end of the Memorial in Jerusalem (Bogaert 1988, 169–170). The *Megillat Ta’anit* knows of the feast of Hanukkah (it has a section dedicated to it).

Regarding this argument, the unique addition to the Vulgate of Judith could also be mentioned. At the very end of the Vulgate version of the story, in fact, a narrative statement is found saying that the celebration of Judith’s victory was added to the Jewish holy days (Jdt 16:31).[10] The author of this gloss, whether Jerome or someone else (some commentators consider it a late addition and not from Jerome

8 “Il es donc raisonnable de penser que l’auteur du livre de Judith a inscrit la fête de Hanukka comme en filigrane, en vue d’une lecture à cette occasion.” See Bogaert 1984, 69.

9 See Schmitz and Engel 2014, 56. Regarding this work, it should also be mentioned that a seventh-century CE commentary exists.

10 *Dies autem victoriae huius festivitatem ab Hebraeis in numero dierum sanctorum accepit et colitur a Iudaeis ex illo tempore usque in praesentem diem* (“But the day of the festivity of this victory is received by the Hebrews in the number of holy days, and is religiously observed by the Jews from that time until this day”).

or his source), clearly speaks of a festival celebrating "this victory" (*victoriae huius*), expression already found in the Vulgate reading of Jdt 16:24.[11] It is clear from the context that "this victory" refers to that of the Israelites over the Assyrians in general, although for several commentators it is linked to Judith. In any case, it remains clear that in both the *Megillat Ta'anit* and the Vulgate, nothing is explicitly stated regarding the rededication of the temple and its altar. Realizing these difficulties, Bogaert, in his second study, adds nuance to his proposal stating that, "La Dédicace est inscrite en filigrane du livre de Judith, mais elle ne constitue pas l'événement majeur du livre" (Bogaert 1988, 167).

The fact that the liberation of Bethulia takes place in the emblematic month of Av, according to the implicit calendar of Judith, seems to us convincing. The same applies to the arguments put forward by both Van Goudoever and Bogaert concerning the "megillah-festive" character of the Book of Judith, even though, unlike the Scroll of Esther, Judith is not explicitly linked to any specific feast. However, when one "catapults" the argument to the Middle Ages, a time when deuterocanonical texts are rediscovered and reworked anew, Judith, notably reworked, is explicitly linked to Hanukkah. Moreover, the Vulgate of Judith seems to have been the *Vorlage* of at least two of the Medieval Hebrew versions of the story. Through it, a new food custom during the celebration of Hanukkah, which stands in several Jewish circles to this day, is introduced.[12] Not surprisingly, engravings of Judith with the head of Holofernes decorating the *hanukkioth*, the nine-branched candelabra that is the central symbol of Hanukkah, date from at least this time. It remains unclear how early Judith came to be associated with Hanukkah and, more importantly, how Judith came to be associated with this festival.

Andre-Marie Dubarle, the first to thoroughly study the Medieval Hebrew texts of Judith, thinks that this association is late and artificial (Dubarle 1966, I, 109). Having not been included in the Hebrew canon, the heroine disappears from the rabbis' view early in the post-New Testament period. Judith, in fact, is not mentioned either in the Mishnah, the Talmud, or any other rabbinic sources. According to the state of the research, "if the Hanukkah *sheelta*, a homily on Jewish law and ethics, ascribed to Rav Ahai (680–752 CE) is authentic, then the earliest extant Hebrew tale telling of Judith dates back to the eighth century (Gera 2014, 74, fn. 21)." With the *sheelta*, we are already at early Middle Ages. Particularly interesting is Rashi's statement on his commentary on the Babylonian Talmud (*Shabbat 23a*) regarding women lighting candles in Hanukkah: "for they were central in that

---

11 Jdt 16:24 Vg: *erat autem populus iucundus secundum faciem sanctorum et per tres menses gaudium huius victoriae celebratum est cum Iudith* / Greek Jdt 16:20 καὶ ἦν ὁ λαὸς εὐφραινόμενος ἐν Ιερουσαλημ κατὰ πρόσωπον τῶν ἁγίων ἐπὶ μῆνας τρεῖς, καὶ Ιουδιθ μετ᾽ αὐτῶν κατέμεινεν.

12 See in this regard, Gera 2014, 333–334; Weingarten 2010, 45–46. See also Bogaert 1999, 25–40.

miracle." This only makes sense if such a miracle during Hanukkah was performed by a woman. Judith's name, however, is not found in Rashi but in a commentary by his grandson Rashbam or Rabbi Samuel Ben Meir (12th century) on another Talmudic passage (*Megilla 4a*). Rashbam explicitly states in his commentary that "Just as the miracle of Purim came about through Esther, the miracle of Hanukkah came about through Judith" (Gera 2010, 35).

Our earliest securely datable mentions of Judith in connection with Hanukkah, however, are found on three piyyutim or liturgical poems from the eleventh century that were recited in the Synagogue during this feast: *Odekha ki anafta bi* by Joseph ben Salomon of Provence; *Eyn Moshia wegoel* by Menachem ben Machir of Ratisbon; and *Ahohem shemony* by Rabbi Isaac ben Samuel. These piyyutim are important for attesting to the early date of the Judith midrashim that they relate to (which are transmitted only in later MSS) and, therefore, to Judith's link with the feast of Hanukkah (Gera 2010, 34–36). Although it is not possible to reconstruct a history of Judith's association with Hanukkah due to a lack of studies, the book itself offers us some hints in this regard.

To begin, in Hebrew, the very name of the protagonist, Judith, can, in fact, mean "Jewess", but also a female person from Judea, and, particularly interesting, it is the feminine form of the name "Judah." This name, not merely of the patriarch and the southern part of Israel, is the name of the famous Jewish warrior of the Hasmonean times: Judas Maccabee (Gera 2014, 355). Several internal elements in Judith, in fact, pave the way for a close connection with the events regarding the Maccabees: the theme of the Hellenistic ruler cult, which supports the idea of Nebuchadnezzar being a cipher for Antiochus IV, the Greek ruler linked to the Maccabean crisis that emblematically demanded such cult; the book's repeated references to the temple and its altar and the mentions of its rededication; the celebration of a feast for Judith's victory taking place in Jerusalem; and the remarkable resemblance between the figure of Holofernes and that of Nicanor, who is beheaded in a battle with Judas and whose head is taken to Jerusalem and displayed outside the city (see 1Macc 7:47). This last account above all has many points of contact with the story of Judith. No less significant appears Judith's points of contact with the story of Esther. According to some commentators, Judith leaves some traces in the reshaping of Esther in the Greek additions C and D of the book (114–78 BC) (Gera 2014, 12). Thus, as the Megillat Esther becomes the text for the festival of Purim, Judith's links with the Maccabees, similarly, in the course of time, comes to be associated with Hanukkah, and her book becomes, in some circles, the megillah for this festival.

5 Conclusion

Inspired by Mikhail Bakhtin's concept of the chronotope, we were able to show that there are — at least — two different chronotopes in the Book of Judith: one related to the years and the threat to the temple, the other to an underlying calendar implicit in the narrative that runs from Kislev to Kislev. The moment these chronotopes merge, they open a window for the attentive reader to jump in and connect the story of Judith to the celebration of Hanukkah, which takes place in the month of Kislev. Whether or not this association was intended with regard to Judith's production, certain elements of the story itself seem to pave the way, and the two chronotopes created by the book's blending of time and space play a unique role in this.

Bibliography

Bakhtin, Mikhail M. 1981. *The Dialogic Imagination: Four Essays*, translated by Caryl Emerson and Michael Holquist. Austin: University of Texas Press.

Bal, Mieke. [2]1997. *Narratology: Introduction to the Theory of Narrative*. Toronto: University of Toronto Press.

Bogaert, Pierre-Maurice. 1984. "Le Calendrier du livre de Judith et la Fête de Hanukka." *RTL* 15(1): 67–72.

Bogaert, Pierre-Maurice. 1988. "Le 'rouleau' de Judith. Hanukka et le vingt-quatre du mois d'Ab." In *La commémoration. Colloque du centenaire de la Section Religieuse de l'École Pratique des Hautes Études 91*, edited by Philippe Gignoux, 163–171. Louvain / Paris: Peeters.

Bogaert, Pierre-Maurice. 1999. "La Halaka alimentaire dans le livre de Judith." *In Nourriture et repas dans les milieux juifs et chrétiens de l'antiquité. Mélanges offerts au Professeur Charles Perrot.* LeDiv 178. Edited by M. Quesnel, Y.-M. Blanchard and C. Tassin, 25–40. Paris: Éditions du Cerf.

Candido, Dionisio. 2020. "Giuditta. Nuova versione, introduzione e commento. I libri biblici." *Primo testamento 32*. Cinisello Balsamo MI: Paoline.

Dennerlein, Katrin. 2009. *Narratologie des Raumes*. Narratologia 22. Berlin: De Gruyter. https://doi.org/10.1515/9783110219920.

Döring, Jörg, and Tristan Thielmann, eds. [2]2008. *Spatial Turn: Das Raumparadigma in den Kultur- und Sozialwissenschaften*. Bielefeld: Transcript Verlag. https://doi.org/10.1515/9783839406830.

Dubarle, André-Marie. 1966. *Judith: Formes et sens des diverses traditions*. Tome I, *Études*, Tome II, *Textes*. AnBib 24,1–2. Rome: Institut biblique pontifical.

Genette, Gérard. 1966–1972. *Figures I–III*. Paris: Éditions du Seuil.

Gera, Deborah Levine. 2014. *Judith. Commentaries on Early Jewish Literature*. Berlin: De Gruyter. https://doi.org/10.1515/9783110323962.

Gera, Deborah Levine. 2010. "The Jewish Textual Traditions." In *The Sword of Judith. Judith Studies Across the Disciplines*, edited by Kevin R. Brine, Elena Ciletti and Henrike Lähnemann, 23–39. Cambridge: Open Book Publishers. https://doi.org/10.11647/OBP.0009.

Herman, David. 2004. *Story Logic: Problems and Possibilities of Narrative*. Lincoln: University of Nebraska Press.

Herman, David, Manfred Jahn, and Marie-Laure Ryan, eds. 2005. *Routledge Encyclopedia of Narrative Theory*. London: Routledge.
Herman, David. 2009. *Basic Elements of Narrative*. Malden, MA: Wiley-Blackwell.
https://doi.org/10.1002/9781444305920.
Jong, Irene de. 2014. *Narratology and Classics: A Practical Guide*. Oxford: Oxford University Press. https://doi.org/10.1093/acprof:osobl/9780199688692.001.0001.
Koosed, Jennifer L., and Robert Paul Seesengood. 2022. *Judith*. Wisdom Commentary 16. Collegeville: Liturgical Press.
Korytiaková, Martina. 2023a. "The Biblical Literary Tradition behind 'Nabouchodonosor who ruled over the Assyrians' in Judith 1:1." *JSCS* 56: 85–98. https://doi.org/10.2143/JSCS.56.0.3292864.
Korytiaková, Martina. 2023b. "The Two Tents: The Interpretation of Judith's and Holofernes' Spaces and Their Functions in the Book of Judith." *StBiSl* 15(2): 151–186.
Korytiaková, Martina. 2024a. "τὸ κωνώπιον in the Book of Judith as a Motif in Narrative Space." *Biblica* 105: 37–58. https://doi.org/10.2143/BIB.105.1.3293256.
Korytiaková, Martina. 2024b. *The Concept of Space in the Book of Judith: A Contribution to the Narrative Analysis of Old Testament Texts*. SEPT 3. Turnhout: Brepols.
Lotman, Jurij M. 1977. *The Structure of the Artistic Text*, translated by Gail Lenhoff and Ronald Vroon. Michigan Slavic Contributions 7. Ann Arbor: University of Michigan.
Nünning, Ansgar. 2009. "Formen und Funktionen literarischer Raumdarstellung: Grundlagen, Ansätze, narratologische Kategorien und neue Perspektiven." In *Raum und Bewegung in der Literatur: Literaturwissenschaft nach dem Spatial Turn*, edited by Wolfgang Hallet and Birgit Neumann, 33–52. Bielefeld: Transcript Verlag.
https://doi.org/10.1515/9783839411360-002.
Pier, John. 2005. "Chronotope." In *Routledge Encyclopedia of Narrative Theory*, edited by David Herman, Manfred Jahn, and Marie-Laure Ryan, 64–65. London: Routledge.
Riffaterre, Michel. 1996. "Chronotopes in Diegesis." In *Fiction Updated: Theories of Fictionality*, edited by Calin-Andrei Mihailescu and Walid Hamarneh, 244–256. Toronto: University of Toronto Press.
Ronen, Ruth. 1986. "Space in Fiction." *Poetics Today* 7: 421–438. https://doi.org/10.2307/1772504.
Ryan, Marie-Laure. 1991. *Possible Worlds, Artificial Intelligence and Narrative Theory*. Bloomington: Indiana Univ. Press.
Schmitz, Barbara, and Helmut Engel. 2014. *Das Buch Judit*. HThKAT 20. Freiburg: Herder.
Schmitz, Barbara. 2021. "Urban Spaces and Prayer in the Book of Judith." In *Prayer and the Ancient City: Influences of Urban Space*, edited by Annette Weissenrieder, Jörg Rüpke, and Maik Patzelt, 290–307. Tübingen: Mohr Siebeck.
Scholz, Bernhard F. 2003. "Bakhtin's Concept of 'Chronotope': The Kantian Connection." In *Mikhail Bakhtin*, Vol. 2, *Sage Masters of Modern Social Thought*, edited by Michael E. Gardiner, 145–172. London: Sage.
Stummer, Friedrich. 1947. *Geographie des Buches Judith*. BWR 3. Stuttgart: Verlag Katholisches Bibelwerk.
Van Goudoever, Jan. 1959. *Biblical Calendars*. Leiden: Brill.
Weingarten, Susan. 2010. "Medieval Hanukkah Traditions: Jewish Festive Foods in their European Contexts," *Food and History* 8(1): 41–62. https://doi.org/10.1484/J.FOOD.1.100973.
Zenger, Erich. 1981. *Das Buch Judit*. JSHRZ I/6. Gütersloh: Gütersloher Verlagshaus Gerd Mohn. https://doi.org/10.14315/9783641247904.
Zoran, Gabriel. 1984. "Towards a Theory of Space in Narrative." *Poetics Today* 5: 309–335. https://doi.org/10.2307/1771935.

Bob Becking

Time and Space in the Aramaic Documents from Elephantine

Abstract: In this contribution, the Aramaic words for the units of time in the documents from Persian period Elephantine are analyzed. These Aramaic documents show an awareness of the aspects of time and its divisions. No grand design or philosophical idea, however, can be detected behind the texts. This is mainly due to the fact that documents present everyday texts, sometimes with a legal content. People just lived their lives in the time-span allotted. Chronotopes are rare in these texts. Other elements of Bakhtin's theoretical scheme, however, such as dialogism and polyphony, are clearly present in the narrative and the sayings of Aḥiqar. On the other hand, reading these texts that present a world of peaceful co-existence of various ethnic groups in an age when so many groups and nations stand hostile towards each other evokes a *chronotopos* for the present reader and a desire to travel through time and space to a more righteous age.

1 Introduction

We all experience time, or better, we are able to connect our experiences with this intangible and irreversible dimension. In order to understand this fluid dimension and have a grip on it, we divide it into neat portions: from seconds and shorter to millenniums and beyond. Despite these measurements, the fabric of time remains an enigma. At the same time, we all are aware of the fact that we live in a three-dimensional space, which is easier to understand. In theoretical physics, ideas about a time-space continuum have been developed and inspired by the relativity theory of Albert Einstein. A few decades after Einstein, the Russian literary theorist Mikhail Bakhtin proposed the concept of chronotopes. If I understand him correctly, Bakhtin states that different literary genres operate with different configurations of time and space. In each genre, the proportions are different (Bakhtin 1981, 84–258; Claassens 2003; Bemong and Borghart 2010).

At Elephantine — an island on the Nile — a multi-ethnic community lived within the power structure of the Persian Empire. Aramaic and Demotic texts give some insights into the daily life of this community (Becking 2020). The documents are written in various genres: letters, lawsuits, memoranda, and various other literary compositions. I will read some of these documents in which words for time occur, hoping to find traces of chronotopes in them.

https://doi.org/10.1515/9783112240366-004

2 Words for Time in the Aramaic Documents

2.1 *Day ywm*

The word is generally used as an indication of a time period of about 24 hours.

2.1.1 In Reflections on the Past

I will start my investigation with a letter.

> [1][Greetings], the [T]emple of YHW in Elephantine.
> To my son Shelomam [fr]om your brother Osea. (Blessings) of welfare and strength [I sent you. [2]And now], from the day (*ywm*) that you went on that way, my heart is not good. Likewise, your mother. Now, blessed be you [by YHW the God [3]that He may let] me [be]hold your face in peace.
> Now, from the day that you went out from Egypt, allotment has not been g[iven *to us/you here.* [4]And when] we complained to the official about your allotment here in Migdol, thus was said to us, saying:
> "About this, [*you, complain* [5]before] the scribes, and it will be given to you."
> Now, when you will come to (Lower) Egypt . . .[. . .[6]. . .] your [allotment which has been withheld, all of it.
> Now, how is the household doing and how was your leaving? If [. . .] will be [7] [. . .w]ell/p]eace and there is no damage. Be a man. Do not weep until you come [. . . .] (PPadua = *TAD* A3.3:1–7)

In this letter, Oshea bewails the absence of his brother Shelomam. The noun "brother" should not be read in a biological kinship sense (Bledsoe 2021, 298–302). The same person is labeled son in this document. The connection between Oshea and Shelomam was most probably that of a working relationship. Shelomam apparently left his home some time ago. The real reason for Oshea's regret is of a financial nature, which becomes clear from line 3 that the *prs*, "allotment for Shelomam" had been withheld. The Aramaic noun *prs*, "portion; payment; salary", refers to the reward in kind or money paid by the Persians for the duties of, for instance, the Yehudites. The day on which Shelomam left is not specified, but its mention refers to a concept of time in which "the past" was an element. Parallel to that, Shelomam is connected to two localities. He had left Migdol in Lower Egypt and, on the day of the writing, resided somewhere else. This *chronotope* marks the financial problem.

A comparable relation between time and space is present in the text of the request to rebuild the demolished temple of Yaho. In their letter to Bagohi, the Yehudite leaders claim:

> And from the days of the king(s) (*wmn ywmy*) of Egypt our fathers had built that Temple in Elephantine the fortress and when Cambyses entered Eg^{ypt} — that Temple, built he found it. And the temples of the gods of Egypt, all (of them), they overthrew, but anything in that Temple one did not damage (*TAD* A4.7:13–14 // A.4.8:12–13.).

I will not start a discussion on the historical value of this claim (see Becking 2022) but only note that the Yehudites had a clear awareness that events had taken place in the past.

A shorter period of time is referred to by the expression *wd'znh ywm'*, "until this day". In the same request for the rebuilding, it is stated that:

> and until this day, we are wearing sackcloth and are fasting (*TAD* A4.7:20 // A.8:19; see also *TAD* A4.7:21 // A.4.8:20).

This example indicates that the Yehudites were mourning from the day of the demolition up to the day on which the request was sent. In the undated document on a loan of silver, Gemeriah promises that he will pay a monthly rent:

> until the day that I pay it to [you] (*TAD* B4.2:3.10).

That day is not fixed. The length of a loan period seems to have been flexible; I assume that it was related to the welfare of the loaner (Porten 2011, 257). In the context of this document, the expression "until the day" refers to a forthcoming but unknown period of time.

2.1.2 Daily, Continually

In a report on a conflict that ends with a request for help, the expression *bkl ywm*, "on every day; daily", occurs:

> It was on every day that [. . .] he complained to the investigators. (*TAD* A4.2:2–3)

The names of the complaining party or the accused are not mentioned. It is clear that the observation that this happened 'day after day' implies a concept of time in which repetition during a longer period plays a role. The words form a parallel to the Hebrew *yôm yôm*, 'day after day', in a positive appreciation of God's beneficial acts. The expression mentioned is paralleled by the words *bkl 'dn*, 'all the time', in the request for the rebuilding. In case Bagohi would react in a positive way:

> we shall pray for you at all times (*TAD* A4.7:26 // A4.8:25).

2.1.3 Days to Celebrate

In the letter formerly known as the “Passover-letter”, two days are mentioned:

Recto

1 [. . .]Jedaniah and his colleagues of the Yehudite f[orce], [from] your brother Hanania[h]. May God [. . .].
2 [. . .] And now, this year, year 5 of Darius the king, from the king has been sent to Arsh[ames . . .]
3 [. . . . .] you will count fou[r . . . . . .]
4 [. . . . . of]fer. You will count from day 15 up to day 21 of [. . . . . .]
5 [. . . . .] be undefiled and be complied work [. . . . .]
6 [. . . . .] you will not drink; and anything that is leavened, you shall not [. . .]

Verso

7 [. . . . .] setting of the sun until day 21 of Nisa[n . . . .]
8 [. . . . . b]ring to your chambers and seal (it) between the days [. . .]
9 [ ]
10 [. . . . . . .] my power Jedaniah and his colleagues of the Yehudite force, your brother Hananiah, so[n of . . .]

(Papyrus Berlin P. 13464; *TAD* A4.1; see a recent picture at http://elephantine.smb.museum/record/ID100463; the papyrus was originally thought to be related to the Passover-festival; see Arnold 1912; criticism at Gass 1999; Becking 2022, 24–28; Moore 2024, 308–310; the proposal of Barnea 2024, to connect the letter to a *yashna*-festival is too speculative.)

Remarks on the text

- In their edition, Porten and Yardeni (1986) translate the end of line 1: “May God/the gods [seek after] the welfare of my brothers”, which is probably based on the salutation formulae in other letters. There is, however, not much space for such an addition.
- The demonstrative pronoun *z’* in line 2 clearly has a deictic function referring to the then actual year (Muraoka and Porten, 2003, § 41a).
- Grelot suggests that the object of (non-)drinking in line 6 would have been *škr*, ‘beer’. He refers to some passages in Mishnaic law that indicate that the drinking on Passover of *zythos*, an Egyptian beer, was forbidden, Mishnah Pesachim 3.1: “These items are a transgression on Pesach: Babylonian *kutach*, Median beer, Edomite vinegar, Egyptian ale (זתום), bran water from dyers, working dough from cooks, and glue from scribes” (Grelot 1954, 361–362; see also Porten 1968, 82, 129; Rohrmoser 2014, 384–385). This argument is, however, not convincing.
- The first sign in line 10 has generally been read as an *’āleph*. Hence the first word was read *’ḥy*, “my brothers”, as an indication for “Jedaniah and his col-

leagues"; see the edition by Porten and Yardeni. Except for the fact that it is uncertain whether *'ḥy* is a noun in the plural with a first-person singular suffix (Folmer 1995, 211; Muraoka and Porten 2003, § 12). The sign on the photograph differs too much from the other *'āleph*'s in the text. In my view, the sign should be read as a *kaph* leading to the word *kḥy*, 'my power', indicating the role of Hananiah in the Persian rule. As far as I can see, the noun *kḥ*, well known in Biblical Hebrew, is not attested elsewhere in Ancient or Persian period Aramaic inscriptions. In the Aramaic of the Targumim, the noun occurs a few times; see Targ Ps 16:3; 22:31; 71:18; 80:3; Job 36:19 and Ruth 3:15

The absence of words like *psḥ*, "Passover", or *mṣwt*, "unleavened bread", in the parts of the letter that survived the ages indicates that an exact reference to a specific festival cannot be established. We are left with relative uncertainty. Nevertheless, the letter makes clear that on behalf of the Persian administration, instructions were given for a Yehudite festival. A day for it was established.

2.1.4 Tomorrow (and yesterday)

In a document from the Mibtaiah "archive" regulating the grant to build a wall, expressions occur that indicate the day after the present one and a day after that occurs:

> Tomorrow (*mḥr*) or the next day (*ywm 'ḥrn*), I shall not be able to restrain you from building upon that wall of yours. (*TAD* B2.1:6; see also B2.1:8 and B2.3:18–20,26; B2.4:8,13; B2.6:17,20,22,26; B3.1:7,9,10,12,13; B3.8:21; B5.1:4; D7.19:12–13; CG 45:6; see Lozachmeur 2006, 216–17)

Both expressions indicate an awareness that time continues after the present moment. A relation with the spatial dimensions is not clear. An ostracon written by a certain Islah, most probably a woman, reads:

> Behold, I will send vegetables tomorrow.
> Meet the boat tomorrow on Sabbath, so that they will not get lost.
> By the life of Yahô, if not, (then) I will take your life.
> Do not rely on Meshullemeth or Shemaiah.
> Now, send me barley in return.
> Now, by the life of Yahô, if not, (then) you will be responsible for the account.
> (*TADAE* D7.16:1–9; see Porten 1968, 126; Porten 1969; Grabbe 2004, 221; Rohrmoser 2014, 331–333; Granerød 2016, 192–193; Bledsoe 2021, 249–250)

This ostracon indicates that on the day of the Sabbath, some trade in grocery ware obviously existed. It might, however, be that this was a case of emergency. The meeting place, "the boat", is a spot where the sender and the receiver of this letter are not present at the moment. The sender hopes to meet the receiver there. On an ostracon, a certain Micaiah receives two messages. Nathan, son of Gemariah, summons him:

> Now, come tomorrow (*mḥr*) without fail (*TAD* D7.20:2).

While Jedaniah reminds him:

> Now, I sent to you yesterday (*'tml*) in the name of Hodaviah, son of Zechariah, saying: "Come this day!" but you did not come (*TAD* D7.20:7–10).

The word yesterday (*'tml*) occurs in a variety of ostraca (E.g. *TAD* D7.33:1–4; D7.44:8–9; D7.47:10; CG 52, 55, 57, 71, 78, 79, 82, 99, 125, 165?, 167, 226, 263, X7, J3, J4, J6; see Lozachmeur 2006). The concept of yesterday is also phrased as:

> One day before (*ywm* 1 *qdm*) (CG 118:4; see Lozachmeur 2006, 271–272).

The word "tomorrow" is attested on an ostracon from the early fifth century:

> Lo, tomorrow I have to go to my house
> (*TAD* D7.1:9–10; see also CG 18, 20, 37, 42, 45, 57, 69, 89, 98, 102, 110, 121, 152, 157, 187, 189, 203, J2, J3, J5, J7; see Lozachmeur 2006; Lemaire 2011, 365).

The use of the words "yesterday" and "tomorrow" indicates an awareness of the chain of days and the understanding that nightfall is not the end of time. These texts can be categorized as "missives" (Lemaire 2022, 45). The words "yesterday" and "tomorrow" are important indicators that these missives should not be kept for long. After completion of the action, the text could be forgotten or overwritten as palimpsest.

2.1.5 On One Day

In the document of wifehood between Esḥor, son of Ṣeḥa, and Mibtaiah, daughter of Mahseiah, some regulations are made in case the marriage ends in a divorce or in case Esḥor, son of Ṣeḥa, declares, "I hated my wife Mibtaiah". (On this expression, see e.g. Nutkowicz 2007; Botta 2009, 59–60; Botta 2013; Nutkowicz 2015, 114–117; Granerød 2016, 49–51, 295). Mibtaiah is allowed to take her dowry (*mhr*) with her "from straw to string". The action must take place quickly and without hesitation:

> In one day in one stroke.
> (*TADAE* B2.6:28; see also the document of wifehood by Ananiah B3.8:24)

The connection with the dimension of space lies in the fact that Mibtaiah is summoned to move from one house to another.

2.1.6 Everlasting

In the regulation between Dargamana, the Khwaresmian, and Mahseiah, the son of Jojada, it is stated that Mahseiah gave a house to his daughter Mibtaiah. One of the stipulations was that Mibtaiah should be the owner forever:

> You have right to it from this day and forever (*'d 'lm*) and (so do) your children after you. To whomever you love you may give (it). I have no other son or daughter, brother or sister, or woman or other man (who) has right to that land but you and your children forever (*TAD* B2.3:9–11).

The expression 'from this day and forever' also occurs in a document of wifehood (B2.6:3) and in a document concerning the withdrawal of goods (B2.8:6–7; see also B2.9:9–10; B2.11:7; B3.12:23; B5.5:4; B6.1:4; with Botta 2009, 41–42). In the Aramaic version of the Bisitun Inscription, a blessing for a loyal king is formulated:

> Ahuramazda will b[less . . . be a]bundant and your days will be long-lasting.
> (*TAD* C2.1 (XI):72).

This blessing assumes the concept that time will be superfluous in the future. A location for this blessed life is not given.

2.1.7 Twenty and Thirty Days

A document on the loan of grain contains the following complex clause:

> And if I do not pay and give you that emmer which above is written when the
> ration is given [me] from the (store-)house of the king, afterwards I, Anani, shall
> be obligated and shall give you silver, a penalty of one, 1, karsh of pure silver. Afterwards, I,
> Anani, shall pay and give you the penalty which is above written
> within 20, that is twenty, days, without suit (*TAD* B3.13:5–8).

In other words, Anani solemnly promises to pay off his debts when receiving his portion from the king's storehouse. In case he fails to do so, he will pay one karsh of pure silver within the given period of twenty days. The document regulating the sale of an abandoned property to Ananiah contains the following guarantee clause:

> And if another person institute (suit) against you or institute (suit) against son or daughter of yours, we shall stand up and cleanse (it) and give (it) to you within 30 days (*TAD* B3.4:19–20; see Botta 2009, 108–111).

The period of 30 days within which the property will be given in case of a suit indicates the relatively quick action by the sellers — the Caspian Bagazushta and his wife — and functions as a guarantee to the buyer. Both documents make clear that period for a potential lawsuit was regarded as a relatively short period of twenty or thirty days. The same clause is probably present in the broken lines in a document from Syene written by Mauziah (*TAD* B7.1:7–7; see also B8.7:8).

2.1.8 Old of Days

In his bequest made up before his death, Anani remarks about a gift to his daughter:

> I, Anani, gave it to Jehoishma my daughter at my death in affection. Just as she supported me while I was old (*sb*) of days — I was unable (to use) my hands, and she supported me — also I gave (it) to her at my death (*TAD* B3.10:16–18).

The expression *'nh ymyn sb* indicates the final phase of human life. The word is probably a dialect form of the more common *šb* or *śb*, "to be old" (see Ezra 6:8). It is tempting to connect this expression with the epithet *attîq yômayyā*, "the Ancient of Days" in Dan 7:9,13,22. Being "dead" can be seen as having arrived in a place beyond the earthly realm.

2.1.9 When it is Proper Time

The noun *'dn*, "set time", occurs a few times in the Aramaic documents. In a document regulating the division of slaves from the heritage of their father, Nathan, between the two brothers Mahseiah and Jedaniah, one of the arrangements made is:

> Moreover, there is Tabi by name, the mother of these lads, and Lilu her son whom we shall not yet divide (between) us. When (the) time will be (*kzy 'dn yhwh*), we shall divide them (between) us and, (each) person his share, we shall take hereditary possession, and a document of our division we shall write between us, without suit. (*TAD* B2.11:12–14; Botta 2009, 113–116)

In a document authorizing the repair of a boat of Mithrades, it is remarked:

> . . . the Carians, thus said: "The boat which we hold-in-hereditary-lease — time has come (*'dn hwh*) its needs to [. . .]" (*TAD* A6.2:3)

In both texts, the noun *ʿdn* refers to a point of time in the future when certain acts will be undertaken. On occasion, the noun *ʿdn* has the meaning "always; all times", for instance, in the salutations of the letter to Bagohi requesting his support for the rebuilding of the temple of Yahô:

> The welfare of our lord] may the God of Heav[en] seek after [abundantly] at all times, [and] favor may He g[ra]nt [you before Da]rius the king [and the princes more than now [a thousand times], and] long [life] may He give you, and happy and strong may you be at all times (*bkl ʿdn*). (*TAD* A4.7:2–3 cf. A4.8:2–3)

Here, the noun *ʿdn* refers to an enduring future. A relation with space is absent. In the final section of both documents, it is promised that if Bagohi reacts in a supportive way, an offering for him will be made in the rebuilt temple (Becking 2022, 196).

2.1.10 Result

In the Aramaic documents from Elephantine, the word "day" is mainly used in its concrete sense. Next to that, the texts give evidence of the awareness of continuity: before and after the present day, there have been days, and there will come days. Periods of days — in the past as well as in the future — are presented as a conceivable measurement. Clear examples of chronotopes have not been found.

2.2 Month

The year was divided into 12 months.

2.2.1 Month Names

Some of these months are known by name:

Egyptian	Babylonian/Aramaic	
Tybi/Tobi *tʿwby* Athyr *ḥtḥwr*	Shebat *šbṭ*	Jan–Feb
Mechir, *mḥr* Choiak *kyḥk*	Adar *ʾdr*	Feb–March
	Nisan *nys[n*	March–April

(continued)

Egyptian	Babylonian/Aramaic	
	Iyar *ʾyr*	April–May
Phamenoth *pmnḥtp*	Siwan *sywn*	May–June
Painy *pʾwny*	Tammuz *tmwz*	June–July
Parmouti *prmwty*	Ab *ʾb*	July–Aug
Pachons *pḥns*	Elul *ʾlwl*	Aug–Sept
Epiph *ʾpp*	Tishri *tšry*	Sept–Oct
	Marcheshvan	Oct–Nov
Thoth *tḥwt* Mesore *mswrʿ*	Kislev *kslw*	Nov–Dec
Phaophi *pʾpy*	Tebeth *ṭbt*	Dec–Jan

These month names are known from a few dozen attestations of the formula: "on the Xth of month Y", see for instance, "on the 20th of Adar" in the heading of a letter (*TAD* B3.11:1). All these references are evidence for the fact that — at least in scribal circles — the division of the year into months was a daily awareness and that this division of time helped the administration to control the continuous stream of this dimension to secure trade and interhuman relations, among other things. The use of both Persian or Babylonian and Egyptian month names — and in many cases in synchrony — is a hint of a double awareness (Moore 2020). On the one hand, the scribes realized that they were a lower part of the Persian pyramid of power (vertical awareness) and, on the other hand, that they were still part of the local community (horizontal solidarity)

2.2.2 Monthly Rent

In the undated document on a loan of silver, Gemeriah promises that he will pay a monthly interest of 5 %:

1. . . . You gave me silver,
2. [3 shekels, 1+]1 (= 2) [q(uarters)] by the stone(-weight)s of Ptah, 6 silver, 1 sh(ekel) to the 10 I and it will increase upon me (at the rate of) silver,
3. 2 hallurs to silver, 1 sh(ekel) for the month until the day that I pay it to [you].
4. And the interest on your silver will be 7 hallurs for 1 month.
5. And the month in which I shall not give you interest, it will be capital and shall increase. And I shall pay it to you month by month
6. from my allotment which they will give me from the treasury

7. (*TAD* B4.2:1–6; see also B3.1:3–7).
Although it is uncertain how long Gemeriah had to pay the interest, the payment fell due after the period of one month, time and again

2.2.3 Continuous Months

In a document referring to the obligation to take a judicial oath in the context of stolen fish, the unknown thief swears to give back the stolen good:

> If I do not give you within [x] day[s . . . give you] the [penalty (of)] 1 qab of barley per 1 portion all the months and years (*TAD* B7.1:7–8).

In other words, the repayment will be continuous. The expression 'month and years' refers to an ongoing period in the near future. A comparative concept of time is present in a recently published letter:

> Month by month an off⌈ic⌉[ial . . .]
> (PBerlin 13445 E – PBerlin 13448/8; Moore 2022, text 1.1).

The context is, however, unclear. The reduplicated noun expresses a recurring concept of time. The action veiled by the document will take place continuously (see Moore 2022, 33).

2.2.4 Conclusion

The division of the year into months must have been to get a grip on various events. It is remarkable that both the Egyptian and Babylonian calendars were in use and that, in the majority of cases, equations between the two systems were made (see Porten 1990; Stern 2012).

2.3 Year

2.3.1 Regnal Years

On occasion, the documents refer to the regnal years of Persian kings. For instance, a document on the exchange of inherited shares is dated:

> Year 27 of king Darius (*TAD* B5.1:1).

Apparently, Darius I is meant here, implying a reference to the year 495 BCE. Comparable references are found to the reigns of the following kings:

- Xerxes (*TAD* D20.3:3).
- Artaxerxes I (e.g. *TAD* B2.2:1–2; B2.3:2; B2.4:1; B3.1:1; B3.2:1; B3.3:1; B2.7:1).
- Darius II (e.g. *TAD* B3.7:1; B3.8:1; A4.1:2; B3.9:1; B2.10:1; A4.7:4,19 = A4.8:4,19).
- Artaxerxes II (*TAD* B3.10:1; B3.11:1)
- Amyrtaeus (*TAD* B5.5:1).

Amyrtaeus had thrown off the Persian yoke and declared himself king of Egypt in 404 BCE, although Artaxerxes denied this claim. By implication, the document dates to the year 400 BCE.

All these connections make clear that at least the administrative elite were aware of the fact that the time in the greater world was related to the reigning Persian king. The habit continued after the decay of the Persian power. The absence of documents from the post-Persian period — except the one mentioning Amyrtaeus — makes it impossible to estimate how long this practice continued.

2.3.2 Old Age

In the bequest by which Ananiah, son of Azariah, arranges the gift of a room to his wife Tamet, an idiomatic expression for old age occurs twice in a stipulation on the inheritance:

> But if you die at the age of 100 years (*brt šnn* 100), it is my children whom you bore me (that) have right to it after your death. And moreover, if I, Anani, die at the age of 100 years (*brt šnn* 100), it is Pilti and Jehoishma, all (told), my children, (who) have right to my other portion (*TAD* B3.5:16–18).

The expression "daughter/son of 100 years" refers to a faraway future. The expression is also attested in a document of wifehood (*TAD* B6.3:2) and in a document regulating the usufruct of an estate (*TAD* B3.7:18–20).

2.4 Lifetime

Intriguing is the mention of a longer period of Meshullam as an older man making up his will:

> I thought of you in my lifetime (*bḥyy*). (To be) free I release you at my death and I release Jeh(o)ishma by name your daughter, whom you bo(r)e me (*TAD* B3.6:3–5).

The "you" character is his wife, the former handmaiden Tapamet, whom he married but who lived a confined life. The word 'lifetime' indicates the awareness of the length of human life (See also *TAD* B2.3:3; B3.10:2–3; B3.11:11). In the present document, Yehoishma is referred to three times as "your daughter, whom you bore me." (*TAD* B3.6:4–5,6,7–8) This expression can be interpreted in two ways: either Meshullam was the biological father of Yehoishma, or, being born from a slave girl, Yehoishma did not fall under the legal responsibility of her biological father — presumably Ananiah — but was seen as part of the larger household of Meshullam. The reference to 'death' implies a chronotope: this will be a different country than the world of the living. In 449 BCE, a document of wifehood was made up arranging the relation between Meshullam and Tamet/Tapamet (*TAD* B3.3; see, e.g., Porten 1968, 205–213; Porten and Szubin 1982; Botta 2009, 59–86, 87; Nutkowicz 2015, 27–30, 44–45; Granerød 2016, 49–51).

2.5 Absent Words

The following words for time are absent in the Aramaic documents from Elephantine:

- Minute
- Hour
- Week
- Decade
- Century

The word "hour" is, however, attested in a Demotic document from 486 BCE:

> They had not finished putting ⌈. . .⌉ on the quay by this 8th hour (*wnwt*) of year 36, Payni, day 17. (I) was going to send (word) of the accounts of the things which were found.
> (PLoeb 1; Spiegelberg 1928, 13–21; Porten 2011, 296–298 (C4):15–17)

The word 'sabbath' occurs a few times but does not yet refer to a weekly day of rest (see Becking 2008).

2.6 Summary

The documents from Elephantine witness the units of time that were known in those days. The concept of "hour" was known in those days. In Mesopotamian texts the noun d a n n a (Sumerian) or *bēru* (Akkadian) occurs that refers to the "twelfth part of a circle" and was used to indicate a period of two hours. Apparently this time unit did not play a role in the daily doings of Elephantine.

3 Reflections on Time in Aḥiqar

In Elephantine, the oldest version of Aḥiqar has been found (*TAD* C.1.1. Original edition: Sachau 1911. Recent translations: Grelot 1972, 427–452; Lindenberger 1983; Kottsieper 1990; Niehr 2007). I will not discuss the complicated question of the order of the columns (see Niehr 2007, 5) nor the role that the erased customs account could play in this discussion (see Yardeni 1994). The document consists of two parts: (1) a narrative around the sage Aḥiqar focusing on the topics of power and loyalty and (2) a collection of proverbs and sayings. I read both parts as elements of one coherent text (see also Bledsoe 2021). The traditions regarding Aḥiqar are almost universal. Demotic fragments from the first millennium BCE are known (Cairo papyrus published by Sobhy 1930; Papyrus Berlin 23729 edited by Zauzich 1976). The tale and the sayings have been translated into various languages, including Arabic to a recently recorded version in neo-Aramaic.

3.1 Novella

The Aḥiqar novella is set at the court of the neo-Assyrian king Esarhaddon (Wigand 2022). Although the Aramaic name *'ḥyqr*, "my brother is noble", is attested in a few Neo-Assyrian and Neo-Babylonian inscriptions (See Weigl 2010, 1; Berlejung and Radner 1998, 63; Oshima 2017, 144–145), in the al-Yahudu documents (Pearce and Wunsch 2014, 8–9.39), a court official by that name from the reigns of Esarhaddon and Ashurbanipal is not known, which makes the Aḥiqar of the wisdom-tradition a fictitious character (Already von Soden 1936; with Niehr 2007, 9; Kratz 2012–2013; Wigand 2022, 33–34). The actors Esarhaddon and Sennacherib, as well as Nabušumiškun, are persons known from history (Wigand 2022, 35–36). Esarhaddon and Sennacherib had been kings of the neo-Assyrian empire. Nabušumiškun was a son of Marduk-apla-idinna who made a career at the Assyrian court. Concerning the Neo-Babylonian name *nabû-šum-iškun*, "Nabu established the name" (see Porten, Zadok, and Pearce 2016), the name also occurs in a contract from Elephantine (*TAD* B2.2:19) and in Neo-Babylonian inscriptions as the name of a son of Merodakhbaladan (von Weiher 1984; Niehr 2007, 8; Weigl 2010, 2). The aim of the Aḥiqar-novella, however, is not to (re)construct an episode at the palace of Nineveh. As Bledsoe has correctly argued, these historical figures are remembered in the story for their symbolic role (Bledsoe 2015; see also Holm 2014; Wigand 2018, 128–132; Schipper 2018; Wigand 2022, 58–71). The kings form a kind of chiffre for the foreign rulers from Persia, and Aḥiqar – both novel and proverbs – should be read from this perspective.

3.2 References to Time in the Aḥiqar Novella

The novella does not contain many references to time.

- Three times the noun *šb*, "old", occurs. Twice Aḥiqar characterizes himself as "old", which is the cause of his proposal to install his nephew Nadin as royal scribe in his place (Aḥiqar 1:6; 2:17; Wigand 2022, 38–39; Bledsoe 2021, 94). Later on, Esarhaddon instructs Nabušumiškun: '[. . . kill him] this [Aḥ]iq[ar], the old man (*šb'*), the wise scribe' (Aḥiqar 3:35; Wigand 2022, 43–44).
- Wigand (2022, 144–146) refers to an interesting parallel in the Demotic Petition of Petese to the motivation and the proposal of Aḥiqar:

  > I have become old! May this favor be shown to me before Pharaoh. I have a relative . . .
  > (P. Rylands 9 V:20–VI:3; Vittmann 1998, 130–131)

- The word *ywm*, "day", occurs in the report of the journey of Nabušumiškun to Aḥiqar:

  > After three more d[a]ys, lo! [. . . he found me] (Aḥiqar 3:39–40; Wigand 2022, 44–45).

  This indication most probably has a symbolic value comparable to the three-day period in stories from the Hebrew Bible (See, e.g., Gen 31:22; 34:25; 40:20; Exod 19:11; Num. 7:24; Judg 20:30; 1Sam 20:19; 2Sam 1:2; 1Kgs 3:18; 2Kgs 20:8; Esth 5:1; Hos 6:2; Bledsoe 2021, 97). The duration of the trip of Nabušumiškun from one place to another is a clear example of a *chronotope*: the reader of the story has to travel this distance in a shorter period.
- The expression *ywmn 'ḥrnn*, "later days", occurs twice and in a narrative parallel. First, Aḥiqar refers to acts in the past when he was hiding Nabušumiškun:

  > Until at [an]other time and in later days I presented you before Sennacherib (Aḥiqar 4:49–50; Wigand 2022, 45–47; Bledsoe 2021, 93).

  Then he asks for a favour in return. He asks Nabušumiškun:

  > Do not kill me! Bring me to your house until later days (Aḥiqar 4:49–50).

- The noun *qdmn*, "formerly", is attested in the self-presentation of Aḥiqar to Nabušumiškun:

I am Aḥiqar who formerly rescued you from an undeserved killing (Aḥiqar 4:52).

The past is still present in Aḥiqar's appeal to the golden rule (Wigand 2022, 65; Bledsoe 2021, 96, 300–302, 380–381).

3.3 The Sayings

The sayings of Aḥiqar contain a tendency to loyalty, prudence, modesty, and adaptation (Folmer 2017; Wigand 2018; Bledsoe 2021, 280–326). This might imply that the educated and leading classes of the various ethnic and/or religious groups in Elephantine were trained in a lifestyle and worldview characterized by the acceptance of the Persian power and openness to negotiating the identity with 'the other'. I will present a set of characteristic sayings.

3.4 References to Time in the Sayings of Aḥiqar

The sayings contain only a few reflections on the concept of time.

- The noun *ywm*, "day", is used figuratively in the proverb:

  [My] son, do not damn the day until you see [nig]ht (Aḥiqar 6:80).

  I follow the reading of TAD C, 36 (with Niehr 2007, 42: [*ly*]*lh*; contra Weigl 2010, 79–80: [*sw*]*ph*, "end"). The meaning of this line is easily established. Human life (*ywm*) might be worrisome and in need of a negative assessment, but the night may bring even worse circumstances (Weigl 2010, 80–82).

  The word group *ywm rwḥ*, "day of wind; storm", refers to a moment in which wickedness will be repaid:

  [A town] of wicked men will split asunder on the day of storm
  (Aḥiqar 7:104; see Weigl 2010, 207–212).

  The word *ywm*, "day", could also refer to a moment like "once upon a time":

  [. . . said] one d[a]y to the wild ass (Aḥiqar 13:203).

  The identity of the speaker in this animal proverb is unknown.
- The more general word *ʿdd*, "time", occurs in the sense of the final moment of a human life:

  A righteous of people: at his time all his attackers will perish (Aḥiqar 7:103).

This saying expresses the consoling idea of reciprocity: evildoers will find their end in just time (see Weigl 2010, 237–239).

– Words like week, month, and year are absent in the sayings.

3.5 Conclusion on Aḥiqar

In this wisdom text, time does not play a very important role. The basic theme of the sayings — how to survive the position of a middleman between power and people — is not connected to time and its measurements or to time in relation to space.

4 To End With

The Aramaic documents from the Persian period Elephantine show an awareness of the aspects of time and its divisions. No grand design or philosophical idea can be detected behind the texts. People just lived their lives in the time span allotted. Chronotopes are rare. Other elements of Bakhtin's theoretical scheme, however, such as dialogism and polyphony (Bakhtin 1981), are clearly present in the narrative about and the sayings of Aḥiqar (see Bledsoe 2021). On the other hand, reading these texts that present a world of peaceful co-existence of various ethnic groups in an age when so many groups and nations stand hostile towards each other evokes a *chronotope* for the present reader and a desire to travel through time and space to a more righteous age.

Bibliography

Arnold, William R. 1912. "The Passover Papyrus from Elephantine." *JBL* 31:1–33. https://doi.org/10.2307/3259988.

Bakhtin, Mikhail M. 1981. *The Dialogic Imagination: Four Essays*. Austin: University of Texas Press.

Barnea, Gad. 2024. "P. Berlin 13464, Yahwism and Achaemenid Zoroastrianism at Elephantine." In *Yahwism under the Achaemenid Empire: Professor Shaul Shaked in Memoriam*, BZAW 548, edited by Gad Barnea and Reinhard G. Kratz, 1–34. Berlin: De Gruyter. https://doi.org/10.1515/9783111018638-001.

Becking, Bob. 2008. "Sabbath at Elephantine: A Short Episode in the Construction of Jewish Identity." In *Empsychoi Logoi—Religious Innovations in Antiquity: Studies in Honour of Pieter Willem van der Horst*, AJEC 73, edited by Alberdina Houtman, Albert de Jong, and Magda Misset-Van de Weg, 177–189. Leiden: Brill. https://doi.org/10.1163/9789047433224_017.

Becking, Bob. 2020. *Identity in Persian Egypt: The Fate of the Yehudite Community of Elephantine.* University Park: Penn State Press.

Becking, Bob. 2022. "'That Evil Act': A Thick Description of the Crisis around the Demolition of the Temple of *Yahô* at Elephantine." In *Elephantine in Context: Studies on the History, Religion and Literature of the Judeans in Persian Period Egypt*, FAT 155, edited by Reinhard G. Kratz and Bernd U. Schipper, 183–207. Tübingen: Mohr Siebeck. https://doi.org/10.1628/978-3-16-160997-8.

Berlejung, Angelika, and Karin Radner. 1998. "Aḫi-iaqar." In *The Prosopography of the Neo-Assyrian Empire.* Vol. 1/I, edited by Karen Radner. Helsinki: The Neo-Assyrian Text Corpus Project; The Finnish Foundation for Assyriological Research.

Bemong, Nele, and Pieter Borghart. 2010. "Bakhtin's Theory and the Literary Chronotope: Reflections, Applications, Perspectives." In *Bakhtin's Theory of the Literary Chronotope: Reflections, Applications, Perspectives*, edited by Nele Bemong, Pieter Borghart, Michel De Dobbeleer, Kristoffel Demoen, Koen De Temmerman, and Bart Keunen, 3–16. Gent: Academia Press. https://doi.org/10.26530/OAPEN_377572.

Bledsoe, Seth A. 2015. "Conflicting Loyalties: King and Context in the Aramaic Book of Ahiqar." In *Political Memory in and after the Persian Empire*, ANEM 13, edited by Jason M. Silverman and Caroline Waerzeggers, 239–268. Atlanta: SBL Press.

Bledsoe, Seth A. 2021. *The Wisdom of the Aramaic Book of Ahiqar: Unravelling a Discourse of Uncertainty and Distress.* JSJ.S 199. Leiden: Brill. https://doi.org/10.1163/9789004473126.

Botta, Alejandro F. 2009. *The Aramaic and Egyptian Legal Traditions at Elephantine: An Egyptological Approach.* LSTS 64. London: T & T Clark.

Botta, Alejandro F. 2013. "Hated by the Gods and your Spouse: Legal Use of אנש in Elephantine and its Ancient Near Eastern Context." In *Law and Religion in the Eastern Mediterranean: From Antiquity to Early Islam*, edited by Anselm C. Hagedoorn and Reinhard G. Kratz, 105–29. Oxford: Oxford University Press. https://doi.org/10.1093/acprof:oso/9780199550234.003.0006.

Claassens, L. Juliana M. 2003. "Biblical theology as dialogue: Continuing the conversation on Mikhail Bakhtin and Biblical theology." *JBL* 122:127–144. https://doi.org/10.2307/3268094.

Folmer, Margaretha L. 1995. *The Aramaic Language in the Achaemenid Period: A Study in Linguistic Variation.* OLA 68. Leuven: Peeters.

Folmer, Margaretha L. 2017. "De Achikar Traditie." In *Wijsheid*, Amsterdamse Cahiers voor Exegese van de Bijbel en Zijn Tradities 31, 73–83. Bergambacht: 2VM.

Gass, Erasmus. 1999. "Der Passa-Papyrus (Cowl 211): Mythos oder Realität?" *BN* 99:55–68. https://doi.org/10.71715/bn.v99i.97692.

Grabbe, Lester L. 2004. *A History of Jews and Judaism in the Second Temple Period.* Vol. 1. LSTS 47. London: T & T Clark.

Granerød, Gard. 2016. *Dimensions of Yahwism in the Persian Period: Studies in the Religion and Society of the Judaean Community at Elephantine.* BZAW 488. Berlin: De Gruyter. https://doi.org/10.1515/9783110454314.

Grelot, Pierre. 1954. "Études sur le 'Papyrus Pascal' d'Éléphantine." *VT* 4:349–384. https://doi.org/10.1163/156853354X00299.

Grelot, Pierre. 1972. *Documents araméens d'Égypte.* Littératures Anciennes du Proche-Orient 5. Paris: Éditions du Cerf.

Holm, Tawny L. 2014. "Memories of Sennacherib in Aramaic Tradition." In *Sennacherib at the Gates of Jerusalem: Story, History, and Historiography*, CHANE 71, edited by Isaac Kalimi and Seth Richardson, 293–323. Leiden: Brill. https://doi.org/10.1163/9789004265622_010.

Kottsieper, Ingo. 1990. *Die Sprache der Ahiqarsprüche.* BZAW 194. Berlin: De Gruyter. https://doi.org/10.1515/9783110846348.

Kratz, Reinhard G. 2012–2013. *"Mille Ahiqar: 'The Words of Ahiqar' and the Literature of the Jewish Diaspora in Ancient Egypt." Al-Abhath* 60–61:39–58.

Lemaire, André. 2011. "Judean Identity in Elephantine: Everyday Life according to the Ostraca." In *Judah and the Judaeans in the Achaemenid Period: Negotiating Identities in an International Context*, edited by Oded Lipschits, Gary Knoppers, and Manfred Oeming, 365–374. Winona Lake: Eisenbrauns. https://doi.org/10.1515/9781575066493-016.

Lemaire, André. 2022. "The Ostraca of Elephantine: A Further Light on the Judeans in Elephantine." In *Elephantine Revisited: New Insights into the Community and its Neighbors*, edited by Margaretha Folmer, 45–54. University Park: Eisenbrauns. https://doi.org/10.1515/9781646022083-008.

Lindenberger, James M. 1983. *The Aramaic Proverbs of Ahiqar.* Baltimore: Johns Hopkins University Press.

Lozachmeur, Hélène. 2006. *La collection Clermont-Ganneau: Ostraca, épigraphes sur jarre, étiquettes de bois.* 2 vols. Paris: De Boccard.

Moore, James D. 2020. "The Persian Administrative Process in View of an Elephantine ʾAršāma Decree (TAD A6.2)." *Semitica et Classica* 13:49–62. https://doi.org/10.1484/J.SEC.5.122980.

Moore, James D. 2022. *New Aramaic Papyri from Elephantine in Berlin.* Studies on Elephantine 1. Leiden: Brill. https://doi.org/10.1163/9789004505568.

Moore, James D. 2024. "Administering Cult at Elephantine." In *Yahwism under the Achaemenid Empire: Professor Shaul Shaked in Memoriam*, BZAW 548, edited by Gad Barnea and Reinhard G. Kratz, 305–336. Berlin: De Gruyter. https://doi.org/10.1515/9783111018638-010.

Muraoka, Takamitsu, and Bezalel Porten. 2003. *A Grammar of Egyptian Aramaic: Second Revised Edition.* HdO 1.32. Leiden: Brill. https://doi.org/10.1163/9789004294257.

Niehr, Herbert. 2007. *Aramäischer Aḥiqar.* JSHRZ.NF 2.2. Gütersloh: Gütersloher Verlagshaus. https://doi.org/10.14315/9783641248307.

Nutkowicz, Hélène. 2007. "Concerning the Verb *śn'* in the Judaeo-Aramaic Contracts from Elephantine." *JSS* 52:211–25. https://doi.org/10.1093/jss/fgm002.

Nutkowicz, Hélène. 2015. *Destins de femmes à Eléphantine au Vè siècle avant notre ère.* Paris: Harmattan.

Oshima, Takayoshi M. 2017. "How 'Mesopotamian' was Ahiqar the Wise? A Search for Ahiqar in Cuneiform Texts." In *Wandering Arameans: Arameans Outside Syria: Textual and Archaeological Perspectives*, Leipziger Altorientalistische Studien 5, edited by Angelika Berlejung, Aren Maeir, and Andreas Schüle, 141–167. Wiesbaden: Harrasowitz.

Pearce, Laurie E., and Cornelia Wunsch. 2014. *Documents of Judean Exiles and West Semites in Babylonia in the Collection of David Sofer.* Cornell University Studies in Assyriology and Sumerology 28. Bethesda: CDL Press.

Porten, Bezalel. 1968. *Archives from Elephantine: The Life of an Ancient Jewish Colony.* Berkeley: University of California Press.

Porten, Bezalel. 1969. "The Religion of the Jews of Elephantine in Light of the Hermopolis Papyri." *JNES* 28:116–121. https://doi.org/10.1086/371997.

Porten, Bezalel. 1990. "The Calendar of Aramaic Texts from Achaemenid and Ptolemaic Egypt." In *Irano-Judaica II: Studies Relating to Jewish Contacts with Persian Culture Throughout the Ages*, edited by Shaul Shaked, 13–32. Jerusalem: Ben-Zvi Institute for the Study of Jewish Communities in the East.

Porten, Bezalel. 2011. *The Elephantine Papyri in English: Three Millennia of Cross-Cultural Continuity and Change.* 2nd rev. ed. Atlanta: SBL Press.

Porten, Bezalel, and Ada Yardeni. 1986. Textbook of Aramaic Documents from Ancient Egypt. Vol. I. Letters ; Appendix: Aramaic letters from the bible. Winona Lake, Ind. : Eisenbrauns.

Porten, Bezalel, and Henri Zvi Szubin. 1982. "'Abandoned Property' in Elephantine: A New Interpretation of Kraeling 3." *JNES* 41:123–131. https://doi.org/10.1086/372930.
Porten, Bezalel, Ran Zadok, and Laurie Pearce. 2016. "Akkadian Names in Aramaic Documents from Ancient Egypt." *BASOR* 375:1–12. https://doi.org/10.5615/bullamerschoorie.375.0001.
Rohrmoser, Angela. 2014. *Götter, Tempel und Kult der Judäo-Aramäer von Elephantine: archäologische und schriftliche Zeugnisse aus dem perserzeitlichen Ägypten.* AOAT 396. Münster: Ugarit-Verlag.
Sachau, Eduard. 1911. *Aramäische Papyrus und Ostraka aus einer jüdischen Militär-Kolonie zu Elephantine: altorientalische Sprachdenkmäler des 5. Jahrhunderts vor Chr.* Leipzig: JC Hinrichs.
Schipper, Bernd U. 2018. "Joseph, Ahiqar, and Elephantine: The Joseph Story as Diaspora Novella." *Journal of Ancient Egyptian Interconnections* 18(1):71–84.
Sobhy, George P.G. 1930. "Miscellanea." *JEA* 16:3–5, Pl. VII.
von Soden, Wolfram. 1936. "Die Unterweltsvision eines assyrischen Kronprinzen. Nebst einigen Beobachtungen zur Vorgeschichte des Aḥiqar-Romans." *ZA* 43:1–31. https://doi.org/10.1515/zava.1936.43.1-4.1.
Spiegelberg, Wilhelm. 1928. *Drei demotische Schreiben aus der Korrespondenz des Pherendates, des Satrapen Darius' I., mit den Chnumpriestern von Elephantine.* Berlin: Akademie der Wissenschaften.
Stern, Sasha. 2012. *Calendars in Antiquity: Empires, States, and Societies.* Oxford: Oxford University Press.
Vittmann, Günter. 1998. *Der demotische Papyrus Rylands 9.* ÄAT 38. Wiesbaden: Otto Harrassowitz Verlag.
Weigl, Michael. 2010. *Die aramäischen Achikar-Sprüche aus Elephantine und die alttestamentliche Weisheitsliteratur.* BZAW 399. Berlin: De Gruyter.
von Weiher, Egbert von. 1984. "Marduk-apla-uṣur und Nabû-šum-iškun in einem spätbabylonischen Fragment aus Uruk." *BaM* 15:197–224.
Wigand, Ann-Kristin. 2018. "Politische Loyalität und religiöse Legitimierung: Überlegungen zur Textpragmatik der aramäischen Achiqarkomposition." *WdO* 48:128–132. https://doi.org/10.13109/wdor.2018.48.1.128.
Wigand, Ann-Kristin. 2022. *Achikar in Elephantine: Die aramäische Achikarkomposition im Kontext des perserzeitlichen Elephantine.* ORA 50. Tübingen: Mohr Siebeck. https://doi.org/10.1628/978-3-16-161354-8.
Yardeni, Ada. 1994. "Maritime Trade and Royal Accountancy in an Erased Customs Account from 475 B. C. E. on the Aḥiqar Scroll from Elephantine." *BASOR* 293:67–78. https://doi.org/10.2307/1357278.
Zauzich, Karl-Theodor. 1976. "Demotische Fragmente zum Ahikar-Roman." In *Folia Rara Wolfgang Voigt LXV. diem natalem celebranti ab amicis et catalogorum codicum orientalium conscribendorum collegis dedicata*, edited by Herbert Franke, Walther Heissig, and Wolfgang Treue, 180–185. Wiesbaden: Franz Steiner Verlag.

Moritz F. Adam

Ambiguous Spaces and Timeless Ideas: On the Openness of Time and Space in the Book of Ecclesiastes

Abstract: This article investigates the construction and representation of time and space in the book of Ecclesiastes, which markedly departs from broader trajectories in the literature of Second Temple Judaism. While Jewish texts of the Persian and early Hellenistic Periods commonly anchor meaning in identifiable historical settings, establish links across time, and draw on culturally embedded "realms of memory", Ecclesiastes cultivates an intentionally decontextualized and ambiguous literary and intellectual framework. The present discussion situates these questions of the study of ancient Jewish literature within larger theoretical conversations about the production of space and temporality, and the distinction between memory and history, especially in the work of Pierre Nora. Against this backdrop, it is demonstrated that Ecclesiastes neither participates in nor actively recalls specific culturally salient realms of memory. Rather, the book is shown to offer reflections which are universalizing, abstract, and detached from specific temporal or spatial reference points. By foregrounding the ambiguity of the book's argument, this article shows how Ecclesiastes opens a reflective space in which key ethical and epistemic tensions of ancient Jewish literature are explored, but left open deliberately, thus opening up a distinctive hermeneutical potential in this unusual contribution to discourses of its time.

One of the pertinent features of the book of Ecclesiastes is that it proactively occludes, conceals, and ambiguates contextual features which may be suspected to have triggered or circumscribed the diverse set of reflections that are attested in it. Ecclesiastes takes an interest in global, totalizing questions of knowledge, meaning, and the human condition which are characterised specifically by not being constrained by or tied to any particular time or space. It challenges a premise, which in the Hebrew Bible and its wisdom literature is most notably established in the book of Proverbs, namely the orientation of theological and moral reflection within the bounds of an individual life, and moves further specifically by enquiring what the יִתְרוֹן, literally "that which remains", is in all the work at which humans toil under the sun (Eccl 1:3), under which, moreover, there is nothing new (1:9) in the first place.

The present discussion enquires into three problems especially. After some theoretical preliminaries, it considers the references to places and contexts, which are shown to be ambiguous, typological, and ultimately outside of any sense of recov-

https://doi.org/10.1515/9783112240366-005

erable context or history of events. Second, an interest will be taken in the relationship between timelessness, eternity, and patterns in Ecclesiastes' temporal conceptions. Third, broader questions will be asked about the place of this strange and idiosyncratic biblical book within the broader dynamic of Second Temple Judaism and its literary text production.

1 Prolegomena: Time and Space as Hermeneutical Constituents

Within the history of scholarship, it is far from obvious to regard conceptions of time and space — in any literature — as subjects worthy of discussion in their own right. For much of the history of thought, they were the canvases on which events, people, and problems were painted, they were circumstances, rather than objects of enquiry. Time and space were thought about in a derivative, rather than generative manner, until such conceptions as Ernst Bloch's (1977, 22–38; 1985, 209–219) notion of the *contemporaneity of the non-contemporaneous* ("die Gleichzeitigkeit des Ungleichzeitigen") or the question whether a linear, ever-progressing time has consequences on the construction of meaning, as encountered in the work of Mircea Eliade (1959, esp. 51–92.141–162) or Franz Rosenzweig (1921, 119–321), were raised. With respect to space, especially the work of Henri Lefebvre (1991, esp. 69–168) contributed to a distinction between natural space and social space, allowing to understand representations of space to carry social function and to be contingent upon historical, economic, cultural, and political concerns. In this sense, space was no longer merely a canvas or a circumstance, but something which is "produced". This type of production can describe the actual, physical configuration of spaces, i.e. how they are shaped by buildings, objects, and the like, but also how the perception of places and space can in itself create meaning.

With respect to Jewish literature, especially that of the Second Temple Period, corresponding questions could follow. Particularly curious within this arrangement is the non-contemporaneity between developments in the production of space and those in the arrangement of time, which can further the argument that conceptions of time and space in ancient Jewish writing were related, yet not in all cases mutually interdependent. New questions of identity formation and theological development already in the Persian period engendered a broader, universalist horizon before which biblical outlooks could unfold. Jewish literature availed itself of a broad range of localities, in Jerusalem, in the diaspora, later in transcendental spaces, though no longer consistently organised around a narrower arrangement of king, people, cult, and country as had been the case in the pre-exilic spatial horizons (Collins 1983, 1–26; Goodman 1996, 1–16; Najman 2014; Newman 2018, esp. 23–52; Schiffman 1991, 33–119; Weinfeld 2005, esp. 200–266, and many others). Further, also writing and literature itself, as holy texts, became — to use Heinrich Heine's term — a "portative fatherland" for early Judaism (Heine 1964, 128). At the same time, the diversity of Judean perspectives, shaped by the exile, by the continued significance of Jerusalem and the Land, by wider experiences of diaspora, and by cultural influences especially from Egypt, Greece, and the Ancient Near East, did not allow for a lowest common denominator in neither form nor ideas within postexilic literature at large as well as within most individual works. Instead, even when texts contained a setting and a locally bound plot, focuses remained blurred.

Conceptions of time, on the contrary, only shifted later, around the Hellenistic period, due to other influences and with different conversation partners. For the preceding history of Judaism, smaller exceptions notwithstanding, time is consistently a time for something or a time of something (cf. Grund and Janowski, 2009, 502–535 [Lit.]). Notably, the Hebrew language knows no words corresponding to the abstract English terms "past", "present", or "future". Their primary unit of measuring time was that of a generation (cf. broadly Chester 2012, 31–51; DeVries 1975; Pioske 2018; Stern 2003). The biblical texts' focuses, insofar as the discussion of temporal circumstances featured — usually setting the scene for some kind of content or plot — rested upon considering the lifetime of one or multiple central protagonists, who served as reference points (cf. Exod 3:15; Lev 17:7; Ps 33:11; 49:12; 77:9; 79:13; 85:6; 89:2; 102:13; 106:31; 135:13; 146:10; Isa 34:17; Joel 3:20, and various others; cf. for a broader discussion on this shift Adam 2025, 163–178). Still in the Persian period, biblical texts such as Chronicles or Ezra and Nehemiah availed themselves of lists and took an interest in a genealogical continuity of the returnees to Jerusalem, while across genres exemplarity remained a key structural principle of biblical literature (Najman and Reinhardt, 2019, 1–37; Reed 2009, 185–212; Uusimäki 2021, 19–48; Wright 2008, 165–182). Even broader, conceptual concerns were tied to or conveyed through more or less literarily stylised characters, rather than being established as systems, ideas, or first principles. Changes which arrived in contact with Greek and with new temporalities can be detected in literature especially with the advent of the apocalyptic tradition (Ben-Dov 2018, 289–303; DiTommaso 2021, 53–88; Koch 2003, 35–68; Stuckenbruck 2018, 160–180), and an interest in calendricality, the arrangement of time through regular structures, such as successions of years in sevens or multiples thereof, broader ideas of regularity and determinism, and a sense of total history encompassing the beginning to the end (cf. Kosmin 2018). While some broader concerns for eternity and laws of nature, or expectations of new creation are encountered in late prophetic texts, such as Jer 31–33 or Isa 65:17–25, the move of departing from meaning-making bound to and constructed within a referential history consisting of a string of at times exemplarised individuals only really occurred in the late 4th century with texts such as the Book of the Watchers (1En 1–36) or the Astronomical Book (1En 72–82). The abstract and timeless orientation of the observations and arguments encountered in the book of Ecclesiastes is triggered, as the following discussion will show on the grounds of a set of representative examples, and it is this broader shift within temporal thinking in Jewish literature from which the present discussion especially departs.

A final theoretical conversation partner, whom to engage can be productive, is a discussion specifically on the *representation* of time, as well as things in time, in both thought and literature. Through the close ties between literary productivity and identity formation in ancient Judaism, the engagement of its texts with exemplarised individuals, yet ones bound in time, could move in two directions. On the one hand, exemplarised characters such as Moses, David, or Solomon could point beyond themselves, and convey context-transcending meaning which was literarily actualised in them.[1] On the other, the practice of engaging these exemplars, for instance in so-called "pseudepigraphic" works, allowed the authors of such writings simultaneously to look backwards and forwards. The stories of these biblical figures, which were formative for Israelite identity and generative for succeeding engagement, rewriting, interpretation, and creativity, created *realms of memory* (*lieux de mémoire*), to which later readers, recipients, or writers could look back in various ways and from different perspectives, while the accessibility and vitality of these traditions enabled them, too, to look forwards upon these realms' continuing hermeneutical potential.

This mode of understanding the formation of biblical traditions as engagements with and literary productivity within collective cultural and religious memory is essential for much ancient Jewish literature and accordingly discussed widely in scholarship (cf. Grund 2008, 41–62). An intriguing and productive distinction, however, which has bearing on Ecclesiastes as a different kind of text that is less detectably situated in realms of memory, is provided by the French historian Pierre Nora, whose work is situated within the academic tradition of *nouvelle histoire* (Nora 1989, 7–24). Crucially, Nora distinguishes in the understanding of meaning across time between two categories, memory and history, with memory carrying many of the connotations of ancient Jewish traditions just described.

> Memory is life, borne by living societies founded in its name. It remains in permanent evolution, open to the dialectic of remembering and forgetting, [. . .] vulnerable to manipulation and appropriation, susceptible to being long dormant and periodically revived. History, on

1 Cf. here my forthcoming article on "Ambiguity, Author-Function, and the Blurring of Historical Referentiality in Hellenistic Jewish Literature".

> the other hand, is the reconstruction [. . .] of what is no longer, [. . .] a representation of the past. Memory, insofar as it is affective and magical, only accommodates those facts that suit it; it nourishes recollections that may be out of focus or telescopic, global or detached, particular or symbolic — responsive to each avenue of conveyance or phenomenal screen, to every censorship or projection. History, because it is an intellectual and secular production, calls for analysis and criticism.
>
> Memory is blind to all but the group it binds [. . . it] is by nature multiple and yet specific; collective, plural, and yet individual. History, on the other hand, belongs to everyone and no one, whence its claim to universal authority. Memory takes root in the concrete, in spaces, gestures, images, and objects; history binds itself strictly to temporal continuities, to progressions and to relations between things (Nora 1989, 8–9).

Nora is dismissive of the category of history in his system and suggests that the kind of historical systematisation he describes, since it is representative, universal, and temporarily broad, suppresses how in societies realms of memory anchor meaning and identity (Nora 1989, 9–11). His critique of historicism doubtless has merit in respect to how history ought to be written or how memory ought to be preserved. If his distinction itself is read historically, however, that is as an interpretatively productive disambiguation of existing sources that can be investigated with respect to the mode in which they observe the world, time, and spaces in it, further hermeneutical horizons arise, including for the study of Jewish antiquity. As will be shown in the following, the book of Ecclesiastes, for instance, does not tie itself to pertinent realms of memory as are encountered in apocalyptic or also liturgical texts, among others, that associate themselves with and rethink known points in history or culturally meaningful religious practices (cf. Newman 2020, 315–434). Rather, Ecclesiastes indeed writes, unusually for the Hebrew Bible, literature that belongs to everyone and no one, and binds itself to wider temporal continuities.

With Nora, therefore, important conclusions follow from this. Ecclesiastes, no matter the width and pertinence of the problems it concerns itself with, nor the sophistication, nuance, and depth with which it undertakes its reflective endeavours, does not recollect, invoke, or represent people, places, times or things, but employs exemplarity without explicit or unambiguous reference points. It binds history through principles, not through memory.

2 Spatial Ambiguities

In line with the broader issues just established, the consultation of a series of textual examples from the book of Ecclesiastes can both illustrate how the book conceives of and describes spaces in which it situates its argument, and how these representations indicate its abstract, decontextualised framework.[2] The first of these is Eccl 8:10–14:

10 וּבְכֵן רָאִיתִי רְשָׁעִים קְבֻרִים וָבָאוּ וּמִמְּקוֹם קָדוֹשׁ יְהַלֵּכוּ וְיִשְׁתַּכְּחוּ בָעִיר אֲשֶׁר כֵּן־עָשׂוּ גַּם־זֶה הָבֶל׃	10 And then I saw the wicked buried (or: draw near) and they came [to rest], they went out of the holy place and were forgotten (or: praised) in the city in which they had acted thus. This, too, signifies transience.
11 אֲשֶׁר אֵין־נַעֲשָׂה פִתְגָם מַעֲשֵׂה הָרָעָה מְהֵרָה עַל־כֵּן מָלֵא לֵב בְּנֵי־הָאָדָם בָּהֶם לַעֲשׂוֹת רָע׃	11 Since a judgement against an evil deed is not carried out swiftly, the heart of the sons of men grows full inside them to do evil.
12 אֲשֶׁר חֹטֶא עֹשֶׂה רָע מְאַת וּמַאֲרִיךְ לוֹ כִּי גַּם־יוֹדֵעַ אָנִי אֲשֶׁר יִהְיֶה־טּוֹב לְיִרְאֵי הָאֱלֹהִים אֲשֶׁר יִירְאוּ מִלְּפָנָיו׃	12 While a sinner does evil a hundred times and prolongs [his life], I know, however, that it will be well for the god-fearing ones, who are in fear before him.
13 וְטוֹב לֹא־יִהְיֶה לָרָשָׁע וְלֹא־יַאֲרִיךְ יָמִים כַּצֵּל אֲשֶׁר אֵינֶנּוּ יָרֵא מִלִּפְנֵי אֱלֹהִים׃	13 And it will not be well for the wicked, and his days will not be prolonged like a shadow, because he does not fear before God.
14 יֶשׁ־הֶבֶל אֲשֶׁר נַעֲשָׂה עַל־הָאָרֶץ אֲשֶׁר ׀ יֵשׁ צַדִּיקִים אֲשֶׁר מַגִּיעַ אֲלֵהֶם כְּמַעֲשֵׂה הָרְשָׁעִים וְיֵשׁ רְשָׁעִים שֶׁמַּגִּיעַ אֲלֵהֶם כְּמַעֲשֵׂה הַצַּדִּיקִים אָמַרְתִּי שֶׁגַּם־זֶה הָבֶל׃	14 There is a transient thing which occurs on the earth, that there are righteous people to whom things are happening according to the deeds of the wicked and there are wicked people to whom things are happening according to the deeds of the righteous. I said that this also [signifies] transience.[3]

This passage is, among the overall fairly sparse references to places and spaces in the book of Ecclesiastes, one of the most yielding. It describes movements and perceptions of people around the מָקוֹם קָדוֹשׁ, the "holy place", which supplies a setting, namely a broadly cultic setting, which is juxtaposed with questions about morally becoming behaviour.

There exist two broader problems in this passage. One is found rather at first glance, the other requires some immersion into text critical questions.

Interpreters have long struggled with this passage, since one is confronted with a narrative progression of the pericope which appears to be incoherent. On the one

2 The following discussion on Ecclesiastes reflects a number of wider findings which I expand in greater depth in my monograph, *Time and Tradition. Temporal Thinking in Ecclesiastes in the Context of Emerging Apocalypticism and the History of Ideas in the Hellenistic Period* (Adam 2025).
3 All renditions of the Hebrew text in the English language are my own translations.

hand, it portrays — in common fashion for the book of Ecclesiastes — the experiential observation that the deed-consequence nexus, which pervades much of ancient Israelite thinking (Koch 1983, 57–87), falls short in light of sinners either not being held accountable for their actions and even prolonging their lives. According to the monologist, this facilitates an inclination in people to stray away from righteous behaviour since evil deeds appear to be carried out with impunity (vv. 10 –12a.14). At the same time, there is an interjection in the middle of the pericope (vv. 12b–13) which seems to reaffirm basic assumptions of a retributive notion of justice. Rather expectedly, conservative propositions have been advanced which regard these different elements of the passage sufficiently irreconcilable as to be necessarily redactionally secondary (Braun 1973, 152; Lamparter 1975, 110; Lauha 1978, 157; Lepre 1975, 108; Zapletal 1911, 189). Others have rather proposed that vv. 12b–13 are a quotation of a traditional wisdom saying (Bonora 1992, 133; Derousseaux 1970, 343; Gordis 1968, 287–288; Hertzberg and Bardtke 1963, 174; Lange 1991, 159; Zimmerli 1983, 106). The excision of the supposed secondary elements of the passage, however, is not possible on the level of language.[4]

What one is confronted with in essence, then, is the exegetical problem that — without auxiliary tools such as narrative framing — the text seems rather blatantly to contradict itself. On the one hand, it is asserted that the speaker is acquainted with retributive notions of justice, on the other he appears to contradict this knowledge[5] based on experiences which he relates. If, however, literary-critical operations cannot be adduced to make the text conform to modern standards of coherence (cf. more broadly Teeter and Tooman 2020, 94–129), different hermeneutical options are called for. These especially have bearing on the rhetoric of the argument in question. The juxtaposition of an experience and a contrary reference to an expected system has the effect that the text ceases to be propositional. It cannot urge the reader either to take the experience at face value or blindly to regard the system of retribution as universally applicable.

---

4 This would leave the subordinate clause of v. 12 without a main clause. Further, the style of vv. 12b–13 contains comparably rare elements which are otherwise distinctively characteristic of the wider passage, such as the use of אֲשֶׁר in a causal sense, which is also found in v. 11.

5 Already the rephrasing of the verse in *Targum Qoheleth* shows that the interpretative difficulty is not restricted to modern readers. The Targum seeks to resolve the issue by transposing it in an eschatological reading: "And when a sinner does evil a hundred years, and space is given him from the Lord in order that he may repent, yet is it revealed to him by the Holy Spirit, and I know that it will be well in the world to come with those that fear the Lord, that fear before him, and do his will." (transl. Ginsburg 1861, 514). Even earlier, crucially, the LXX seems to restrict the extent in time to which the experiential statement applies, reading ὃς ἥμαρτεν, ἐποίησεν τὸ πονηρὸν ἀπὸ τότε καὶ ἀπὸ μακρότητος αὐτῷ·, "He who sinned (*nota bene* past tense) did evil from then and a long time before."

Herein lies the disconnect between the primary text and its reading in modern exegetical studies, which seem to assume that exegesis must draw out from a source not a problem, but a solution, a correct answer to be recovered rather than a vital, intellectually available question whose answer need not have been implied in the text. In other words, their exegetical endeavours show individual possible — and notably varied — responses to the problem with which the monologist wishes to confront his readers. By resorting to the use of what is commonly labelled incoherent, paradoxical, or contradictory expressions, however, the book of Ecclesiastes primarily accomplishes to alert the reader to the limits of encompassing the entirety of one's experience in an ethical system (to the contrary, cf. Rudman 2001). The richness of this approach lies precisely in this openness, which allows for the text to be relatable to readers of various backgrounds and circumstances. It is a move to uncouple the text from context, while continuing to embed it in traditions to which contemporary readers would have been able to relate.

Specifically because the episode at hand is situated at the temple, which is referred to only by the paraphrasing expression מְקוֹם קָדוֹשׁ, "holy place", readers may bring to the text assumptions which are based in their knowledge of tradition, much of which in the case of ancient Judaism is associated with cultic concerns. Due to this association, the problem at hand is made relevant to them, despite no further context whatsoever being provided. Readers do not learn who the people in question are, what they do, or on the basis of which moral system their actions are judged as wicked. But because this association of an ethical discourse with a cultic setting in Eccl 8:10 is so loose, and because the place in question is left as vague as it is, the monologue is free to operate critically with the problem it poses without clashing with the tradition itself or the relationship in which readers find themselves with this tradition through more specific, culturally bound realms of memory. It does not need to construct propositional meaning but can engage in a more abstract dialectical consideration. Other Jewish literature, whose construction of meaning is more closely tied to memory in Nora's sense, described above, could not engage in self-reflection like this precisely because of this difference.

The ambiguity of Eccl 8:10 goes even further. There are two verbal forms in this verse which have led scholars to propose emendations to the Masoretic text. The first one is the form קְבֻרִים, a Qal passive masculine plural participle from the root קבר. The proposition in this case is to read alternatively by way of metathesis קְרֵבִים, from the root קרב, "to draw near" (e.g. Loader 1979, 98–99; Schoors 2013, 623), since the connection between burial and holy places is not attested anywhere in ancient Jewish literature, while the verb קרב is the most common technical term in Hebrew for participating in temple worship (cf. e.g. within the book Eccl 4:17). What is accomplished by the proposed emendations — notwithstanding the question whence the problem emerged in the linguistic or transmission history of the text —

is that in the opening verse of the passage readers encounter in one word the two central orientations of the pericope at large, namely the question of the connection between sinfulness and premature death on the one hand, and the question of one's acclaim in spite of wickedness on the other. It is precisely this overlap which has made the emendation appealing to modern critical readers, and speaks to the playfulness with which the two focuses of the passage can come together in the process of reading. A second case is similarly intriguing. The form וְיִשְׁתַּכְּחוּ, a Hitpael imperfect 3rd person masculine plural form of the root שׁכח ("and they were forgotten"), causes difficulty in light of ancient versional evidence. Contrary to the Masoretic Text, one encounters in the Septuagint the translation καὶ ἐπῃνέθησαν ἐν τῇ πόλει, "and they were *praised* in the city", with ἐπῃνέθησαν – a 3rd person plural aorist passive indicative of ἐπαινέω, "to praise" — corresponding to the Hebrew form ישתבחו from שָׁבַח II., "to praise", — which is also attested in some Hebrew manuscripts, and has compelled commentators to emend the Hebrew accordingly (e.g. Backhaus 1993, 252; Lauha 1978, 154; Michel 1989, 220). Here, too, the text critical problem is in essence a microcosm of the wider pericope, which deals with the deed-consequence nexus on the one hand, and the question of death and oblivion on the other.

The openness and ambiguity of the book of Ecclesiastes, as exemplified in this pericope, is encountered almost in a suspended space. Small terms, such as "holy place" give broad indications as to the setting of the book, but otherwise it stands entirely apart from traceable people or events. Nothing is described, least of all the places in which the monologist says to have witnessed or experienced various matters which caused the succeeding reflections. Many pericopes in Ecclesiastes, between which other literary forms are also encountered, begin with the verb רָאִיתִי, "I saw" (Eccl 1:14; 3:16; 4:15; 5:13,18; 6:1; 7:15; 8:9,10; 9:13; 10:5), and the following reflections are often introduced with the verb אָמַרְתִּי, "I said" (Eccl 2:1,2; 3:17,18; 6:3; 7:23; 8:14). That which Ecclesiastes says to have seen, however, pertains exclusively to human activities, their fleetingness, and some moral problems, never an identifiable context in which they take place, nor indeed an identifiable time or a set of identifiable people.

For the book of Ecclesiastes, its discussions are about the problems upon which it reflects, not where they arose, who or which events they might have been tied to — although in some instances reasonable guesses are possible. The book shows *that* there are problems to knowledge and meaning within and beyond human lives.

A very similar example to the one in Eccl 8:10–14 is Eccl 4:17–5:6. This pericope, too, is introduced by a reference to a cultic setting, again without any further detail, and a succeeding, much broader problem which is unfolded in this rather indescript space. The pertinent questions for the current discussion are expanded especially in 4:17–5:2:

4:17 שְׁמֹר רגליך כַּאֲשֶׁר תֵּלֵךְ אֶל־
בֵּית הָאֱלֹהִים וְקָרוֹב לִשְׁמֹעַ מִתֵּת
הַכְּסִילִים זָבַח כִּֽי־אֵינָם יוֹדְעִים
לַעֲשׂוֹת רָֽע׃
5:1 אַל־תְּבַהֵל עַל־פִּיךָ וְלִבְּךָ אַל־
יְמַהֵר לְהוֹצִיא דָבָר לִפְנֵי הָאֱלֹהִים
כִּי הָאֱלֹהִים בַּשָּׁמַיִם וְאַתָּה עַל־
הָאָרֶץ עַל־כֵּן יִהְיוּ דְבָרֶיךָ מְעַטִּים׃
2 כִּי בָּא הַחֲלוֹם בְּרֹב עִנְיָן וְקוֹל
כְּסִיל בְּרֹב דְּבָרִים׃

4:17 Watch your foot as you go to the house of God;
and coming near to listen is better than to offer the
dullard's sacrifice, for they do not know that they
do evil.
5:1 Do not make haste upon your mouth, and your
heart do not bring quickly to put forth a word before God, for God is in the heavens, and you are
upon the earth, therefore your words shall be few.
2 For a dream comes with much business; but the
voice of a dullard with many words. [. . .][6]

This reference is more explicit and employs a term which in Late Biblical Hebrew is regularly used for the Jerusalem temple, specifically in Ezra-Nehemiah and Chronicles, and at least loose reference is made — though in a deprecating manner — to sacrificial practices. The associations of the expression בֵּית (הָ)אֱלֹהִים, "house of God", however, are broader, and it is also employed, beyond references to non-Israelite cultic places that can safely be neglected here, also in the episode of Jacob's dream at Bethel (Gen 28:17), which, too, accentuates a spatial distinction of God and humanity. Especially since dreaming is invoked in a critical manner in this passage in Ecclesiastes, which especially cautions against excessive speech and critically engages dreaming as a mode of revelation (Adam 2025, 96–119), the use of this specific term, בֵּית הָאֱלֹהִים, is striking. The intertextual nexus, which evokes images of the Second Temple at Jerusalem — in which at this time also apocalyptic speculation took hold, which, too, drew upon dreams as a revelatory means (Collins 2016; Segal 2016; Stone 2003, 167–180) — as well as this foundational story of the origins of Israel, is evident to informed readers, but the association is rather gentle, so that rhetorically Ecclesiastes need not position itself against other biblical traditions more explicitly.

A similar recourse to places, though in a different literary setting and to partially different ends, occurs also in the royal travesty (Eccl 1:12–2:26), especially in Eccl 2:4–6:

6 In English translations, the verses in this chapter are numbered differently than in the Hebrew text. The verse numbers used here correspond with the Hebrew.

4 הִגְדַּלְתִּי מַעֲשָׂי בָּנִיתִי לִי בָּתִּים נָטַעְתִּי לִי כְּרָמִים׃	4 I made great my works great; I built houses and planted vineyards for myself.
5 עָשִׂיתִי לִי גַּנּוֹת וּפַרְדֵּסִים וְנָטַעְתִּי בָהֶם עֵץ כָּל־פֶּרִי׃	5 I made gardens for myself, and orchards, and I planted in them trees with all kinds of fruit.
6 עָשִׂיתִי לִי בְּרֵכוֹת מָיִם לְהַשְׁקוֹת מֵהֶם יַעַר צוֹמֵחַ עֵצִים׃	6 I made water pools for myself, to water from them the forest of growing trees.

In these verses, the spaces in which the monologist situates himself, are even more abstract. The use of the Persian loanword פַּרְדֵּס, which is etymologically related to the modern English word "paradise", even raises cultural associations beyond Israel (Adam 2024). Ultimately, however, the description of a lavish life, which the monologist says initially to have striven for and then abandoned, operates in no real space at all. It is a foil against which Ecclesiastes establishes the ultimate transience and fleetingness of life. The places in question, the houses, vineyards, gardens, orchards, pools and forests do not point to anything or anywhere. Rather, the fact that they do not point to anything beyond themselves is key to the argument of this chapter. They are ambiguous, timeless, and even more hermeneutically available to be transposed to any time or context which a reader may choose than the localities of the previously considered pericopes which at least loosely allowed for association with established spaces of Jewish tradition. In a number of instances, moreover, the royal travesty directly borrows from a diverse set of Egyptian, Greek, and Ancient Near Eastern cultural influences (Adam 2025, 50–58), thus blurring its picture even further.

In a curious way, the notions of place and space are similar to the Song of Songs. In its anthology of secular love poetry, it praises love between man and woman that is removed from the conventions and pressures of society. The characters, a man and a woman, are at times placed in physical spaces, though consistently ones that are so far exemplarised as to be untraceable. Its notion of space, too, is ambiguous, diverse, and profoundly varied (cf. Hagedorn 2015, 207–233).[7]

Finally, the most bound and explicit references to a place are the handful of verses which refer to Jerusalem. These are exclusively confined to the royal travesty, besides the book's superscription (Eccl 1:1,12,16; 2:7,9). In none of the verses in question, however, do these references contribute meaningfully to the arguments

7 The arrangement of toponyms around the city of Jerusalem, which stands in the center of attention and appears in eight verses, spreads in a roughly balanced manner into all four cardinal directions (Jericke 2005, 39–58). Scholarship has further accentuated that the manner in which space is more broadly conceptualized traverses the public and the private, the physical and the imagined, or the real and the fantastic. The interplay of these notions in language situates the text often in a liminal space.

which are being advanced. The book of Ecclesiastes, like the Song of Songs and the book of Proverbs, stylises itself as "Solomonic literature" (Bolin 2017, esp. 20–35; Dell 2021, 321–336) and superficially invokes through these references to Jerusalem its authorial fiction (cf. Schipper 2019, 65). It is noticeable, however, that none of the details provided in the purportedly autobiographical account of the royal travesty corresponds meaningfully with any detail that is related about Solomon in 1Kgs 1–11 or 2Chr 1–9. Importantly, when places are invoked in the book's reflections outside the royal travesty, Jerusalem is not explicitly mentioned. In the abstract discussion of Eccl 8:10–14 — discussed above —, which is loosely set in a cultic context, the book only speaks of "the city".[8] While, of course, Jerusalem is in view here, the book of Ecclesiastes does not speak of the city by name except for its framing references to Solomon, which authorise the book but remain otherwise unconnected.

More broadly, there are a number of intriguing observations which arise from the manner in which the book of Ecclesiastes conceives of places and spaces. When places are referred to, usually loosely and without any details whatsoever that could situate them in a history of events, they are consistently public spaces, but the concerns described which the monologist observes in them and reflects upon are focused on individuals, albeit exemplarised ones. Ecclesiastes is concerned with the transience of the legacy of individual lives (first in Eccl 1:2–3), of a kind of everyman, not with collective, let alone national or religious concerns. In Lefebvre's terms, places are only produced through the abstract problems that are set in them, they have nothing about themselves and no independent qualities in the book other than the problems which are unfolded in them. These settings are not at all furnished, there are no details, no descriptions, and even the few contextualisations around Jerusalem and the temple appear occasional. Beyond places and spaces, the book of Ecclesiastes obscures any context that may have given rise to its reflections. Even the somewhat traceable, though, of course literarily stylised Solomonic attribution is not explicit, but avails itself of the somewhat cryptic name "Qoheleth" as a cypher.[9]

It is essential that the arguments which are advanced in the book of Ecclesiastes are consistently ambiguous and open (cf. further Ingram 2006), rather than propositional, as the discussion especially of Eccl 8:10–14 has shown. In the absence of a situation in traceable places, without anything more than is absolutely necessary to invoke a connection between the reader and the text through known spaces, such as cultic ones, arguments can unfold in the book that are left hermeneutically open and alert to questions, rather than answers. In this way, the reflections of

8 On cities more broadly and their significance in the Hebrew Bible, cf. Aitken and Marlow 2018.

9 The question of the meaning of the name Qoheleth is as old and varied as the study of the book which is named after him. For a summary of the discussion, cf. e.g. Schoors 2013, 30–36.

Ecclesiastes stand in a suspended space — though one that is generally identifiable as Jewish — and are available in such a way that its problems, which are not context-specific, can be transposed to any other place or time to which they may speak.

3 Abstract Time and Total Histories

Beyond this discussion of place and space, there are a number of issues in Ecclesiastes, specifically with respect to the book's conceptions of time, which help to further the present argument. A particularly illuminating passage is the reflection about the cyclic motions of natural things in Eccl 1:4–11:

4 דּוֹר הֹלֵךְ וְדוֹר בָּא וְהָאָרֶץ לְעוֹלָם עֹמָדֶת׃	4 A generation comes, and a generation goes, and the earth stands in time.
5 וְזָרַח הַשֶּׁמֶשׁ וּבָא הַשָּׁמֶשׁ וְאֶל־מְקוֹמוֹ שׁוֹאֵף זוֹרֵחַ הוּא שָׁם׃	5 The sun rises, and the sun sets, and it hastens to its place, rising [again] there.
6 אֶל־דָּרוֹם וְסוֹבֵב אֶל־צָפוֹן סוֹבֵב ׀ סֹבֵב הוֹלֵךְ הָרוּחַ וְעַל־סְבִיבֹתָיו שָׁב הָרוּחַ׃	6 Going to the south, and turning to the north, round and round goes the wind, and all around the wind returns.
7 כָּל־הַנְּחָלִים הֹלְכִים אֶל־הַיָּם וְהַיָּם אֵינֶנּוּ מָלֵא אֶל־מְקוֹם שֶׁהַנְּחָלִים הֹלְכִים שָׁם הֵם שָׁבִים לָלָכֶת׃	7 All streams flow to the sea, and the sea is not full. To the place whence the streams flow, there they return.
8 כָּל־הַדְּבָרִים יְגֵעִים לֹא־יוּכַל אִישׁ לְדַבֵּר לֹא־תִשְׂבַּע עַיִן לִרְאוֹת וְלֹא־תִמָּלֵא אֹזֶן מִשְּׁמֹעַ׃	8 All things are weary, man cannot speak [of it]. The eye is not sated from seeing, and the ear is not filled by hearing.
9 מַה־שֶּׁהָיָה הוּא שֶׁיִּהְיֶה וּמַה־שֶּׁנַּעֲשָׂה הוּא שֶׁיֵּעָשֶׂה וְאֵין כָּל־חָדָשׁ תַּחַת הַשָּׁמֶשׁ׃	9 What has been will be, and what was done will be done, and there is nothing new under the sun.
10 יֵשׁ דָּבָר שֶׁיֹּאמַר רְאֵה־זֶה חָדָשׁ הוּא כְּבָר הָיָה לְעֹלָמִים אֲשֶׁר הָיָה מִלְּפָנֵנוּ׃	10 Is there a thing which says [of itself], 'see, this is new'? It has existed already in the times which have taken place before us.
11 אֵין זִכְרוֹן לָרִאשֹׁנִים וְגַם לָאַחֲרֹנִים שֶׁיִּהְיוּ לֹא־יִהְיֶה לָהֶם זִכָּרוֹן עִם שֶׁיִּהְיוּ לָאַחֲרֹנָה׃	11 There is no remembrance for the former ones, and also for the latter ones that will exist, there will be no remembrance for them with those who will be after them.

Much of the discussion of time in the book of Ecclesiastes has been focused on the objects of temporal thinking. Mette Bundvad (2015, esp. 45–82) has introduced an important distinction between world time and human time, that is a wider, ever-flowing progression of the circumstances and surroundings to which humanity is subjected, and a narrower development of experiences and meaning within a human lifetime that is ultimately realised to be transient before this horizon of a total history. An important further dimension is that there is importance specifically to the function of such temporal thinking that allows not only to describe the book's argument analytically, but to understand it before the wider history of ideas in the Hellenistic period (thus more extensively Adam 2025, esp. 161–225).

Eccl 1:9 is an especially important case in which the book uses idiosyncratic language that is otherwise fully unattested in Hebrew. The expressions מַה־שֶּׁהָיָה, literally "that which was", and שֶּׁיִּהְיֶה, literally "that which will be" are the earliest attestations in the Hebrew language of temporal categories which have not an object as their reference point, such as בִּימֵי + an attributive genitive, or express a relative past compared to a reference time, e.g. שִׁלְשֹׁם, literally "the day before yesterday", which is at times used figuratively to describe things in the past. Ecclesiastes reflects a new temporality, a sense of total history, which can be spoken of as one, rather than as a sum of constituent parts, i.e. generations, as is otherwise the case in biblical literature. Comparable shifts around the time of Ecclesiastes' composition in the 3rd century BCE are encountered especially in such literature which is influenced by the advent of apocalyptic thinking, e.g. the earliest parts of the Enoch corpus, the book of Jubilees, or 4QInstruction (Bakker 2023, 106–139; Ben-Dov 2018, 289–303; DiTommaso 2021, 53–88; Goff 2022, 429–452; Stuckenbruck 2018, 160–180). The main interlocutor for this development in the history of ideas is of Greek origin, as Paul Kosmin has shown in his discussion of new time reckonings in the Seleucid Empire, which can in this period be understood also to have had an effect on Israel and its world of thought:

> [The] Seleucid Era was a continuous, unbroken count of years. Its epoch, or Year 1 was placed in 312/311 BCE [. . .]. At Seleucus I's death in 281 BCE, his son and successor, Antiochus I, did not restart the count, and the subsequent kings let it continue unbroken. Accordingly, the Seleucid Era's time reckoning was uninterrupted, irreversible, paratactic, cumulative, endless, and directional. It did not represent a king's reign or office of state. It did not depend on or respond to actions in the real world. It was decoupled from things, objects, and events. It belonged to a separate order than the phenomena it dated. It was a regular, numericalized measure of ever-deepening duration. Put simply, it rolled (rolls) on and on (Kosmin 2018, 21–22).

This mode of an uninterrupted, irreversible, paratactic, cumulative, and endless, flow of history is encountered also in Ecclesiastes, and especially exemplified in the opening poem of Eccl 1:4–11. Besides a variety of other aspects, this sentiment is represented in its notion of space, too. Especially the first half of the poem describes the regular, cyclical flow of patterns in nature, which are introduced as an underlying framework, as a moving, yet ever-constant stage on which human lives play out and disappear again. This is an interest in nature and an unqualified description of nature *as such*. It does not point beyond itself, it has no beginning or end, no tie to any specific places, people, or events, nothing where time and natural progressions in time point beyond themselves.

In this sense, for instance, there is a difference between this articulation and other Jewish traditions which took an interest in the cosmos and in natural order. The description of the luminaries in the Priestly creation account in Gen 1, or the pronouncement of an eternal divine covenant with day and night in Jer 33, also consider natural, unchanging patterns, but they introduce them only inasmuch as they point beyond themselves, as they signify times and seasons in creation or point to the relationship between God and his people in salvation history. Here, on the contrary, a sense of the flow of time is introduced which considers such patterns genuinely in their own right, as an epistemically limiting principle which relegates the position of generations, lives, experiences, ideas or meaning and makes them הֶבֶל, “transient”.

This total history and abstract underlying time, which the book of Ecclesiastes, in contradistinction to other biblical literature, takes as its ontological first principle, engenders the following departure of the book’s argument from context, from explication in a history of events, and from specificity with respect to the places and people whom the monologist observes and reflects upon. If time progresses unchangingly, any moral reflection, any observation, any event or any thought is primarily dependent on being open rather than closed, on being contingent upon a progression of circumstances of which human experience can only grasp parts, while the only remaining certainty is that any conclusion is based on a partial picture and any effect is transient, set before a wider cyclical, yet changing horizon of total history within which — with Heraclitus — πάντα ῥεῖ, “everything flows” (Jarick 2000, 79–99).

In this sense, there exists a link between the book’s orientation in time and space, and the openness of its arguments. While the book acknowledges that certain things have their proper times (cf. Eccl 3:1–8), it concludes that one cannot know or place them (cf. Eccl 3:9–15), and the only course of action which is ultimately recommended is to eat, drink, and enjoy oneself (Eccl 2:24a; 3:12; 3:22a; 5:17; 8:15a; 9:7–9a; 11:7–12:1a; Whybray 1982, 87–98). Any investigation into specific things in specific places or times are foremost characterised by their fleetingness, so that within this mode of thinking there is no longer any need for specificity or propositionality. On the one hand, the book observes continuing patterns of reality that are independent from anything specific in time, thus relegating the importance of context, on the other, this wider horizon — together with a sceptical view about being able to know anything about God's actions and plans towards humanity acting from outside of experienceable reality — creates an epistemic uncertainty that makes it difficult to say anything with certainty beyond the observation that all is transient.

4 The Place of Ecclesiastes in Second Temple Judaism

The book of Ecclesiastes often looks like the odd one out within the Hebrew Bible, but also within Second Temple Literature. Many of its problems and perspectives, whose spatial and temporal orientations have just been discussed, feel idiosyncratic and different from other ancient Jewish texts. In many ways, however, its concerns and questions are not too different from other literature of its time, only the mode in which it undertakes its reflections and presents its arguments. While Ecclesiastes is not engaged much as a book in Second Temple Judaism — as are only very few books in this period, which binds tradition to exemplary figures rather than closed compositions — its ideas are repeatedly taken up, developed, and discussed, at times with substantial linguistic proximity, in a number of texts, such as 4QInstruction, Ben Sira (Marböck 1997, 275–301), or 2Baruch (Henze 2008, 28–43).

In order to understand, now, the place of Ecclesiastes in Second Temple Judaism, the taxonomy of memory and history introduced above can help to understand better which aspects of its outlook make the book stand out so much relative to its contemporaries.

Since Ecclesiastes' notion of time was not constituted as a first principle by a string of generations, people, and events in time, but understood a broader continuity of uninterrupted, irreversible, paratactic, cumulative, endless, and directional total history, this new temporality made context and location less important, since their relevance would be relegated anyway on the grounds of the book's main observation, the ultimate transience of all things in human time before the wider horizon of world time. While much writing in the Second Temple period, especially liturgical, pseudepigraphic, and apocalyptic literature, tied itself vertically across time to people, places, or historical events (e.g. Najman 2012, 497–518; Newman 2020, 415–434), which are reimagined and filled with new content and thus served as *lieux de mémoire*, binding early Judaism in formative traditions, the book of Ecclesiastes reads mostly horizontally. The book contains many and varied allusions and a loose sense of referentiality which places it within Jewish *discourses*, as can be seen through the broad intertextual nexus in which it presents itself (more broadly, cf. Dell and Kynes 2014). It takes an interest in the problems encountered in Jewish tradition inasmuch as they are problems, less than that they are part of this tradition. The specificities, the places, people, and events, which served Jewish writing at the time and pointed beyond themselves as foundational realms of memory, Ecclesiastes acknowledges but regards them as ultimately transient, too. Its interest is rather in the here established sense historical, and binds itself strictly to temporal continuities, to progressions and to relations between things. Ecclesiastes reimagines past and present not only as relevant for present and future — as do eschatological outlooks in apocalyptic literature or attempts at a bridging and re-actualising of history in liturgy and prayer (e.g. Newman 1999) — but conceives of problems and questions in them in a timeless, broader manner that can be decoupled from the history of Israel. While some references to Jerusalem, the temple, or Solomon serve to alert readers to the relevance of Ecclesiastes' broader reflections and to authorise the text within the tradition of Jewish literature, attempts at reading vertically in a clearer sense through ties to specific contexts are avoided. This orientation in worldly space and time is supplemented by its radically immanent perspective, its agnosticism about the divine and transcendental (Eccl 3:11; 7:14,24; 8:17), or its hesitancy about dreaming (cf. Eccl 4:17–5:6 above). While such thinking is at times tied in scholarship to Greek philosophy (e.g. Braun 1973; Gericke 2015, 1–7; Rudman 2001, 25–32; Schwienhorst-Schönberger 1996; Sneed 2023, 1–19) — *nota bene* the same cultural context whence Ecclesiastes gets its notions of time and history — the problems the book discusses are especially deeply entangled within Jewish thought, albeit in a more abstract manner.

5 Conclusions

In his theses on the philosophy of history, Walter Benjamin wrote that "history is the subject of a structure whose site is not homogenous, empty time, but time filled by the presence of the now (in German "Jetztzeit")" (Benjamin 1968, 261). This understanding of history, which in Nora's terms may perhaps better be characterised as "memory", drives reflections upon the past which seek to actualise it through realms of memory, to reimagine it and to establish its relevance from contexts for the concerns of the present and those who avail themselves of it. Such a history is constituted by the places, people, and events in it, by lines being drawn across it, and by meaning being constructed through recourse to, descriptions of, and reflections upon it, and is characteristic for most reflections upon space and time in ancient Judaism.

In this sense, and in comparison with its literary contemporaries, Ecclesiastes is indeed the odd one out. It does not describe the places and spaces in which its observations are situated, it does not place itself in a history of events, rather, it seeks to occlude or ambiguate any context, strives for a plurality of possible readings and interpretations even up to the smallest parts of its argument, and seeks to be abstract, timeless, and hermeneutically open literature. It does so before a horizon of new temporality, which it could draw from due to changes to temporal reckoning in the Seleucid Empire, and its innovative distinction between time as such as an ongoing, ever-flowing, detached course of total history, and the transience of human lives, of meaning, and of only partially testable intellectual systems, which causes a necessary epistemic uncertainty. Ecclesiastes does not construct for itself or evoke the realms of memory that are distinctively characteristic for much of the vital text production which characterises Second Temple Judaism, but it bears immense relevance for it through its rather more horizontal reading and its abstract reflections upon pertinent questions. It therefore shares an intellectual history with many of its contemporaries upon which it drew and which drew upon it in turn.

The preceding discussion has considered wider trends in the study of space and time in Second Temple Judaism and introduced new theoretical perspectives into this discourse, drawing especially on the French academic tradition of *nouvelle histoire*. Through the discussion of representative textual examples from the book of Ecclesiastes, it was shown how the ambiguity in the book's arguments works, on which levels of reflection it manifests itself, and how this ambiguity is tied in specifically with the Ecclesiastes' reticence to explicate, describe, situate, and clarify the places in which its experiential reflections are set. Further, the new, totalising horizons of temporal thinking in Ecclesiastes were sketched, and it was demonstrated which modes of reflection about time serve as a background for the consideration of knowledge, meaning, and the human condition in time. It is hoped that this discussion can help to integrate the book of Ecclesiastes further into pertinent discourses of Second Temple Judaism, profile its intellectual arrangement, explain how its interlocutors are found rather more in a history of ideas than a history of events, and situate its reflections upon space and time as an unusual, yet productive interlocutor for the study of Jewish tradition, thought, and literature.

Bibliography

Adam, Moritz F. 2024. "Paradise in Second Temple and Hellenistic Judaism." In *Encyclopedia of the Bible and Its Reception*, edited by Constance M. Furey et al. Vol. 23. Berlin: De Gruyter.

Adam, Moritz F. 2025. *Time and Tradition: Temporal Thinking in Ecclesiastes in the Context of Emerging Apocalypticism and the History of Ideas in the Hellenistic Period*. Tübingen: Mohr Siebeck.

Aitken, James K., and Hilary F. Marlow, eds. 2018. The City in the Hebrew Bible: Critical, Literary, and Exegetical Approaches. London: T&T Clark.

Backhaus, Franz Josef. 1993. *"Denn Zeit und Zufall trifft sie alle" Studien zur Komposition und zum Gottesbild im Buch Qohelet*. Frankfurt a. M.: A. Hain.

Bakker, Arjen F. 2023. *The Secret of Time: Reconfiguring Wisdom in the Dead Sea Scrolls*. Leiden: Brill. https://doi.org/10.1163/9789004537798.

Ben-Dov, Jonathan. 2018. "Apocalyptic Temporality: The Force of the Here and Now." *Hebrew Bible and Ancient Israel* 5(3):289–303. https://doi.org/10.1628/186870316X14805954607759.

Benjamin, Walter. 1968. *Illuminations*. New York: Schocken Books.

Bloch, Ernst. 1977. "Nonsynchronism and the Obligation to its Dialectics." *New German Critique* 11:22–38. https://doi.org/10.2307/487802.

Bloch, Ernst. 1985. "Über Ungleichzeitigkeit, Provinz und Propaganda." In *Tendenz – Latenz – Utopie*, 209–219. Frankfurt a. M.: Suhrkamp.

Bolin, Thomas M. 2017. *Ecclesiastes and the Riddle of Authorship*. New York: Routledge.

Bonora, Antonio. 1992. *Il libro di Qoèlet*. Rome: Città Nuova.

Braun, Rainer. 1973. *Kohelet und die frühhellenistische Popularphilosophie*. Berlin: De Gruyter. https://doi.org/10.1515/9783110832815.

Bundvad, Mette. 2015. *Time in the Book of Ecclesiastes*. Oxford: Oxford University Press. https://doi.org/10.1093/acprof:oso/9780198739708.001.0001.

Chester, Andrew. 2012. *Future Hope and Present Reality*. Vol. 1. Tübingen: Mohr Siebeck. https://doi.org/10.1628/978-3-16-152282-6.

Collins, John J. 1983. *Between Athens and Jerusalem: Jewish Identity in the Hellenistic Diaspora*. New York: Crossroad.

Collins, John J. 2016. *The Apocalyptic Imagination. An Introduction to Jewish Apocalyptic Literature*. 3rd ed. Grand Rapids, MI: Eerdmans.

Dell, Katharine J., and Will Kynes, eds. 2014. *Reading Ecclesiastes Intertextually*. London: T&T Clark.

Dell, Katharine J. 2021. "Solomon and the Solomonic Collection." In *The Oxford Handbook of Wisdom and the Bible*, edited by Will Kynes, 321–336. New York: Oxford University Press. https://doi.org/10.1093/oxfordhb/9780190661267.013.20.

Derousseaux, Louis. 1970. "Qohélet et l'authentique crainte de Dieu" In *La crainte de Dieu dans l'Ancien Testament*, 337–346. Paris: Éditions du Cerf.

DeVries, Simon J. 1975. *Yesterday, Today, and Tomorrow: Time and History in the Old Testament*. London: SPCK.

DiTommaso, Lorenzo. 2021. "Time and History in Ancient Jewish and Christian Apocalyptic Writings." In *Dreams, Visions, Imaginations. Jewish, Christian and Gnostic Views of the World to Come*, edited by Matthias Konradt, Judith Lieu, Laura Nasrallah, Jens Schröter, and Gregory E. Sterling, 53–88. Berlin: De Gruyter. https://doi.org/10.1515/9783110714746-004.

Eliade, Mircea. 1959. *Cosmos and History: The Myth of the Eternal Return*. New York: Harper and Brothers.

Gericke, Jaco. 2015. "A Comprehensive Typology of Philosophical Perspectives on Qohelet." *VeEc* 36:1–7. https://doi.org/10.4102/ve.v36i1.1358.

Goodman, Martin. 1996. "Sacred Space in Diaspora Judaism." In *Studies on the Jewish Diaspora in the Hellenistic and Roman Periods*, edited by Benjamin Isaac and Aharon Oppenheimer, 1–16. Tel Aviv: Tel Aviv University; Ramot Publishing.

Ginsburg, Christian D. 1861. *Coheleth: Commonly Called the Book of Ecclesiastes: Translated from the Original Hebrew, with a Commentary, Historical and Critical*. London: Longman, Green, Longman, and Roberts.

Gordis, Robert. 1968. *Koheleth, the Man and his World*. 3rd ed. New York: Schocken Books.

Grund, Alexandra. 2008. "‚Des Gerechten gedenkt man zum Segen' (Prov 10,7). Motive der Erinnerungsarbeit in Israel vom sozialen bis zum kulturellen Gedächtnis." In *Die Macht der Erinnerung*, edited by Bernd Janowski and Ottmar Fuchs. JBTh 22. Neukirchen-Vluyn: Neukirchener Verlag, 41–62.

Grund, Alexandra, and Bernd Janowski. 2009. "‚Solange die Erde steht . . .' Zur Erfahrung von Raum und Zeit im Alten Israel." In *Der Mensch im alten Israel. Neue Forschungen zur alttestamentlichen Anthropologie*, edited by Bernd Janowski and Kathrin Liess. HBS 59. Freiburg i. Br.: Herder, 487–535.

Hagedorn, Anselm C. 2015. "Place and Space in the Song of Songs." *ZAW* 127:207–233. https://doi.org/10.1515/zaw-2015-0012.

Heine, Heinrich. 1964. "Geständnisse (1854)." In *Heinrich Heine, Sämtliche Werke*, vol. 13, edited by Hans Kaufmann, Munich: Kindler.

Henze, Matthias. 2008. "Qoheleth and the Syriac Apocalypse of Baruch." *VT* 58:28–43. https://doi.org/10.1163/156853307X204600.

Hertzberg, Hans Wilhelm, and Hans Bardtke. 1963. *Der Prediger – das Buch Esther*. Gütersloh: Gütersloher Verlagshaus.

Ingram, Doug. 2006. *Ambiguity in Ecclesiastes*. London: Bloomsbury.

Jarick, John. 2000. "The Hebrew Book of Changes: Reflections on *hakkol hebel* and *lakkol zeman* in Ecclesiastes." *JSOT* 90:79–99. https://doi.org/10.1177/030908920002509006.

Jericke, Detlef. 2005. "Toponyme im Hohenlied." *ZDPV* 121:39–58.

Koch, Klaus. 1983. "Is there a Doctrine of Retribution in the Old Testament?" In *Theodicy in the Old Testament*, edited by James L. Crenshaw, 57–87. Philadelphia: Fortress Press.

Koch, Klaus. 2003. "Das Geheimnis der Zeit in Weisheit und Apokalyptik um die Zeitenwende." In *Wisdom and Apocalypticism in the Dead Sea Scrolls and in the Biblical Tradition*, edited by Florentino García Martínez, 35–68. Leuven: Peeters.

Kosmin, Paul J. 2018. *Time and Its Adversaries in the Seleucid Empire*. Cambridge, MA: Harvard University Press. https://doi.org/10.4159/9780674989634.

Lamparter, Helmut. 1975. *Das Buch der Weisheit. Prediger und Sprüche*. 3rd ed. Stuttgart: Calwer-Verlag.

Lange, Armin. 1991. *Weisheit und Torheit bei Kohelet und seiner Umwelt*. Frankfurt a. M.: P. Lang.

Lauha, Aarre. 1978. *Kohelet*. Neukirchen-Vluyn: Neukirchener Verlag.

Lefebvre, Henri. 1991. *The Production of Space*. Oxford: Blackwell.

Lepre, Cesare. 1975. *Qohelet: Traduzione ritmica dall'originale ebraico e note*. Bologna: Libreria Antiquaria Palmaverde.

Loader, James A. 1979. *Polar Structures in the Book of Qohelet*. Berlin: De Gruyter. https://doi.org/10.1515/9783110846539.

Marböck, Johannes. 1997. "Kohelet und Sirach: Eine vielschichtige Beziehung." In *Das Buch Kohelet: Studien zu Struktur, Geschichte, Rezeption und Theologie*, edited by Ludger Schwienhorst-Schönberger, 275–301. Berlin: De Gruyter. https://doi.org/10.1515/9783110805963.275.

Michel, Diethelm. 1989. *Untersuchungen zur Eigenart des Buches Qohelet*. Berlin: De Gruyter. https://doi.org/10.1515/9783110874396.

Najman, Hindy. 2012. "The Vitality of Scripture Within and Beyond the 'Canon'." *JSJ* 43:497–518. https://doi.org/10.1163/15700631-12341237.

Najman, Hindy. 2014. *Losing the Temple and Recovering the Future: An Analysis of 4 Ezra*. Cambridge: Cambridge University Press. https://doi.org/10.1017/CBO9781139051651.

Najman, Hindy, and Tobias Reinhardt. 2019. "Exemplarity and Its Discontents: Hellenistic Jewish Wisdom Texts and Greco-Roman Didactic Poetry." *JSJ* 50:1–37. https://doi.org/10.1163/15700631-15051303.

Najman, Hindy. 2025. *Scriptural Vitality: Rethinking Philology and Hermeneutics.* Oxford: Oxford University Press. https://doi.org/10.1093/9780191898037.001.0001.

Newman, Judith H. 1999. *Praying by the Book: The Scripturalization of Prayer in Second Temple Judaism*. Atlanta, GA: Scholars.

Newman, Judith H. 2018. *Before the Bible: The Liturgical Body and the Formation of Scriptures in Early Judaism*. New York: Oxford University Press. https://doi.org/10.1093/oso/9780190212216.001.0001.

Newman, Judith H. 2020. "The Participatory Past: Resituating Eschatology in the Study of Apocalyptic." *Early Christianity* 10:415–34. https://doi.org/10.1628/ec-2019-0027.

Nora, Pierre. 1989. "Between Memory and History. Les Lieux de Mémoire." *Representations* 26:7–24. https://doi.org/10.2307/2928520.

Pioske, Daniel D. 2018. *Memory in a Time of Prose: Studies in Epistemology, Hebrew Scribalism, and the Biblical Past.* Oxford: Oxford University Press. https://doi.org/10.1093/oso/9780190649852.001.0001.

Reed, Annette Yoshiko. 2009. "The Construction and Subversion of Patriarchal Perfection: Abraham and Exemplarity in Philo, Josephus, and the Testament of Abraham." *JSJ* 40:185–212. https://doi.org/10.1163/157006309X355187.

Rosenzweig, Franz. 1921. *Der Stern der Erlösung*. Frankfurt a.M.: J. Kauffmann Verlag.

Rudman, Dominic. 2001. *Determinism in the Book of Ecclesiastes*. Sheffield: Sheffield Academic Press.

Schiffman, Lawrence H. 1991. *From Text to Tradition: A History of Second Temple and Rabbinic Judaism*. Hoboken, NJ: Ktav Publishing.

Schipper, Bernd U. 2019. *Proverbs 1–15*. Minneapolis: Fortress Press.

Schoors, Antoon. 2013. *Ecclesiastes*. Leuven: Peeters.

Schwienhorst-Schönberger, Ludger. 1996. *'Nicht im Menschen gründet das Glück' (Koh 2,24): Kohelet im Spannungsfeld jüdischer Weisheit und hellenistischer Philosophie*. Freiburg i. Br.: Herder.

Segal, Michael. 2016. *Dreams, Riddles, and Visions: Textual, Contextual, and Intertextual Approaches to the Book of Daniel*. Berlin: De Gruyter. https://doi.org/10.1515/9783110330991.

Sneed, Mark R. 2023. "Qohelet as Divine Hedonist. A Philosophical and Rhetorical Approach." *VT* 73:1–19. https://doi.org/10.1163/15685330-bja10131.

Stern, Sacha. 2003. *Time and Process in Ancient Judaism*. Oxford: Littman. https://doi.org/10.1017/S0041977X05210054.

Stone, Michael E. 2003. "A Reconsideration of Apocalyptic Visions." *HTR* 96:167–180. https://doi.org/10.1017/S0017816003000385.

Stuckenbruck, Loren. 2018. "Eschatology and Time in 1 Enoch." In *Apocalyptic Thinking in Early Judaism*, edited by Cecilia Wassen and Sidnie White Crawford, 160–180. Leiden: Brill. https://doi.org/10.1163/9789004358386_009.

Teeter, D. Andrew, and William A. Tooman. 2020. "Standards of (In)coherence in Ancient Jewish Literature." *Hebrew Bible and Ancient Israel* 9(2):94–129. https://doi.org/10.1628/hebai-2020-0009.

Uusimäki, Elisa. 2021. *Lived Wisdom in Jewish Antiquity: Studies in Exercise and Exemplarity*. London: Bloomsbury.

Weinfeld, Moshe. 2005. *Normative and Sectarian Judaism in the Second Temple Period*. New York: T&T Clark.

Whybray, Roger Norman. 1982. "Qoheleth, Preacher of Joy." *JSOT* 23:87–98. https://doi.org/10.1177/030908928200702300.

Wright III, Benjamin G. 2008. "Ben Sira on the Sage as Exemplar." In *Praise Israel for Wisdom and Instruction: Essays on Ben Sira and Wisdom, the Letter of Aristeas and the Septuagint*, 165–82. Leiden: Brill. https://doi.org/10.1163/ej.9789004169081.i-364.36.

Zapletal, Vicenz. 1911. *Das Buch Kohelet, kritisch und metrisch untersucht, übersetzt und erklärt*. 2nd ed. Freiburg i. Br.: Herdersche Verlagsbuchhandlung.

Zimmerli, Walther. 1983. "'Unveränderbare Welt' oder 'Gott ist Gott': Ein Plädoyer für die Unaufgebbarkeit des Predigerbuches in der Bibel." In *Wenn nicht jetzt, wann dann? Aufsätze für Hans-Joachim Kraus zum 65. Geburtstag*, edited by Hans-Geord Geyer, 103–14. Neukirchen-Vluyn: Neukirchener Verlag.

Frank Ueberschaer

עולם in the Book of Ben Sira and Its Translations

Abstract: This article examines the meaning and use of the word olam in the Book of Ben Sira. It argues that the book is on the cusp of a shift in the meaning of the term and seems to give the word its own meaning in the sense of a statement of quality.

In his article on the keyword עולם published almost forty years ago in ThWAT, Horst Dietrich Preuß also discusses the book of Ben Sira. For the brevity required, he does so in relative detail. In the last sentence, he acknowledges the book:

> Mit allem steht Sirach deutlich in einer Situation des Übergangs im Blick auf die Füllung des Begriffs *'ôlām*, wobei altes weiterwirkt, neues sich anbahnt, und manche Textbelege deutlich zwischen alt und neu schillern und nicht eindeutig bestimmbar sind.[1]

Preuß argues that in the Book of Ben Sira, there is evidence for עולם having both the most widespread temporal meaning in the biblical writings and a spatial connotation (Preuß 1986, 1157; see Stadel 2016, 61–68), though it is already clear in his account that the temporal meaning is by far the most frequent. In principle, there is nothing to add to this, and yet it is worth going through the evidence again, especially when dealing with the diversity of the textual versions because, in the Book of Ben Sira, not even parallel texts within the Hebrew textual tradition provide the same choice of words throughout. Thus, the keyword עולם can be attested in one Hebrew manuscript but not in another Hebrew manuscript, even in the same verse, and instead reads either a different word or a completely different text. Together with the non-Hebrew text versions, further insights can thus be gained into the understanding of the term עולם in the textual world of the book.

In the Hebrew texts of the Book of Ben Sira, the word עולם is attested a total of 48 times. There is a striking distribution. Only 15 occurrences are found in the proverbs of the book, and the rest are in the two final sections: three occurrences in the cosmology (Sir 42:15–43:33), 13 occurrences in the Praise of the Ancestors (Sir 44–50), and 14 occurrences in the final chapter, chapter 51, which is statistically conspicuous in that it contains a poem with the refrain כי לעולם חסדו in Sir 51:12.

Even if this statistic should be treated with caution because only around two-thirds of the Hebrew text of the book has been preserved — with the gaps in the

1 Preuß 1986, 1157. Christian Stadel argues the same in Stadel 2016, 61–68.

text being located in the sections with proverbs — it is nevertheless remarkable that in the biblical book of Proverbs, the keyword עולם is only used six times in a total of 915 verses,[2] while the preserved Hebrew parts of Ben Sira alone already count 913 verses. This situation is not different from that of the other wisdom writings of the Hebrew Bible: Qohelet has seven occurrences in 222 verses; Job has three occurrences in 1070 verses. The relatively high density of the keyword עולם, therefore, makes the book of Ben Sira special from a spatio-temporal perspective.[3]

In order to trace the levels of meaning and connotations of the use of עולם, the evidence in the Book of Ben Sira will be investigated under three aspects:

1. Evidence with clearly temporal meaning
2. עולם as *nomen rectum* in constructus compounds
3. Text-historically interesting instances

1 עולם in Temporal Meaning

In 26 of the 48 occurrences, עולם clearly has a temporal meaning. However, the sheer number suggests a meaningfulness that it does not actually have because, out of these 26 references, 14 references are included from the same sentence in the verse Sir 51:12 in Ms B. If one, therefore, counts the 14 repetitions of the refrain כי לעולם חסדו as only one single reference, the proportion is 13:33, which means that around 40% of the references have a clearly temporal meaning.[4] This can be concluded from the context, which means the temporal meaning is usually proved by temporal information in the immediate textual context.

In 7:36, it is about the end of a process in time. Ms A reads:

בכל מעשיך זכור אחרית ולעולם לא תשחת:	In all your actions remember the end/result, ולעולם you will not come to ruin.

2 Prov 8:23; 10:25,30; 22:28; 23:10; 27:24. All evidence is clearly to be understood in the temporal sense.

3 This investigation focuses on the term עולם; therefore, it will concentrate on the extended Hebrew texts of the book of Ben Sira. On several other terms which are used in the book of Ben Sira, see e.g. Wilch (1969, 138–143) and Bussino (2021, 339–368) on עת, Calduch-Benages (2021, 369–386) on καιρός resp. עת in Sir 18:19–26, Egger-Wenzel (2021, 403–426) on קץ and Beentjes (2021, 387–401) on אחרית. Interestingly, there is a lack of a study on the term עולם, which has also been stated by Beentjes (2021, 388).

4 In addition, there are the two verses, Sir 4:23 and 40:17, which are interesting in terms of textual history.

The admonition to remember the end is surely a good example in which אחרית must be understood in the sense of "result" or "consequence" (cf. Beentjes 2021, 391); nevertheless, it refers to a result in a temporal process and, therefore, finally to an end. In this context, the second stichos appears in a synthetic parallelism membrorum. The keyword עולם is, therefore, to be understood temporally, and the Greek and Syriac text versions confirm that this was also done in antiquity:

36 ἐν πᾶσι τοῖς λόγοις σου μιμνῄσκου τὰ ἔσχατά σου, καὶ <u>εἰς τὸν αἰῶνα</u> οὐχ ἁμαρτήσεις.	In all your words, remember your end, and you will not ever sin.
36 ܒܟܠܗܘܢ ܥܒܕ̈ܝܟ ܗܘܝܬ ܕܟܝܪ ܚܪܬܐ. <u>ܘܠܥܠܡ</u> ܠܐ ܬܚܛܐ.	In all your works keep in mind the end and you will never sin.

The majority of Greek textual witnesses are even more specific and remind the reader of their own end.

In 16:13, עולם is used with the preposition ל again. Ms A reads:

13 אל° ימלט בגזל עול ולא ישבית תאות צדיק <u>לעולם:</u>	He will not let the ungodly escape with the spoil, and he will not end the desire of the righteous לעולם.
re mg: לא	

On its own, לעולם could also be translated as "for the world", "with reference to the world", "in the direction of the world", but the narrower context speaks against this. In v. 12, the passage is introduced with a statement about God:

12 כרב רחמיו כן כמפעליו איש תוכחתו ישפט:	As his compassion is abundant so also is his punishment. Each one will be judged according to their deeds.

This is followed by several proverbs in which the perspective on the future, which is introduced in the second stichos of v. 12, is continued by *yiqtol* forms, while *qatal* forms refer to the past and things known to the biblically educated. לעולם thus carries the meaning "forever" or, in the negation, "never".

The Peshitta changes the subject in its translation (from God to hope) but otherwise follows the Hebrew text literally:

13 ܠܐ ܢܦܠܛ ܠܥܒ̈ܕܝ ܫܘܩܪܐ ܘܠܚܛܘ̈ܦܐ. ܘܠܐ ܢܒܛܠ ܣܒܪܗܘܢ ܕܙܕܝ̈ܩܐ ܠܥܠܡ.	And he will not let perpetrators of falsehood and plunderers escape and the hope of the just will not be idle for ever.

In contrast, the Greek translation provides no equivalent to לעולם:

13 οὐκ ἐκφεύξεται ἐν ἁρπάγματι ἁμαρτωλός, καὶ οὐ μὴ καθυστερήσει ὑπομονὴ εὐσεβοῦς.	A sinner will not escape with booty, and the endurance of the pious will never fail.

Although the negation with οὐ μή could be interpreted in this direction,[5] the phrase οὐ μή does not replace לעולם in other instances, signifying the Greek translation may have been based on a Hebrew text without the temporal indication לעולם. If this is the case, לעולם could be a later, clarifying addition. This indicates a temporal use of לעולם because the *yiqtol* form ישבית can only be understood futural in context.

In 39:20, two further prepositions are used that can also have a locative meaning in themselves but are to be understood here as temporal.

20 מעולם ועד עולם יביט ⟦ ⟧ [°°°°°° מספר] לתשועתו: אין קֹטֹןֹ ומעט עמו ⟦ ⟧ ואין נפלא וחזק ממנו:	He has always and forever observed, and no one can measure his victory. There is nothing small or little with him, and nothing more wonderful or more powerful than him.
20 ἀπὸ τοῦ αἰῶνος εἰς τὸν αἰῶνα ἐπέβλεψεν, καὶ οὐθέν ἐστιν θαυμάσιον ἐναντίον αὐτοῦ.	From age to age he watched, and nothing is a wonder before him.
20 ܠܝܬ ܕܩܠܝܠ ܘܣܓܝ ܩܕܡܘܗܝ܂ ܘܠܝܬ ܕܝܩܝܪ ܘܥܣܩܐ ܠܘܬܗ.	There is no(thing) which is little and much for Him nor is there (anything) which is heavy and difficult for Him.

In Ms B (9r:6), it reads: מעולם ועד עולם יביט. The following stichos is destroyed in Ms B, and the Greek and Syriac texts each offer their own versions of this part of the verse. In the Peshitta, however, this applies to the entire verse, while the Greek text corresponds to the Hebrew and provides a temporal translation with αἰών.

In any case, however, the context speaks in favor of a temporal interpretation. It is about the fact that there is nothing that God does not have in view. In itself, this would also allow a spatial interpretation of עולם at this point since only examples are mentioned that happen in space or that are arranged spatially in relation to each other: It is about "all flesh" (כל בשר) that stands opposite him (נגדו), about things not hidden (נסתר) that are "before his eyes" (מנגד עיניו) (v. 19); it is about small and strong things (v. 20), and finally about the fact that everything fulfills its purpose and therefore one is not to be valued better than the other (v. 21). With this statement, v. 21 closes the link to v. 16: everything is sufficient (v. 16) and effective (v. 21) "in its time" (בעיתו), as it says in both verses. However, the framework also

---

5 Blass, Debrunner, and Rehkopf 2001, 316–317 (§365), defines οὐ μή with a verb in the indicative future tense as the "most definite form of the negating statement about what is to come" ("bestimmteste Form der verneinenden Aussage über Zukünftiges").

provides the interpretative horizon for the understanding of עולם: It is about the two outermost temporal extensions that are conceivable for both time directions in the notion of a linear course of time.[6]

At the beginning of his cosmology in Sir 42:15–43:33, Ben Sira praises God's greatness, insight and wisdom. In 42:21, he says about God: אחד הוא מעולם.

M 21 גבורת חכׄמׄ[תו תכן ⟦ ⟧]	His mighty wisdom [. . .],
אחד הׄ[ו]א [מע]ולם	[of] old, he is one and the same.
[לא נאסף [ולא נאצל ⟦ ⟧]	He is not added to nor subtracted from
[וׄלׄא צריך/צרך לכ]וׄל מבין	and he does not need any instructor.
B 21 ג[בורת֯ ח֯כ֯מ֯]תו תכן ⟦ ⟧	He has measured his mighty wisdom,
אחד הוא מעולם°:	from of old, he is one.
ל[א נא֯ס֯ף֯ ו]לא נאצל ⟦ ⟧	He has not added to or subtracted from,
ולא צריך° לכל מבין:	he has no need for any instructor.
mg re: גבורות	
mg li: מהעולם	
mg li: צרך	
21 τὰ μεγαλεῖα τῆς σοφίας αὐτοῦ ἐκόσμησεν,	He set in order the splendors of his wisdom;
ὡς ἔστιν πρὸ τοῦ αἰῶνος καὶ εἰς τὸν αἰῶνα.	since he is one before the age and forever,
οὔτε προσετέθη οὔτε ἠλαττώθη,	he was neither added to nor diminished,
καὶ οὐ προσεδεήθη οὐδενὸς συμβούλου.	and he needed no one as a counselor.
21 ܘܥܫܝܢܘܬܐ ܘܚܟܡܬܗ ܩܝܡܢ ܠܥܠܡ.	Fortitude and wisdom stand firm for Him forever.

The sentence is attested consistently in the Masada manuscript and in Ms B. In the latter, a glossator has added the article as a textual variant in the left margin: מהעולם. The phrase only allows for a temporal understanding, and the versions also follow this. In Greek, the statement is even more pointed by not only focusing on the entire course of time but on the time before time and adding the distant future (πρὸ τοῦ αἰῶνος καὶ εἰς τὸν αἰῶνα). The Syriac, on the other hand, offers only one stichos, which takes vocabulary from the Hebrew text of 42:21 but offers a completely different statement. One recorded keyword is ܠܥܠܡ as an indication of time: "Wisdom stands firm for Him forever."

Most of the instances where עולם has a clearly temporal meaning can be found in the Praise of the Ancestors (Sir 44–50). At the beginning of this section, Ben Sira presents his idea of which people have gone down in history and which have not. In doing so, he categorizes the important figures of the past: There are those who have left a name, who are, therefore, remembered (v. 8), and those who have been forgotten (v. 9). The former include the אנשי חסד in v. 10, with whose descendants

6 Ben Sira thus follows the biblical use of language, cf. Jer 7:7; 25:5; Ps 103:17; 1Chr 29:10, as well as in the formulation with articles in Ps 41:14; 106:48; 1Chr 16:36.

their good has endured (v. 11), and the remembrance of them עד עולם (v. 13), which in this context can only be understood temporally.

Unfortunately, Sir 45:13 is only preserved so fragmentarily in Ms B that nothing can be said about the meaning of עולם from the Hebrew, but the Greek translation allows for further discussion. This is because it renders עולם with the phrase ἕως αἰῶνος and also contrasts it with a temporal phrase in the preceding stichos:

13 לׄ[—] ל [—][⟦ ⟧	[. . .]
[- לׄ] עׄוׄלׄםׄ ל [א —] זר:	never [. . .] stranger.
האׄמׄן [—] לבניו כזה ⟦ ⟧	Entrusted to his children alone in this way,
וכן בניו לׄדׄוׄרׄותם:	and thus his children in their generations.
13 ὡραῖα πρὸ αὐτοῦ οὐ γέγονεν τοιαῦτα,	Before him such beautiful things did not exist
ἕως αἰῶνος οὐκ ἐνεδύσατο ἀλλογενὴς	Until eternity, no alien put them on
πλὴν τῶν υἱῶν αὐτοῦ μόνον	except his sons alone
καὶ τὰ ἔκγονα αὐτοῦ διὰ παντός.	and his descendants in perpetuity.

However, there are many more significant instances in which עולם clearly has a temporal meaning:

In 45:24, Pinchas is promised a כהונה גדולה (great priestly dignity) עד עולם.

The same phrase is used to characterize Isaiah's role in 48:24–25 by saying that he had seen "the end" (אחרית) and had announced עד עולם what was yet to happen[7] — even לפני בואן ("before they appear"). Here, too, עולם is to be understood temporally.

In 47:11, God raises David's "horn" לעולם, gives him the charter of kingship, and establishes his throne.

At the end of the book, in 51:8, Ben Sira speaks of the proofs of God's faithfulness, which is מעולם, that is, from eternity.

Whether the psalm preserved in Ms B following Sir 51:12a (Ms B 20v:12–21r:8) was written by Ben Sira is disputed. However, it cannot be denied that לעולם in the refrain כי לעולם חסדו is to be understood temporally. And even in the blessing in the epilogue of the book, which is attested in Sir 51:30 in Ms B, עולם can only be understood in terms of time:

v:(1221) ברוך ייי לעולם ⟦ ⟧	Blessed is YYY forever,
ומשובח שמו לדר ודר:	and his name is praised by every generation.

7 For Beentjes 2021, 397, this is the argument to understand אחרית in the sense of "future", but this by far underestimates the term in this instance.

2 עולם as Nomen Rectum in Constructus Compounds

In Hebrew, the nomen rectum designates a *nomen regens* in more detail. This first raises the question of what Ben Sira qualifies with עולם and then what he wants to express with it or which aspect of עולם comes into play.

However, firstly, using עולם in constructus connections does not alter the meaning in general. Indeed, the most prominent example is the heading of the Praise of the Ancestors שבח אבות עולם in Sir 44:1 in Ms B 13v:1, in which Ben Sira gives an outline of the history of Israel using the example of outstanding men (and only men) from the beginning of biblical history up to his own present. Whether this heading was written by Ben Sira himself is questionable in view of the textual tradition and the lack of an equivalent in the cosmology of Sir 42:15.[8] However, the phrase apparently was arranged as a heading by the scribe of Ms B: He centered it in the middle of the first line of a new page of Ms B.

But the temporal understanding of עולם is even more certain in connection with other temporal expressions, as, for example, in the expression ימות עולם ("days of eternity") in the version of Ms B (13v:3) in Sir 44:2:

M 2 רב כבוד חלֹּק עליון ⟦ ⟧ וגדלהׄ מי [מות עולם]	Abundant glory the Most High apportioned, greatness, from [the days of old.]
B 2 רב כבוד חלק° עליון ⟦ ⟧ וגדלו מימות עולם: mg re: להם	Abundant glory the Most High apportioned, his greatness from days of old.
2 πολλὴν δόξαν ἔκτισεν ὁ κύριος, τὴν μεγαλωσύνην αὐτοῦ ἀπ᾽ αἰῶνος.	The Lord created much glory, his majesty from eternity.
2 ܣܓܝ ܐܝܩܪܐ ܢܦܠܘܓ ܠܗܘܢ. ܘܟܠܗ ܪܒܘܬܗܘܢ ܥܠ ܕܪܐ ܕܥܠܡܐ.	Much honor we shall assign to them, and all their greatness (will be) upon the generations of the world.

Unfortunately, in this verse, the versions do not correspond to Ms B, and the textual evidence for the attestation of יום thus remains uncertain. However, the temporal understanding of עולם also emerges from the versions because P offers "generations of the past" instead of speaking of days, and G only speaks of eternity without a reference to "days".

Further instances are consistent with this understanding. The connection with דור in 45:26 and the parallelization of ממשלת קץ ("dominion to the end") and אות

8 Rey and Reymond 2024, 284, tend to see traces of the heading in Ms M after all.

עולם in 43:6 also proves the temporal understanding of עולם.[9] The same applies to 42:18:

M 18 תהום ולב חקר ⟦ ⟧	He probes abyss and heart,
ובׄמערמיהם יתבונן	contemplating their intimate parts.
כי ידע עליון דעׄ [ת ⟦ ⟧	The Most High knows all [. . .]
ו] יׄביט <u>אתיות עולם</u>	observing what transpires throughout eternity.
M 19 מחוה <u>חליפׄות</u> [ונהיות ⟦ ⟧	The one declaring what changes [. . .],
ו]מׄ [גׄ] לה חׄקר נׄסׄתׄרות	and the one revealing the depth of hidden things.
B 18 תהום ולב חקר ⟦ ⟧	He probes abyss and heart,
ובכל מערומיהם יתבונן:	contemplating all their intimate parts.
B 19 מחוה <u>חליפות נהיות</u>° ⟦ ⟧	The one declaring what changes what is to be,
ומגלה חקר נסתרות:	and the one revealing the depth of hidden things.
mg re: ונהיות	
18 ἄβυσσον καὶ καρδίαν ἐξίχνευσεν	Abyss and heart he searched out,
καὶ ἐν πανουργεύμασιν αὐτῶν διενοήθη·	and he considered their wonderful feats;
ἔγνω γὰρ ὁ ὕψιστος πᾶσαν εἴδησιν	for the Most High knew all knowledge,
καὶ ἐνέβλεψεν εἰς σημεῖον <u>αἰῶνος</u>	and he saw into the sign of the age,
19 ἀπαγγέλλων τὰ παρεληλυθότα καὶ τὰ ἐσόμενα	relating the things that passed and the things that will be
καὶ ἀποκαλύπτων ἴχνη ἀποκρύφων·	and revealing tracks of hidden things.
18 ܬܗܘܡܐ ܘܠܒܐ ܗܘ ܒܨܐ.	Abyss and heart he scrutinizes;
ܘܟܠܗܘܢ ܬܪ̈ܥܝܬܗܘܢ ܕܒܢܝ̈ܢܫܐ.	and all thoughts of human beings
ܐܝܟ ܫܡܫܐ ܓܠܝܢ ܩܕܡܘܗܝ.	are revealed before Him as the sun
ܡܛܠ ܕܠܐ ܟܣܝܐ ܡܢ ܐܠܗܐ ܡܕܡ.	because nothing is concealed from God.
19 ܘܓܠܝܢ ܩܕܡܘܗܝ ܟܠ ܕܐܬܝܢ ܠܥܠܡܐ.	And all that befalls the world is revealed before Him
ܕܥܒܪ̈ ܘܕܥܬܝܕܝܢ.	(the things) which have passed and which are to come
ܘܓ̈ܠܝܢ ܩܕܡܘܗܝ ܟܠܗܘܢ ܟܣܝ̈ܬܐ.	and before Him are revealed all secrets.

Here, where God's comprehensive knowledge is mentioned and, in this context, the expression אתיות עולם is used in Ms M, the context indicates that the translation with "signs of eternity" is correct (also in G, while P offers a different text) because it then speaks of the change of events (חליפות נהיות) (Sir 42:19).

9 On 43:6, see Bussino 2021, 345, who understands the use of עת and עולם in parallel as "a sort of play".

The phrases בחיי עולם in 37:26 and נוחת עולם ("eternal rest") in 30:17[10] also fall into this category. In the former, it is in the expression itself; in the latter, it is the keyword נאמן that indicates this in 30:17:

17 ⟦ ⟧ טוב למות מחיי שוא B	Better to die than (live) a life of vanity,
ונוחת עולם מכאב° נאמן:	and eternal rest than persistent pain.
טוב למות מחיים רעים ⟦ ⟧	Better to die than (live) an unhappy life,
ולירד שאול°° מכאב עומד:	and go down to Sheol than (endure) a stubborn pain.
mg li: מחיים רעים	
mg li: ולוד ושא׳	
mg li senkrecht: ולֵרֵד לשאול	
17 κρείσσων θάνατος ὑπὲρ ζωὴν πικρὰν	Better death than a bitter life,
καὶ ἀνάπαυσις αἰῶνος ἢ ἀρρώστημα ἔμμονον.	and eternal repose than chronic sickness.
17 ܦܩܚ ܠܡܡܬ ܡܢ ܚܝܐ ܒܝܫܐ .	It is more advantageous to die than (to lead) a bad life
ܘܠܡܚܬ ܠܫܝܘܠ ܡܢ ܟܐܒܐ ܕܩܐܡ .	and to descend to Sheol than (to suffer) pain which lasts.

In 45:15 the phrase ברית עולם is used.

[וי]מלא משה את ידו⟦ ⟧	Moses ordained him,
וימשחהו בשמן הקדש:	and anointed him with holy oil,
ותהי לו ברית עולם ⟦ ⟧	so that the eternal covenant would be his,
ולזרעו כימי שמים:	and his seed's, lasting as long as the heavens exist,
לשרת ולכהן לו ⟦ ⟧	to serve and act as priest for him,
ולברך את עמו בשמו:	to bless his people by his name.
15 ἐπλήρωσεν Μωυσῆς τὰς χεῖρας	Moyses filled his hands
καὶ ἔχρισεν αὐτὸν ἐν ἐλαίῳ ἁγίῳ·	and anointed him with holy oil;
ἐγενήθη αὐτῷ εἰς διαθήκην αἰῶνος	it became for him an everlasting covenant
καὶ τῷ σπέρματι αὐτοῦ ἐν ἡμέραις οὐρανοῦ	and in his seed for the days of the sky,
λειτουργεῖν αὐτῷ ἅμα καὶ ἱερατεύειν	to minister to him and at the same time to be a priest
καὶ εὐλογεῖν τὸν λαὸν αὐτοῦ ἐν τῷ ὀνόματι.	and to bless his people in the name.
15 ܘܣܡ ܥܠܘܗܝ ܡܘܫܐ ܐܝܕܗ.	And Moses laid his hand upon him
ܘܡܫܚܗ ܡܫܚܐ ܕܩܘܕܫܐ .	and he anointed him with ointment of sanctity
ܘܗܘܬ ܠܗ ܠܩܝܡܐ ܕܠܥܠܡ .	and it was for him as covenant which is for ever
ܘܠܙܪܥܗ ܐܝܟ ܝܘܡܬܐ ܕܫܡܝܐ .	and for his offspring as the days of heaven
ܠܡܫܡܫܘ ܘܠܡܒܪܟܘ ܠܥܡܗ ܒܫܡܗ .	in order to serve and to bless his people in his name.

10 It is better to die than a deceptive life / and eternal rest (נוחת עולם) than constant pain.

Here, the term also has a temporal understanding because of the context because this covenant is also attributed to Aaron's descendants, namely as long as there are "days of heaven" (כימי שמים), i.e. as long as heaven exists.

However, this understanding is also suggested in other passages without explicit temporal expressions, e.g. 44:18:

B 18 באות עולם נכרת° עמו ⟦ ⟧ לבלתי תשחית כל בשר:	With a perpetual sign, it was made with him, so that it would not annihilate all flesh.
mg re: כרת	
18 διαθῆκαι αἰῶνος ἐτέθησαν πρὸς αὐτόν, ἵνα μὴ ἐξαλειφθῇ κατακλυσμῷ πᾶσα σάρξ.	Covenants of eternity were added to him lest all flesh be blotted out by a flood.
18 ܡܘܡܬܐ ܕܝܡܐ ܠܗ ܒܫܪܪܐ. ܕܠܐ ܢܐܒܕ ܟܠ ܒܣܪ.܀	Oaths He swore to him truly that not all flesh would perish.

Sirach 44:18 is the third example of the expression אות עולם. It can be found in the portrayal of Noah in the Praise of the Ancestors and is a reference to Gen 9:12:

וַיֹּאמֶר אֱלֹהִים זֹאת אוֹת־הַבְּרִית אֲשֶׁר־אֲנִי נֹתֵן בֵּינִי וּבֵינֵיכֶם וּבֵין כָּל־נֶפֶשׁ חַיָּה אֲשֶׁר אִתְּכֶם לְדֹרֹת עוֹלָם:	God said, "This is the sign of the covenant that I make between me and you and every living creature that is with you, for all future generations:

Although the same wording is not used in Gen, the text in Sir clearly refers to the bow as God's sign of his covenant for generations to come (לְדֹרֹת עוֹלָם). The temporal meaning is, therefore, derived from the reference text.

The same applies to the term חק עולם in Sir 14:17 and 45:7. In 14:17, Ben Sira refers to death as an eternal statute, and in 45:7, it is about Aaron and his descendants, whom God Himself has appointed as an "eternal statute" for Israel. Even if it is singular that Aaron and his descendants are themselves referred to as an "eternal statute", the temporal meaning of עולם is clear from the use of the phrase in the Torah.

In other instances, the understanding of other construction compounds is no longer *clearly* temporal.

When it says in Sir 49:11–12 that Zerubbabel and Joshua had built the temple לכבוד עולם, then this can be well and convincingly understood temporally, but in view of the significance of the temple in Ben Sira's thinking and also in the hopes of the Judaism of his time, the meaning "world" cannot be dismissed out of hand.

This is clearer in the designation of God as אל עולם at the end of the prayer of Sir 36 in v. 22. When it says, "all the ends of the world (כ֯ל אפסי ארץ) will know that you are the אל עולם”, the context does indeed point to God’s world dominion, especially since the prayer is about a request for God’s intervention now and God’s eternity plays no role in this. However, the versions do not share this understanding. They clearly take the term אל עולם in a temporal meaning: G translates ὁ θεὸς τῶν αἰώνων (God of eternity / eternal God), and P renders ܐܢܬ ܗܘ ܐܠܗܐ ܒܠܚܘܕܝܟ ܠܥܠܡ ܥܠܡܝܢ (you are God alone for eternity).

But there may also be other connotations that are expressed by עולם as nomen rectum.

The characterization of David in Sir 47:4, referring back to 1Sam 17, states that he removed a חרפת עולם from Israel by killing Goliath:

B 4 בנעוריו הכה ג֯בור ⟦ ⟧	In his youth, he struck the warrior,
ויסרׄ[חר]פ֯ת֯ ע֯[ו]לם:	and reversed the perpetual disgrace.
בהניפו ידו על קלע ⟦ ⟧	When he raised his hand to his sling,
וישבר תפ֯א֯רת גלית:	he shattered the renown of Goliath.

The use of the expression חרפה in connection with the verb סור goes directly back to David’s speech in 1Sam 17:26:

וַיֹּאמֶר דָּוִד אֶל־הָאֲנָשִׁים הָעֹמְדִים עִמּוֹ לֵאמֹר	David said to the men who stood by him,
מַה־יֵּעָשֶׂה לָאִישׁ אֲשֶׁר יַכֶּה אֶת־הַפְּלִשְׁתִּי הַלָּז	“What shall be done for the man who kills this Philistine,
וְהֵסִיר חֶרְפָּה מֵעַל יִשְׂרָאֵל	and takes away the reproach from Israel?
כִּי מִי הַפְּלִשְׁתִּי הֶעָרֵל הַזֶּה	For who is this uncircumcised Philistine
כִּי חֵרֵף מַעַרְכוֹת אֱלֹהִים חַיִּים׃	that he should defy the armies of the living God?” (NRSV)

However, in 1Sam 17:26, there is no reference to a חרפת עולם, but only to a חרפה that must be removed from Israel. Now, עולם can undoubtedly be interpreted temporally in Sir 47:4, but then the question arises as to why the shame should have been eternal. Therefore, it seems much more likely here that עולם should be understood as a kind of judgment of quality, in which the focus is less on a temporal statement than on the intensity of what is designated by עולם. The term חרפת עולם would then be an immeasurable shame that can no longer be increased.

A look at the history of the text could provide a clue as to the dating of this use of עולם, for neither G nor P offers an equivalent for עולם but read עם in agreement:

4 ἐν νεότητι αὐτοῦ οὐχὶ ἀπέκτεινεν γίγαντα	In his youth, did he not kill a giant
καὶ ἐξῆρεν ὀνειδισμὸν ἐκ <u>λαοῦ</u>	and take away reproach from the people
ἐν τῷ ἐπᾶραι χεῖρα ἐν λίθῳ σφενδόνης	by raising his hand with a sling’s stone
καὶ καταβαλεῖν γαυρίαμα τοῦ Γολιαθ;	and by striking down the arrogance of Goliath?

4 ܒܛܠܝܘܬܗ ܩܛܠ ܠܓܢܒܪܐ.	In his youth he killed a mighty warrior
ܘܐܥܒܪ ܚܣܕܐ ܕܥܡܗ.	and he removed the scorn of his people;
ܐܘܫܛ ܐܝܕܗ ܒܩܠܥܐ.	he laid his hand to the sling
ܘܬܒܪ ܟܠܗ ܫܘܒܗܪܗ ܕܓܘܠܝܕ.	and he broke all arrogance of Goliath.

Thus, there is strong evidence that this reading is original and that the attestation of Ms B is a later internal Hebrew development. This would then only have happened after the translation of P and thus in the 2nd century AD at the earliest.

There is similar evidence in Sir 41:9, where the context is that wicked fathers bring forth such children. In v. 9, the readers are addressed directly and somewhat abruptly. In Ms B (11r:1), it says:

9 ...[א]ם תכשלו לשמחת עולם ⟦ ⟧	If you stumble, it is for שמחת עולם,
.. ואם תמותו לקללה°:	and if you die, it is to be cursed.
li mg: לקללתה	

In contrast to the previous example, there is another Hebrew textual attestation in Ms M, one of the oldest textual witnesses of the book. Instead of שמחת עולם, Ms M offers the reading שמחת עם, thus saying:

9 ... [אם תכשל]ו לשמחת עׄם ⟦ ⟧	If you stumble, it is for the joy of the people,
ואם תמותו לקללה	and if you die, it is to be cursed.

Ms M is not alone with the reading עם; P also attests to it, although both P and G seem to be based on a slightly different textual composition.

9 καὶ ἐὰν γεννηθῆτε, εἰς κατάραν γεννηθήσεσθε,	and if you are born, you will be born for a curse,
καὶ ἐὰν ἀποθάνητε, εἰς κατάραν μερισθήσεσθε.	and if you die, you will be apportioned a curse.

9 ܐܢܬܬܐ ܝܠܕܬܐ ܠܚܕܘܬܐ ܕܥܡܗ.	A child-bearing woman is (a cause) for joy for her people
ܘܐܢ ܢܡܘܬ ܐܒܐ ܒܝܫܐ.	and if an evil father dies, his upright sons will
ܒܢܘܗܝ ܟܐܢܐ ܠܐ ܢܬܐܒܠܘܢ ܥܠܘܗܝ.	not mourn over him.

This means that the reading שמחת עם instead of שמחת עולם is the oldest and most widely attested reading, while the expression שמחת עולם is found exclusively in Ms B. Furthermore, שמחת עם is the reading that makes the most sense in context. Should it be the same misreading in both cases? Or could the same understanding of עולם as an expression of intensification be present in both cases? In this case, the fallen would not become the "eternal mockery" but the great, excessive, at any rate, intense mockery of the people.

Given the dating of the manuscript to the Middle Ages, this would not contradict the aforementioned dating of this understanding of עולם, but Sir 11:33 points in a different chronological direction.

A 33 גור מרע כי רע יוליד למה <u>מום עולם</u> תשא:	Beware the wicked for they engender wickedness, lest you carry an eternal scar.
33 πρόσεχε ἀπὸ κακούργου, πονηρὰ γὰρ τεκταίνει, μήποτε <u>μῶμον εἰς τὸν αἰῶνα</u> δῷ σοι.	Beware of a scoundrel — for he devises wicked things — lest he deliver to you disgrace forever.
33 ܕܚܠ ܡܢ ܒܝܫܐ ܡܛܠ ܕܡܒܘܥ ܒܝܫܐ. ܕܠܡܐ <u>ܡܘܡܐ ܕܥܠܡܐ</u> ܬܩܒܠ.	Fear a wicked person, because he is a well-spring of wickedness lest you incur an eternal stain.

In this verse, Ben Sira warns to beware of evil so that one does not suffer מום עולם. G and P also testify to עולם here and understand the expression as a temporal determination and translate it as "eternal stain". However, there is no reference to temporal aspects in the context. Thus, although this translation is not to be contradicted in principle, a translation in the meaning of "a blemish before the world" could also be considered. This would require a very comprehensive understanding of עולם in the sense of "world", however, which also raises the question of whether עולם should not be better understood as an expression of intensity. This, in turn, would have far-reaching implications because, if this were the case, we would be dealing with a concordant textual attestation of עולם in the versions, and this understanding would already exist for Ben Sira, at least in the context of a constructus compound.

The last example is the phrase שם עולם in Sir 15:6.

A 6 ששון ושמחה ימצא <u>ושם עולם</u> תורישנו:	Joy and delight he will find, and she will make him inherit an eternal name.
B 6 ששון ושמחה °תמצא ⟦ ⟧ וש]ם עולם תורישנו:[	Joy and delight you will, and [she will make them inherit an eternal] name.
mg re: ימצא	
6 εὐφροσύνην καὶ στέφανον ἀγαλλιάματος εὑρήσει καὶ <u>ὄνομα αἰῶνος</u> κατακληρονομήσει.	Gladness and a garland of rejoicing and an everlasting name will he inherit.
6 ܚܕܘܬܐ ܘܪܘܙܐ ܬܡܠܝܘܗܝ. <u>ܘܫܡܐ ܕܥܠܡܐ</u> ܬܘܪܬܝܘܗܝ.	With gladness and rejoicing she will fill him and an eternal name she will let him inherit.

The meaning of the phrase שם עולם cannot be clarified with certainty. In this passage about the encounter between the disciple and Wisdom, v. 6 states that the disciple will find rejoicing and joy, and Wisdom will give him a שם עולם. The textual attestation is consistent in this verse, so the expression is to be regarded as original and ancient.

As a nomen rectum, עולם can be understood in two ways, without these being categorically mutually exclusive. A temporal understanding of עולם would mean that Wisdom would give her faithful disciple an "eternal name", which would then ultimately inscribe him in the history of Israel, as Ben Sira already does in his historical account of outstanding personalities. This understanding is indeed supported by Ben Sira's introduction to the Praise of the Ancestors itself, for in Sir 44:8, he speaks of those who have left a name behind, in contrast to those who have also achieved great things but have nevertheless been forgotten. According to 15:6, Wisdom would, therefore, ensure that her faithful disciple would enter the collective memory of Israel's history in the same way as Abraham, Moses, David, and others in the Praise of the Ancestors.

In view of the examples just mentioned, however, it could also be a qualitative understanding of עולם, and then the verse would be about an important, outstanding name. Likewise, these considerations make it clear that the two are not mutually exclusive because an important name and an outstanding reputation may ultimately also go down in history and be commemorated permanently — so to say, for eternity.

3 Instances of Text-Historical Interest

There are five interesting examples of עולם in terms of their textual evidence. Although the very first example of the Hebrew textual attestation in the structure of the book provides further evidence for עולם as nomen rectum, it is not textually verified, so it shall be discussed here. In Sir 3:18, it says in Ms A:

18 מעט נפשך מכל גדולת עולם	Humble yourself more than all גדולת עולם,
ולפני אֵל תמצא רחמים:	and you will find mercy before God.

For the understanding of עולם, the question intuitively arises as to whether one should not expect a spatial rather than a temporal notion and whether the expression should be translated as "the magnitude of the world". Depending on whether one reads גְדוּלֶת or גְּדוֹלֹת, the instruction would read: "Humble yourself more than all the magnitude resp. all the great things of the world."

The problem is that neither Ms C nor G supports this reading as the oldest translation. Ms C reads:

18 בני גדול אתה כן תשפיל נפשך
ובעיני אלהים תמצא חן.

My son, great as you are, so humble yourself,
and in the eyes of God you will find grace.

The common intention of the statement is recognizable, so two independent formulations of the same maxim can be assumed. Expanding the view by looking at the versions, Ms C is supported by G:

18 ὅσῳ μέγας εἶ, τοσούτῳ ταπείνου σεαυτόν,
καὶ ἔναντι κυρίου εὑρήσεις χάριν·

The greater you are, the more you should humble yourself,
and before the Lord you will find favor.

This corresponds exactly to Ms C, and in the Greek textual tradition, there is no indication of a reading with עולם. There is, therefore, no influence whatsoever, even in later times.
On the other hand, P reads the following:

18 ܒܟܠ ܕܐܝܬ ܪܒ ܒܥܠܡܐ ܐܙܥܪ ܢܦܫܟ.
ܘܩܕܡ ܐܠܗܐ ܬܫܟܚ ܪ̈ܚܡܐ.

In all that is great in the world, be humble,
and before God you will find mercy.

P not only corresponds to Ms A in the first part of the verse but also uses רחמים instead of חן in the second part. From this, it can be concluded that the message of the verse was formulated twice very early and that one version has been preserved in Ms C and G and the other in Ms A and P. The reading גְּדוֹלַת עולם or עולם גְּדוֹלַת would be the more recent one and could therefore correspond to a later stage in the development of the meaning of עולם, which would justify a translation with "world", i.e. with a spatial meaning. In this way, the book of Ben Sira would have a share in this linguistic development in its own textual evolution.

But none of this is mandatory, as the next example shows. Before that, a word about the use of ܥܠܡܐ in P: P consistently translates the Hebrew עולם with the Syriac ܥܠܡܐ, with the exception of those verses in which it is highly probable that P's *Vorlage* is different from the text attested in the presently preserved Hebrew manuscripts. This is important insofar as no conclusions can be drawn from P about the respective meaning of the Hebrew עולם.

In Sir 4:23, there is an attestation in Ms A and C. Again, it is Ms A that testifies to עולם:

23 אל תמנע דבר בעולם
אל תצפין את חכמתך:

Do not withhold your word בעולם,
do not hide your wisdom.

Ms C, on the other hand, reads:

23 אל תמנע דבר <u>בעיתו</u> ואל תקפוץ את חכמתך.	Do not withhold your word at its proper moment, do not stifle your wisdom.

In both stichoi, the difference is only one word. In the second stichos, it is even very small in terms of meaning. However, it shows that the difference is explained less by copying processes than by memorization. In both cases, the scribe is of the opinion that he is expressing the same meaning. This would then also have to apply to the first stichos. However, in this case, עת and עולם have different connotations. Thus, one might assume that there was a phase in time in which the two terms were used with an overlap in meaning. However, it might be more plausible that both versions want to express different aspects of meaning, whereby the version of Ms A can be read as an exaggeration.

A look at the versions shows that both G and P support the reading בעיתו of Ms C and, therefore, P also stands against Ms A here:

23 μὴ κωλύσῃς λόγον ἐν <u>καιρῷ</u> χρείας·	Do not hinder speech in a time of need.
χρείας = Conj. Ra and Zi; Mss read <u>σριας</u> for σωτηριας, possibly mis-writing for χριας (= χρειας)	

23 ܠܐ ܬܟܠܐ ܦܬܓܡܐ <u>ܒܙܒܢܗ</u>. ܘܠܐ ܬܛܫܐ ܚܟܡܬܟ.	Do not hold back a saying in its time and do not conceal your wisdom.

In any case, the instance of 4:23 proves a temporal meaning for עולם.

In Sir 16:7, there are again two Hebrew readings, this time attested by Ms A and Ms B:

7 A אשר לא נשא לנסיכי קדם <u>המורים עולם</u> בגבורתם:	that he did not forgive the ancient princes, המורים עולם / who rebelled עולם in their power.
7 אשר לא נשא לנסיכ̊י קד̇ם 〚 〛 <u>המורדים</u>° ב̊ג̊ב̊ורתם:	For he did not forgive the ancient princes, and against an impious nation wrath is kindled.
mg li: בגב[ו̊ר̊ם̊]	

Ms A again provides the reading with עולם. In the context of the text, the point is that wrath burns and is passed on among the wicked for generations. The text is apparently referring back to Gen 6. Since the word עולם lacks a preposition, it is not an adverbial determination of time or place but the object of the verb מרה because with מרה, the object against which someone rebels is connected as a direct object (accusative). So, the sentence reads: "who rebelled against עולם in their power." Since rebelling against time makes no sense, the text probably talks about rebelling against the world. In the context of Jewish literature from the Hellenistic period, in which the short note in Gen 6 is a well-known subject and is elaborated on several times, the question arises as to whether עולם perhaps even refers to the world order.[11]

Strictly speaking, Sir 40:12 should not be included in the statistics. Although the text is attested in principle in the Masada manuscript, the verse is only preserved with its first letters, so its completion remains hypothetical. Nevertheless, the occurrence of עולם can be made plausible from both the Greek and the Syriac texts, even if these reveal a remarkable difference in the understanding of the word.

M 12 כל משׁ[קר ועולה ימחה ⟦ ⟧ ואמונה לעולם תעמד]	Everything from a bribe [. . .]
12 Πᾶν δῶρον καὶ ἀδικία ἐξαλειφθήσεται, καὶ πίστις εἰς τὸν αἰῶνα στήσεται.	Every gift and injustice will be blotted out, but good faith will stand forever.
12 ܟܠ ܡܢ ܕܚܛܐ ܘܡܕܓܠ ܟܠ ܢܒܛܠ. ܘܟܫܝܪ̈ܝ ܥܠܡܐ ܐܦ ܗܢܘܢ ܢܬܩܝܡܘܢ.	Everyone who sins and lies will come to naught nevertheless the diligent ones of the world, these will abide.

According to the Greek text, it is a juxtaposition of bribery and injustice on the one hand and πίστις (fidelity/trust/consistency) on the other. While bribery and injustice are wiped away, πίστις will endure εἰς τὸν αἰῶνα, forever and ever. On this basis, the phrase ואמונה לעולם תעמד can be reconstructed for the second stichos. The temporal understanding would be unquestionable.

The Syriac text also speaks to the existence of the word עולם in Hebrew but is open to interpretation in its understanding of the word. The Syriac text is also about a juxtaposition, this time of sinners and the diligent or successful. The one will perish, and the other will endure. Here, too, the focus on the future is undeniable. Nevertheless, the Syriac equivalent ܥܠܡܐ appears to have a different meaning, namely a spatial meaning. The Peshitta integrates the Syriac equivalent ܥܠܡܐ as nomen rectum in a constructus compound with the diligent/successful as nomen regens: ܟܫܝܪ̈ܝ ܥܠܡܐ (the diligent ones of the world, these will abide). This allows for a twofold interpretation: it could be both "the constantly diligent" or "the diligent ones of the world". If the latter is the case, P would document the already described expansion of the meaning of the word עולם in late antiquity.

---

11 Besides this, in terms of textual history, the passage is remarkable in that Ms B does not attest the word עולם, and then the same divergence of versions emerges as before in the comparison of Ms A and Ms C. Additionally, G follows Ms B, and, here again, P corresponds to Ms A in that it also attests עולם.

In Sir 40:17, the textual tradition again confirms the temporal understanding of עולם in Sir, with all versions using different temporal expressions.
In this case, Ms B provides the reading with עולם:

17 וחסד <u>לעולם</u> לא ימוט ⟦ ⟧	But piety will not be shaken in eternity,
וצדקה לעד תכון:	and righteousness will be established forever.

This contrasts with the much older Ms M, which offers a unique phrase:

17 חסד <u>בעד</u> לא תכרת ⟦ ⟧	Piety, like eternity, will never perish,
וצדקה לעד תכן	righteousness forever is secure.

The reading of Ms M, כעד, is only documented here. This is likely why it has prompted people to interpret it. This is reflected in the further transmission of the text. In any case, the Greek translation confirms it in its own way, as G reads:

17 χάρις <u>ὡς παράδεισος</u> ἐν εὐλογίαις,	Kindness is like an orchard with blessings,
καὶ ἐλεημοσύνη εἰς τὸν αἰῶνα διαμενεῖ.	but an act of charity will endure forever.

G turns the phrase כעד into the expression כעדן, thus presupposing the consonants of Ms M and adding a Nun. G thus follows the later v. 27[12], in which exactly this reading is found in Ms M.

P takes a different path and reads:

17 ܘܥܒ̈ܕܐ ܕܟܐ̈ܢܐ <u>ܒܙܒܢܐ</u> ܢܬܒܪܟܘܢ.	The works of the upright in time will be blessed
ܘܥܒ̈ܕܐ ܕܙܕ̈ܝܩܐ ܠܥܠܡ ܢܬܩܝܡܘܢ.	and the works of the righteous will be established for ever
ܘܕܡܬܩܪܒ ܠܗܘܢ ܐܝܟ ܐܢܫ ܕܡܫܟܚ ܣܝܡܬܐ.	and he who approaches them is as a person who finds a treasure.

P thus seems to presuppose בעת. This equivalent is found seven times in Sir[13] and in the other translations of P;[14] thus, it is not unusual. Since the readings of G and P can be derived equally from Ms M, the latter is regarded as original not only because of the age of the textual witness.

Finally, the reading of Ms B can also be derived from this. Ms B offers a temporal interpretation, in contrast to the unwieldy textual presentation in Ms M, just like P, and clarifies it as עולם and additionally gives the expression the perspective of temporal extension by choosing ל as a preposition and not adopting כ. The latter

12 Sir 40:27a: יראת אלהים כעדן ברכה (The fear of God is like Eden: a blessing).
13 Sir 3:31; 11:19; 12:5; 32:11; 37:4; 39:28; 51:30.
14 Cf. Job 38:32; Eccl 10:17; Dan 11:40; Neh 9:27.

must also be regarded as original, as it is supported by the Greek ὡς and the Syriac preposition ܐܝܟ, each in its own way.[15] In this case, however, the understanding of עולם is temporal, in contrast to the attestations in Ms A.

4 Conclusions

To summarize, three aspects can be highlighted:

First, Ben Sira clearly has a predominantly temporal understanding of the term עולם, and in this, it essentially corresponds to the "traditional" use of language as attested in the biblical writings. However, a multi-layered usage shines through in some places. This concerns, second, the possibility of understanding עולם in the position of the nomen rectum in constructus compounds as an expression of intensity.

Third, there are also occasional indications of a spatial understanding, even if this only emerges primarily in the later textual tradition. However, since the textual transmission is a central theme in the Book of Ben Sira, and it is a characteristic of this book that it exists exclusively in pluriform manifestation, the book thus becomes, in its own way, a linguistic-historical mirror of the expansion of the meaning of עולם in late antiquity.[16]

Finally, a remark on the statistics mentioned in the beginning. How can the accumulation of the term עולם with its temporal meaning be explained as found in the book of Ben Sira?

First of all, it should be noted that, unlike the Book of Proverbs, the Book of Ben Sira, like Qohelet, is the work of an individual author and, therefore, also of an authorial personality with his own linguistic and intellectual preferences. The keyword עולם, therefore, seems to be an important point in Ben Sira's own thinking, whereas it hardly plays a role for Qohelet. Why is this the case with Ben Sira?

The answer is likely to be found in the frequency of the word in the Praise of the Ancestors. In it, Ben Sira introduces people who are remembered in history. It cannot be said that, in contrast to the forgotten, they achieved anything outstanding. But the fact is that there are people who are forgotten and those who are not. Ben Sira cannot give a reason for this in the introduction to the Praise of the Ancestors. However, his concern is now that his students — and certainly he himself — may be among those who are not forgotten but whose names are

15 In the case of the Syriac, the ܐܝܟ might be explained by a misreading of כ but not of the preposition ל.
16 Cf. m. Ber. 9:2; m. Pesaḥ. 10:6; m. Roš Haš. 1:2 and more frequently.

included in the history of Israel. This may not simply be about a desire for fame but also about ensuring one's own continued existence. At the beginning of his book, in Chapter 3, Ben Sira rejects apocalyptic ideas and involvement with them. He does not know of or believe in the idea of life after death. The continuation of a good reputation and entry into the collective memory of the people is, therefore, the only possibility of a "life after death." Ben Sira thus makes himself the "wisdom teacher of eternity", who repeatedly points out in his teachings that one must pay attention not only to the consequences but also to the effectiveness of one's own actions in history.

Bibliography

Beentjes, Pancratius C. 2021. "Aspects of Time in the Book of Ben Sira: אחרית." In *Notions of Time in Deuterocanonical and Cognate Literature*, edited by Stefan Beyerle and Matthew Goff, 387–401. Berlin / Boston: De Gruyter. https://doi.org/10.1515/9783110705454-018.

Ben-Dov, Jonathan. 2017. "Time and Natural Law in Jewish-Hellenistic Writings." In *The Construction of Time in Antiquity: Ritual, Art, and Identity*, edited by Jonathan Ben-Dov and Lutz Doering, 9–30. New York: Cambridge University Press. https://doi.org/10.1017/9781316266199.002.

Beyerle, Stefan, and Matthew Goff, eds. 2021. *Notions of Time in Deuterocanonical and Cognate Literature*. Berlin / Boston: De Gruyter. https://doi.org/10.1515/9783110705454.

Blass, Friedrich, Albert Debrunner, and Friedrich Rehkopf. 2001. *Grammatik des neutestamentlichen Griechisch: Joachim Jeremias zum 75. Geburtstag.* 18th ed. Göttingen: Vandenhoeck & Ruprecht.

Bussino, Severino. 2021. "Time and Change in the Book of Ben Sira." In *Notions of Time in Deuterocanonical and Cognate Literature*, edited by Stefan Beyerle and Matthew Goff, 339–368. Berlin / Boston: De Gruyter. https://doi.org/10.1515/9783110705454-016.

Calduch-Benages, Nuria. 2021. "The Notion of Time in Sir 18:19–26." In *Notions of Time in Deuterocanonical and Cognate Literature*, edited by Stefan Beyerle and Matthew Goff, 369–386. Berlin / Boston: De Gruyter. https://doi.org/10.1515/9783110705454-017.

Corley, Jeremy. 2021. "Ben Sira and the Sabbath." In *Notions of Time in Deuterocanonical and Cognate Literature*, edited by Stefan Beyerle and Matthew Goff. DCLY 2020/2021, 169–190. Berlin / Boston: De Gruyter. https://doi.org/10.1515/9783110705454-009.

Egger-Wenzel, Renate. 2021. "Die Bedeutung von קץ im Buch Ben Sira." In *Notions of Time in Deuterocanonical and Cognate Literature*, edited by Stefan Beyerle and Matthew Goff, 403–426. Berlin / Boston: De Gruyter. https://doi.org/10.1515/9783110705454-019.

Mermelstein, Ari. 2015. *Creation, Covenant, and the Beginnings of Judaism: Reconceiving Historical Time in the Second Temple Period*. JSJ.S 168. Leiden: Brill.

Preuß, Horst Dietrich. 1986. "עולם." In *Theologisches Wörterbuch zum Alten Testament*, vol. 5, edited by G. Johannes Botterweck, Heinz-Josef Fabry and Helmer Ringgren, 1144–1159. Stuttgart: Kohlhammer.

Rey, Frédérique M., and Eric D. Reymond. 2024. *A Critical Edition of the Hebrew Manuscripts of Ben Sira: With Translation and Philological Notes*. JSJSup. 217. Leiden: Brill. https://doi.org/10.1163/9789004700802.

Stadel, Christian. 2016. “עולם.” In *Theologisches Wörterbuch zu den Qumrantexten*, vol. 2, edited by Heinz-Josef Fabry and Ulrich Dahmen, 61–68. Stuttgart: Kohlhammer.

Wilch, John R. 1969. *Time and Event: An Exegetical Study on the Use of ʿĒth in the Old Testament in Comparison to Other Temporal Expressions in Clarification of the Concept of Time*. Leiden: Brill. https://doi.org/10.1163/9789004676176.

Martina Kepper

The Chronotopes of Ezechiel, Baruch, and Sapientia. Three Case Studies

Abstract: Within the methodological framework of combining Septuagint and Hebrew Bible studies, this paper adopts Mikhail Bakhtin's concept of the chronotope—that is, the intrinsic connectedness of temporal and spatial relations as they are artistically expressed in literature—as a heuristic tool for the analysis of ancient biblical texts. Although originally developed for the analysis of modern narrative fiction, the Bakhtinian chronotope is here applied experimentally to biblical literature in order to assess its explanatory value for theological meaning-making in different textual and linguistic traditions. The methodological potential of this approach is explored through three case studies: the Book of Ezekiel in its Hebrew and Greek textual traditions, the Book of Baruch, and the Wisdom of Solomon. These texts represent diverse historical settings, languages, and stages of textual transmission within the literature of the Second Temple period.

The analysis demonstrates that chronological and spatial references in these writings function primarily as literary-theological constructs rather than as instruments of historical precision. Temporal frameworks and spatial settings structure narrative discourse, qualify events as salvifically significant, and articulate theological conceptions of judgment, restoration, and hope. A comparison of divergent textual traditions—particularly the Masoretic Text and the Greek versions—reveals distinct theological profiles that emerge from differing chronotopic configurations. Chronology thus operates not merely as a historiographical tool, but as a constitutive element of theological reflection. The application of Bakhtin's chronotope offers a productive lens for reassessing exegetical strategies in biblical texts and underscores the value of literary-theoretical approaches for the study of ancient scripture.

This paper attempts to combine at least two different strands of scholarship that are normally separated, namely Septuagint studies and studies referring to the (end-)text of the Hebrew Bible. This is still quite an unusual endeavor. Therefore, a few preliminary remarks may be at hand. Septuagint studies have undergone a massive change in the last decade or two. In the aftermath of the pivotal academic translations released in French, English, and German,[1] a bulk of studies have been

1 See *La Bible d'Alexandrie* 1986; *New English Translation of the Septuagint* 2006, *Septuaginta Deutsch* 2009.

published which focus on the — for convenience[2] — so-called Septuagint. Linguistic studies and philological descriptions of the Septuagint's language as normal instruments of scholarship have led to commentaries on particular books in the text[3] which are analogue to the books of the Hebrew Bible. There is still a debate, however, whether one can even detect a theology specific to the Septuagint (Ausloos and Lemmelijn 2020, 29–46).

Yet it is without a doubt that Septuagint studies have broadened our knowledge about the formation of the authoritative texts and now extend into the canon of the Hebrew and Greek Bible alike. This has opened our eyes to the idea that it is not only the Hebrew scriptures which are a product of a younger stage of the redactional and productive process than previous scholars suggested, but also the specific text forms of individual books of the Hebrew canon can be younger than other text forms, for instance its Greek version.

Concurrently, the methodological issue of whether it is better to interpret the texts of the Hebrew Bible in its historical framework or in a holistic view as literature, accepting its transmitted text through the ages is still going on. Therefore, it is not without difficulty to apply literary methods, such as the theory of chronotope — a method initially developed for fictional novels of the 20th century — for interpreting ancient texts.[4] With this being said, the following observations can be nothing more than test cases in order to examine if describing the chronotope of a certain book can be of heuristic value for analyzing its theological message(s), especially in its different versions.

Applying this analytical device to ancient texts must also have in mind the formation history of biblical texts. Firstly, this alludes to the topos of intertextuality between the Hebrew texts themselves, then between its different forms in Hebrew and Greek, and at last between "younger" and older books. The following three test cases are, therefore, deliberately chosen: first, there is the Book of Ezechiel which extends into at least two different text types in Hebrew and Greek; second, the Book of Baruch, which may be a Greek translation, but with no Hebrew texts passed down to us yet; third, the Book of Wisdom, probably the youngest text which has been canonized and written only in Greek. Therefore, it might be possible to

---

2 For a quite general, but nonetheless critical approach to this term see Greenspoon and Ross 2024.

3 Of course, there are several commentaries for the Book of Ezechiel in its Hebrew version, but up to now, there is no special volume of its Greek version. But we do have commentaries for the Book of Baruch (for instance Steck 1993; Adams 2014) as well as the Book of Wisdom (for instance Engel 1998; Mazzinghi 2019).

4 A similar approach would be applying theories about literature already developed in antiquity as, for instance, Ekphrasis, see Weissenrieder and Kepper 2024. For a comprehensive summary of Bakhtin's approach see the paper of Brum/Schmitz in this volume.

discover similar approaches and maybe even developments between these texts, seeing as the texts chosen cover a certain range of time and language.[5]

1 First Test Case: Ezechiel in the Greek and Hebrew Versions

If any biblical book is predestined to be analyzed in terms of its chronotope, it surely is the Book of Ezechiel. Meticulous dating (see Table 1) extends throughout the book, in both its Masoretic as well as the Greek version(s).[6] Already the very first verse defines a chronotope, it combines a very specific dating with a certain space: a first-person-speaker dates all which follows to "the 30th year, on/in the fourth, on the 5th day of the month" at the "river Kebar". What makes this verse a chronotope is that neither the dating nor the geographic orientation shows any reference to historically valid entities. To start with the spatial orientation, a river called *Kebar* is only mentioned here and is further referred to only within the book itself.[7] Up to the present day we cannot identify its location with certainty.[8] Any etymological considerations about the name as a hint to its meaning or of its place are not helpful either.[9] This is accompanied by a specific date which lacks a point

5 The following observations are not meant to be comprehensive or solve the manifold text-critical or redactional-critical issues, especially in the Book of Ezechiel. The aim of this paper is to elicit if observing the chronotope of a certain book helps to understand why an author wants to tell his story to be happening in a certain time at a certain place. Is it possible to detect certain strategies that hint to an overall view of time as salvific history or are there different strategies of placing certain events in temporal context?

6 Following Lilly (2012) and others, the (proto-)Masoretic text and the Greek tradition, with Papyrus 967 as its oldest representation of the "Old Greek" (Finsterbusch 2013), should be considered as at least two different versions of the book.

7 See Ezek 1:3; 3:15,23; 10:15,20,22; 43:3. For a detailed analysis see Segev and Zilberg (2025).

8 Two clay tablets of the Muraššû archive, written between 443 and 424 BCE, mention a navigable canal Kabari / Kabaru in the vicinity of Nippur, which some scholars tend to identify with the biblical Kebar (Vogt 1958). But this identification is highly disputed, because the canal itself cannot be located beyond doubt (Schnocks 2009). We will find the same pattern of "inventing" certain locations in Bar, see later in this paper.

9 The root כבר is quite rare in the Hebrew Bible: the verb occurs only in Job 35:16 and 36:21 in the meaning of "multiply" but is probably a misreading for כבד. We find the adverb 8 times only in Ecclesiastes, meaning "already". Two abstract nouns כברה in Am 9:9 in the meaning of "sieve" and three times in Gen 35:16; 48:7 and 2Kgs 5:19 in the meaning "some, a little" can be traced. The latter occurrences hint to the fact that the word was already incomprehensible for the LXX translators, as they are just transcribing it.

of reference. The data which is given in the book seems to be absolutely clear but are *de facto* fuzzy.

All of the following datings serve a special purpose, namely, to make sure that certain oracles or events all happen at a given time. The following table shows which events are dated and the differences between the versions:

Event	**LXX^B / P. 967 (where extend)**	**MT**
1:1 The beginning of the Merkavah-Vision	in the 30th year, in the fourth +month, on the fifth of the month	in the 30th year, in the fourth, on the fifth of the month
1:2 Alignment of the fifth month to the fifth year of the Exile	on the fifth of the month — that is the fifth year of the captivity (αἰχμαλωσία) of king Jehojakim	On the fifth of the month — that is the fifth year of the captivity (תולג) of king Jehojakim
3:15,16 Ezechiel's call to be the Watcher of the people	After the seven days	After seven days
8:1 The vision of the defiled Temple	In the sixth year, in the *fifth* +month, on the fifth of the month	In the sixth year, in the *sixth* month, on the fifth of the month
20:1 The elders try to get an oracle but JHWH refuses to speak to them	In the seventh year, in the fifth +month, on the tenth of the month	In the seventh year, in the fifth, on the tenth of the month
24:1 oracle of the cooking pot	In the ninth year, in the tenth month, on the tenth of the month	In the ninth year, in the tenth month, on the tenth of the month
26:1 oracle against Tyre	P. 967: In the *tenth* year, on the first of the month LXX^B: in the *eleventh* year, on the first of the month LXX^A: in the *twelfth* year, on the first of the +first month	In the *eleventh* year, on the first of the month (month missing)
29:1 oracle against Pharaoh and Egypt	P. 967: in the tenth year, in the *twelfth* month, on the *first* of the month LXX^B: in the tenth year, in the tenth month, on the first of the month	In the tenth year, in the *tenth*, on the *twelfth* of the month
29:17 Oracle of Nebuchadnezzar taking over Egypt	In the 27th year, on the first of the first month	In the 27th year, *in the first / beginning*, on the first of the month

(continued)

Event	LXX^{B} / P. 967 (where extend)	MT
30:20 Oracle against Pharaoh	P. 967: In the *tenth* year, in the first month, on the seventh of the month LXX^{B}: in the *eleventh* year. In the first month, on the seventh of the month	In the *eleventh* year, in the first / beginning, on the seventh of the month
31:1 Oracle against Pharaoh	P. 967: in the *tenth* year, in the third month, on the first of the month LXX$^{B:}$ in the *eleventh* year, in the third month, on the first of the month	In the *eleventh* year, in the third, on the first of the month
32:1 The lament for pharaoh	P. 967: in the *twelfth* year, in the *tenth* month, on the first of the month LXX$^{B:}$ in the *eleventh* year, in the twelfth month, on the first of the month	In the *twelfth* year, in the *twelfth* month, on the first of the month
32:17 The lament for the people of Egypt	P. 967: in the *tenth* year, in the first month, on the fifteenth of the month LXX$^{B:}$ in the *twelfth* month, in the first month, on the fifteenth of the month	In the *twelfth* year, on the fifteenth of the month (month missing)
33:21 Message of the fall of Jerusalem	P. 967: In the *tenth* year, in the twelfth month, on the *fifth* of the month of our captivity (αἰχμαλωσία) LXX$^{B:}$ in the *twelfth* year, in the *twelfth* month, on the fifth of our captivity	In the *twelfth* year, in the *tenth* month, on the fifth of the month of our captivity (ונתולגל)
40:1 Beginning of the vision of the new temple	P. 967: In the 25th year of the captivity, in the first month, on the tenth of the month; in the fourteenth year after the city was captured, on that day LXX$^{B:}$ in the 25th year of our captivity, in the first month, on the tenth of the month; in the fourteenth year after the city was captured	In the 25th year of our captivity, on the beginning of the year (ראש השנה), on the tenth of the month, in the fourteenth year after the city was captured, on that same day (verbally: on the "bone" of the day)

Three observations may be of interest: first, the Greek versions as well as MT use a year-to-day pattern.[10] This pattern does not reflect the custom of dating as recorded in contracts or official records of the Achaemenid period. Preserved in, for instance, the Al-Yāhūdu or the Muraššû archives,[11] the pattern is day-to-year, normally calibrated to the reign of the ruler.

Second, despite a lot of minor differences, a major difference between the versions occurs in dating the oracle against Tyre (26:1). From there on, the MT, P. 967 and the LXX-versions differ. The MT shows chronological inconsistencies, as the oracle against Tyre in chapter 26 is dated one year earlier than the oracle against Pharaoh and Egypt in chapter 29.[12] Likewise, P. 967 skips the chronological order by placing the lament over Pharaoh in the twelfth year (32:1), but places the lament for Egypt in 32:17 back in the tenth year.

Third, the last date given is at the beginning of the vision of the New Temple (40:1). Although the dates given in the versions agree, there is a tiny difference: the MT stresses the importance of that "very" day, whereas the Greek traditions do not. Can these observations be interpreted in terms of a chronotope?

1.1 The Year-To-Day-Pattern

The datings of the book of Ezechiel have been a point of contention for a long time. For a start, why is the "30th year" not contextualized?[13] The point of reference is immediately submitted in the following verse: 1:2 counts from the captivity, here of King Jehojakim. This is repeated only in the last dating in the vision of the New Temple (40:1), but here without reference to Jehojakim: P. 967 mentions "the" captivity, MT and LXX "our" captivity.

The following datings are nearly in chronological order. Applying historical value to the dates given, they cover 20 years, from 593 to 573 BCE, which would be the years between the first deportation up to the first years of the Babylonian Exile

10 The Hebrew version mostly lacks the word "month" and mentions only the number, also see 26:1 and 32:17 where even the number of the month is missing.

11 See Weippert 2010, no. 274–282, and also Bob Becking's paper in this volume about the Elephantine papyri.

12 All versions agree in the chronological disorder of dating the oracle against Nebuchadnezzar (29:17) to the 27th year, although the next dating (30:20) turns back to the tenth or eleventh year.

13 Most scholars try to explain it as a reference to Ezechiel's age, as someone needs to reach the age of 30 (Num 4:3,23,30) to become a priest, Ezechiel would therefore be "fit for office" (Bewer 1934, 34, 96–101)

after the fall of Jerusalem.[14] Mainstream scholarship applies a redactional-critical view on the Hebrew text by placing its oldest layers somewhere in the 6th century. This means that they presume that the chronological data given is basically historically accurate.[15]

As mentioned above, the year-to-day-pattern is uncommon to extra-biblical texts which have their *Sitz im Leben* in everyday life, especially in legal contexts when an exact dating is of great importance. The year-to-day pattern, though, has a striking similarity to biblical texts. To note just one example: the beginning of God speaking to Moses is dated in Deut 1:3 "in the 40th year, in the eleventh month, on the first of the month". Here no calibration is given, although it should be clear that, implicitly, the point of reference is the Exodus. Within the framework of the Deuteronomistic History, the 40th year has another special connotation: it is the end of one generation (*dōr*), when God again turns towards a new generation of his people for salvation (Otto 2012, 317).

The beginning of Deuteronomy, therefore, is also a chronotope, and very similar to that in Ezechiel, by dating the "words" Moses said — or the "speeches" he gave — to the people without further reference as well as also giving an itinerary in detail which mentions places that are of no specific connotation.[16]

Strikingly, Deut 1:2–3 uses two different forms of the number "eleven": אחד עשר V. 2 with a total of 11 occurrences in MT, and עשתי־עשר (with a total of 18 occurrences in MT) immediately following in V. 3.[17] When we try to bring these different wordings for the same number in line, we may say that עשתי־עשר is the wording

14 The oracles against Egypt (29:1,17) disturb this chronological order. Whereas the oracle against Tyre in 26:1 is already dated to the 11th year, the date of the oracle against Egypt is placed back in time to the 10th and the second one in the 27th year although the last date in 40:1 is placed in the 25th year. Codex L and the Latin version present the 12th year.

15 See Greenberg 2001, 28–34, and especially Pohlmann 1992, 217: the oldest layers would be the lamentations on the fall of Jerusalem and its king in chapter 19 and the King of Tyre in chapter 31. Main argument for the destruction of Jerusalem in 587 as a *terminus a quo* is the lack of any explanation for the disaster. For different views see Becker 1992, 142–146, opting for a much younger date, or Schöpflin 2002, 345: she opts for Ezek as a pseudepigraphical book from Hellenistic times. For a general overview see Pohlmann 2008; Tooman and Barter 2017. Concerning text historical issues see Schwagmeier 2004, and especially Lilly 2012.

16 See Otto 2012, 313: already Noth noted that the names given show no signs of special quality and do not appear elsewhere. The reference to Suf resembles the blurry spatial data in Ezek 1:1 as well as Bar 1, for details to Deut 1:2 see Rüterswörden 2013, 2.

17 Derived from Akkadian *ištēn* = one (Ges[18], 1027) עשתי־עשר occurs in Exod 26:7,8; 36:14,15; 2Kgs 25:2; Jer 1:3; 39:2; 52:5; Num 7:72; 29:20; Zech 1:7; 1Chr 12:14; 24:12; 25:18; 27:14 (bis), whereas אחד עשר shows up in Gen 32:23; 37:9; Josh 15:51; 1Kgs 6:38; 2Kgs 9:29; 23:36; 24:18; Jer 52:1; Ez 30:20; 31:1.

used in Jer and 2Kgs when dating the fall of Jerusalem on the "eleventh" year of Zedekiah (Jer 1:3; 39:2; 52:5 in accordance with 2Kgs 25:2).

When we take a closer look at the dating of the oracle against Tyre in Ezek 26:1 we see that MT not only dates the oracle one year later than P. 967 and thus confusing its own chronological order, but also uses the exact same wording (עשתי־עשר) for counting, like the years of Zedekiah in Jer and 2Kgs. The other datings to the eleventh year in MT (30:20; 31:1), though, use the other wording אחת עשרה. It seems as if MT favours the idea that the numerical data for this oracle should be connected to the other texts outside of Ezechiel which mention the fall of Jerusalem.[18]

1.2 Chronological Confusions?

This leads to the question why the dating of the oracle against Tyre is important at all. When we compare the different versions, we find that P. 967 dates everything from the oracle against Tyre (26:1) up to the vision of the new Temple (40:1, in the 25th year) to the tenth year,[19] most importantly including the message of the fall of Jerusalem in 33:21. The MT, on the other hand, confuses the chronological order in 26:1 to 29:1, and dates the fall of Jerusalem two years later in the twelfth year. But the alleged confusion of the dates in 32:1 and 17 in contrast to 33:21 is no confusion at all by means of the probably alluded chronotope: the fall of Jerusalem in 33:21 is simply dated earlier than the victory over Israel's enemies but narrated later.

This falls in line with observations that Christoph Rösel (2012) brings up by analysing the following chapters 36–39. His conclusion is that MT was expanded at a very late stage of the transmission of the text. Especially 38:4 and 39:28 as well as 38:8 and 39:3–4 were added to serve as a different interpretation for the episode of Gog from Magog and therefore show signs of redactional work by very late hands.

Most important, Rösel has shown that the ultimate war against Gog from Magog in chapters 38–39 should neither be interpreted mythologically nor historically but against the background of the book itself and therefore, as a literal device to underline the notion of JHWH as easily capable of winning over every ultimate enemy. Literal narration does not necessarily follow chronological order.[20] He concludes, for instance, that by placing the vision of the dry bones in chapter 37 (37 MT = 39 LXX) behind the mythical story of Gog from Magog, every enemy is destroyed before God acts benevolently towards his people. He even interprets the Gog story

---

18 As there is only one word for "eleven" in Greek, this tiny connection cannot be observed in the Greek versions.

19 The one exception would be 32:1.

20 Rösel 2012, 409: we cannot assume "Textfolge [. . .] als zeitliche Abfolge".

in terms of a chronotope without naming it: In Rösel's own words: "Die zeitliche Ferne [temporal distance] des Gog-Geschehens steht gemeinsam mit der räumlichen Ferne [spatial distance] der heranziehenden Feinde zunächst für die Endgültigkeit der beschriebenen Ereignisse." (Rösel 2012, 409). Therefore, MT stresses the *temporal* span between the presence of its addressees as well as the final victory and judgment of the nations which still have not been judged, whereas the Greek versions stress the *spatial* span of destroying first the outermost worldly enemies.

This also falls in line with the observation that the lament for Pharaoh in chapter 32:1 in P. 967 is dated *after* the fall of Jerusalem (although narrated earlier), because the fall of Jerusalem is the (temporal) beginning of God's will to restore Israel which then leads to the (spatial) victory over all evil powers, worldly or mythologically alike.

1.3 The Dating of the Temple Vision (40:1)

The differing dates from 26:1 onwards are not as unimportant as they may seem because they mark the seams between the oracles of doom against Israel, the surrounding enemies, and the envisioned salvific future of Israel which begins either with the fall of Jerusalem (P. 967) or with the oracles against the enemies (MT / part of LXX). The vision of the New Temple, in which this salvific future culminates, is the last date given in the book. Or, so to say: by literally reaching the eschatological place, time/dating stops.

MT has a plus, as the first month that occurs in all versions is contextualized as the very beginning of the year (ראש השנה).[21] The two points of reference are worked together: first, 25 years are counted from the deportation (גלות or αἰχμαλωσία). This system relates the Merkabah Vision in 1:2 to the fall of Jerusalem in 33:21 and the Temple vision here in 40:1. Second, 14 years after, the fall of Jerusalem is mentioned which also hints back to 33:21. As MT dated the fall of Jerusalem in the eleventh year, the dating is arithmetically correct.[22]

However, some other terms in this verse are remarkable: the vision is said to happen at that "very or special day": בעצם היום הזה, obviously stressing that it is important to happen on that "very day". If we look at the Greek version of this

21 ראש השנה becomes the significant term for the New Year in later times but does not occur elsewhere in the Hebrew bible. Obviously, Ezechiel dates the beginning of the year in spring, cf. 45:18ff, not in autumn. This would hint to a luni-solar calendar system. For discussion cf. LXX.E II, 2968.
22 From a textcritical point of view, MT would be a lectio facilior, as p967 dates the fall of Jerusalem in the tenth year. Most modern translations change the datings in chapters 32 and 33 to a chronological order.

dating, it is not that striking at all: ἐν τῇ ἡμέρᾳ ἐκείνῃ is the common rendering of the typical ביום הזה, denoting the present or new day as contrasted to the already mentioned or previous day.[23] In Greek, the pronoun denotes "the one there" with reference to the point of view of the speaker, the one which is already known or what is present.[24]

The Hebrew phrase is different. Literally translated it would be "to the bone" of this day,[25] grammatically this idiom is explained as the essence or true character of that day.[26] So, this day is said to have a special quality in Hebrew, but not in Greek.[27]

If we follow this path, we find that the same Hebrew idiom occurs in 2:3 and 24:2. In 2:3[LXX] Ezechiel is sent to the House of Israel because they separated with God "up to this present day" (ἕως τῆς σήμερον ἡμέρας), which is the standard equivalent for Hebrew עד היום הזה. But in the Hebrew Text, Ezechiel is sent to the Israelites and the nations, because they broke with God "up to this very/special day" (עד־עצם היום הזה). Moreover, in the parable of the cooking pot in 24:2, Ezechiel is ordered to write down the name of the very/special day, when Nebuchadnezzar laid siege to Jerusalem. In both cases the Greek rendering also stresses the importance of that very day: ἕως τῆς σήμερον ἡμέρας, but it does not do so in 40:1. So why was the Hebrew term עצם deliberately chosen in 40:1 to mark that the essence or core of the day is significant for the things that happen on that "very day"?[28]

These "very days" are quite specific, indeed: Noah enters the Ark (Gen 7:13), Abraham and all of his male offspring get circumcised (Gen 17:23–26), the Israelites eat Mazzot the night before the Exodus (Exod 12:17), the sacrifices on the 50th day after Passover and the Day of Atonement (Lev 23:21–28,30), the last words of God to Moses right before his death (Deut 32:48) and the first Passover in the promised Land (Josh 5:11) all happen at this "very day": בעצם היום הזה. Every specific Greek rendering of these passages also stresses the idea of a core day by rendering either ἐν τῷ καιρῷ τῆς ἡμέρας ἐκείνης or ἐν αὐτῇ τῇ ἡμέρᾳ ταύτῃ.[29]

---

23 Cf. GK §136[a].

24 Cf. The Cambridge Greek Lexicon I, 445.

25 There is a manuscript (62') doing so: ὅστια τῆς ἡμέρας.

26 Cf. GK §139[g]: "tropisch für *Wesen*", like נפש is used as describing a person.

27 I am grateful to Frank Ueberschaer who, during the discussion of this paper at the conference, pointed out that the Peshitta does not stress the importance of the "bone" of the day either.

28 See also Lilly 2012, 307–308, who points to the fact that MT presents an "increased use of the eschatological phrase 'on that day'", but without analyzing this any further.

29 Another observation is that day of the Exodus of all troops (Ex 12:51) is also marked as בעצם היום הזה, but rendered in Greek unmarked as ἐν τῇ ἡμέρᾳ ἐκείνῃ like in Ezek 40:1. As the same Hebrew phrase occurs also in Exod 12:41 as a plus of MT, it would be interesting to examine whether the phrase was also inserted into MT at a very young stage.

So, the chronotope of the Hebrew version sets the vision of the New Temple in line with the most important events of the salvific history: from the primeval rescue of Noah to the beginning of cultic agency in the land given to Israel. Although spatially aligned to the river Kebar, the temporal data connects this terminologically to God's rescuing and preserving of his people in the past as narrated in the Torah. We can assume that this sheds light on how the vision is to be understood: as an alignment to a new glorious time to come. And this time starts — if we follow the calculation that the fall of Jerusalem was in the twelfth year — with the lament over Pharaoh and Egypt. So the final victory over the terrestrial enemies, which we may understand as a reference to the hope of the scribes themselves for victory over contemporary enemies, may it be in late Hellenistic or Roman times.

If we compare this to the different chronotope in the Greek version, which according to a lot of scholars preserves the older version of the text,[30] we may sum up that disregarding minor differences the fall of Jerusalem is the starting point of God's benevolent actings towards his people. However, God's restoration of his people should not necessarily be compared to the primeval or ancestral times. On this (future) day in 40:1, there can be seen the New Temple. This is also seen at the River Kebar, which stresses the importance of the community living there. The presence of the addressees is stressed, speaking to a community that is hoping for a return to the land they had to leave. And thus — so we may guess — thinks of itself as the real Israel which will return and live again in the presence of its God at the new temple.[31] This was obviously not hoped for at the end of times but in due future, so that we may dare to call it an eschatological point of view.

If these observations are convincing, using the idea of a chronotope as a device for analyzing the Book of Ezechiel as literature may be of importance and should be open the field for further research.

---

30 Rösel 2012, 405–406: the "Old Greek" as represented in P. 967 is the oldest stratum of Ezechiel. Lilly 2012, 301: The text of Ezechiel, as represented in its oldest forms in P. 967 and B, "present a textual puzzle." Her heuristic starting point would be 12:26–28, a plus in MT according to P. 967, cf. Lilly 2012, 304, 325. She counts no less than 87 variants or "Prophecy Tendenzen" that deal with a different view on the message of Ezechiel. Konkel 1998, 60: "Die Analyse der Textüberlieferung zeigt, dass das Ezechielbuch nicht aus einem Guss ist, und dass in später Zeit — also bis ins 2. Jahrhundert v. Chr. — teilweise noch umfangreich am Buch gearbeitet wurde." Mackie 2015, 218: "These intersecting dynamics of textual interpretation and production mean that studying the involved and often complex phenomenon of scribal expansion in Ezekiel places us deep into the seedbed of what will later become the large and variegated tradition of Jewish scriptural interpretation."

31 Maybe this indicates a connection to the so-called „Gola-orientierte-Redaktion" (Pohlmann 1992).

2 Second Test Case: Baruch 1:11: "The days of heaven upon the earth"

The Book of Baruch is named after the secretary of Jeremiah (Jer 32:11–15; 36; 45)[32]. Up to the third century CE, its 5 chapters were transmitted as an annex to the Book of Jeremiah in both the Septuagint and the Vetus Latina (together with the Letter of Jeremiah as chapter 6 of Baruch). The book starts with a report of a penitential service of the exiles in Babylon (1:1–14). They collected money for the Temple in Jerusalem which they sent there, together with a long penitential prayer (1:15–3:8). The exiles then request for it to be read in the Temple to pray for forgiveness. The second part is a Wisdom poem (3:9–4:4). A speech promising the end of the exile and the return of Jerusalem's children in 4:5–5:9 completes the book. Although pretending to be situated at the beginning of the exile it was probably written sometime during the second century BCE. Whether or not the text may have originally been written in Hebrew or Aramaic or if Greek is its original language is an open question. Also it is unclear if it was meant to follow the short version of Jeremiah or its longer, Hebrew form (LXX.H I 2016, 597–599; Adams 2014, 4–6).

When we try to describe the chronotope of the Book of Baruch, it is astonishingly close to Ezechiel's by using the same, incomplete pattern for the chronological framework: 1:2 dates the service to the 5th year, on the 7th of the month (with no further information which month),[33] with the same point of reference as that in Ezechiel: the very point of time (*kairos*) the Chaldeans burnt down Jerusalem.

However, it is surprising that Baruch is in Babylon at all because it contradicts the data given in the Book of Jeremiah: Baruch was in Judah/Jerusalem together with Jeremiah during the reign of Jehojakim (Jer 36:1,9; 45:2), Zedekiah (Jer 32:1,2), and Gedalja (Jer 43:3) after the first deportation. After his homicide, Baruch was displaced to Egypt (Jer 43:6–7; Steck 1993, 16). In terms of its chronotope, it is necessary, therefore, that the dates given in the Book of Baruch reflect his stay in Babylon only after the destruction of Jerusalem in 587 BCE.

Furthermore, the spatial orientation is as blurry as it is in Ezechiel: the exiles live at the river Sud (1:4), which again is a river not known to us.[34] Although the

32 Translation according to Lexham English Septuagint 1987.

33 ἐν τῷ ἔτει τῷ πέμπτῳ ἐν ἑβδόμῃ τοῦ μηνὸς ἐν τῷ καιρῷ, ᾧ ἔλαβον οἱ Χαλδαῖοι τὴν Ιερουσαλημ καὶ ἐνέπρησαν αὐτήν ἐν πυρί.

34 See Adams 2014, 55 who points to 4Q389 1.7 as a close parallel. Most exegetes try to explain this name either as a reference to the Hebrew word *sod* "assembly", indicating that the exiles in Babylon recognized themselves as the "true" assembly, against the assembly in Judah, normally called *qahal*. Or they think of a common misinterpretation of the letters *dalet* and *resch*, indicating that the River *sur* would have the telling name "leave quickly". One way or the other, the spatial

overall notion that the exiles lived at "the rivers of Babylon" (Ps 137:1) is plausible,[35] the exact place cannot be reconstructed. This incomplete dating with no month mentioned can be compared to Ezek 1:2, where also no month is mentioned. Therefore, the 5th year must relate to the destruction of Jerusalem, which brings the date in line with 2Kgs 25:8 and surprisingly not with Jer 52:12–13.[36] At the end of this first narratological segment (1:14) another temporal reference is given: the penitential prayer should be read as "on the day of the feast and on the days of the season". As Odil Hannes Steck has shown,[37] this phrase reflects Num 28–29 and Neh 8–11 by intending to stress that there was no gap in temple service after the fall of Jerusalem: all feasts took place on the 7th month according to the Torah[38] (New Moon on the first day, the day of Atonement of the 10th day, Sukkot from the 15th day on), thus placing the events from Persian times back to Babylonian times.

Although there is a striking similarity between dating and spacing in Ezechiel and Baruch there are also notable differences: Ezechiel's visions are placed 5 years after the first deportation with, according to his first vision of the Temple in chapters 8–10, a temple defiled by the elders and the king; Baruch's prayer takes place 5 years after the second deportation,[39] implying that the temple was in working order, and of redemptive quality. Looking from the "rivers of Babylon," the text shows a clear strategy of deliberately dating events not for historical accuracy but for literal or liturgical purposes, which we then may call scribal exegesis.

Unfortunately, we do not find more absolute dating in Baruch, but analysing its chronotope nevertheless helps us to understand that both entities — time and space — are thoughtfully connected. Perhaps the most peculiar verse in the penitential prayer is 1:11: While delivering sacrifices, the priests in Jerusalem are asked to pray for Nebuchadnezzar and his son Belshazzar "in order that their days may be like the days of heaven upon the earth".[40]

---

orientation of the book seems to indicate at least a tension between the narration and historically valuable data.

35 Cf. Ezra 8:15,21,31; Dan 8:2–3.

36 Cf. Steck 1993, 19. So it is unlikely that Bar conceptually was written to follow up Jer 52.

37 Cf. Steck 1993, 42–43. The return of the Temple vessels on the 10th of Siwan does not hinder to presume that sacrifices could be delivered even if the temple itself was destroyed.

38 This would be the Day of Atonement and Sukkot.

39 For other possible explanations see Steck 1993, 20. He even reflects on the possibility to understand Bar 1:2 as corresponding to Jer 52:30 MT where a third deportation is mentioned.

40 The NETS translation is not exactly accurate because it skips the preposition ἐπί: *so* "that their days on the earth may be like the days of the sky", as the overall regime of NETS is to be orientated at KJV. LXX.D translates including the preposition: "dass ihre Tage seien wie die Tage des Himmels über der Erde".

The historical inconsistency according to Belshazzar who actually was the son of Nabonidus is also found in Dan 5:22. If this is interpreted in a historical perspective, most commentators stress that this phrase is plausible and in line with Jer 29 where the prophet writes a letter to the exiles encouraging them to pray for the best of Babylon. Even the wording itself should have parallels in other Babylonian prayers, as Kneucker[41] has already assumed. However, texts like the Babylonian prayers or Ps 72:5,17, for example, only refer to the basic idea of praying for a foreign king and his descendants by asking kindly and metaphorically for a long life. Yet, this is not the notion of the exact wording in Baruch, which is unique.

If we take a closer look at the phrase, we may understand it as a chronotope: it's the *days* — the temporal constituent — of the "heaven upon the earth" — the spatial constituent. We do find parallels to the phrase, but they only stress either the temporal or the spatial reference. The temporal formula "days of heaven" can be compared to other formulaic phrases, for instance praising God's promise of an eternal dynasty to David (Ps 89/88: 30).[42] The spatial connotation is part of oath formulas such as Gen 24:1. However, there are no direct parallels to the phrases of "days" and "heaven *upon* the earth."

When interpreted in terms of a chronotope, we do have a clear vertical orientation. The point of reference is not only to Jerusalem, the conventional idea. The perspective changes — we may cite 3:18, the Wisdom poem: Wisdom "has gone up into heaven . . . and brought her down from the clouds". For instance, when compared to Job 28 where vertical down mining-metaphors are used, here we find a vertical up orientation: the praying community looks up. So, we can continue, there we find God's heavenly dwelling; see also 2:16: Lord, look down from your holy house.

The idea of a heavenly sanctuary is in itself conventional. Beate Ego (1998) has already shown the development of this topos in the writings of the Second Temple Period. But in Baruch this is interlaced with further temporal and spatial ideas. The present situation "on earth," as displayed in the prayer for Nebuchadnezzar, is stressed. This can be seen throughout the book in phrases where extent references to events and ideas are already mentioned in other texts of the Torah. For instance,

41 See Kneucker 1879, 217. Steck 1993 even opts for a date for the composition of the book already under Babylonian rule because otherwise a prayer for the Babylonian king would not make any sense. This is a weak argument, though. Although he acknowledges the reference to the Babylonian rule as a literary fiction analogous to the fictional character of Dan 1–5 the interpretation does not in itself justify such an early date. Steck himself points to the similar prayers in Dan 9, Ezra 9, Neh 1 and 9 which altogether are not composed that early.

42 Ps 88:30: ὡς τὰς ἡμέρας τοῦ οὐρανοῦ. For the "eternal covenant", corresponding to an "eternal service", see Sir 45:15: εἰς διαθήκην αἰῶνος καὶ τῷ σπέρματι αὐτοῦ ἐν ἡμέραις οὐρανοῦ λειτουργεῖν αὐτωῷ ἅμα καὶ ἱερατεύειν καὶ εὐλογεῖν τὸν λαὸν αὐτοῦ ἐν τῷ ὀνόματι.

the people were disobedient "from the day that the Lord led our fathers out of the land of Egypt even *until this day*" (2:19). The reference to the presence is repeated in 2:20 ("as this day", cf. 2:6; 2:11; 2:26 "today" in 3:8). This culminates in 3:2: God is said to be "seated forever and we are perishing forever" (τὸν αἰῶνα), vgl. 3:13; 4:1,8.[43]

Seated again is a spatial referent, referring to God's throne in his heavenly sanctuary; *eternal*, on the other side, stresses the temporal dimension of this fact. So, he is likewise the eternal one — which is related to time — and the Holy one — which is related to space. The heavenly Temple which in itself is also eternal. Like the personified Jerusalem prays for its children in 4:22:

> ἐγὼ γάρ ἤλπισα *ἐπὶ τῷ αἰωνίῳ* τὴν σωτηρίαν ὑμῶν, καὶ ἦλθέν μοι *χαρὰ παρὰ τοῦ ἁγίου* ἐπὶ τῇ ἐλεημοσύνῃ, ᾗ ἥξει ὑμῖν ἐν τάχει παρὰ τοῦ αἰωνίου σωτῆρος ὑμῶν.
>
> For I hoped in the Everlasting for your salvation and joy came to me from the Holy One because of mercy that will come to you quickly from our everlasting saviour. (Adams 2014, 45).

As such, these conventional phrases get a different meaning when combined. Understood as a chronotope, the perspective changes: the days of heaven "upon" the earth are not only a more or less applicable citation form in Babylonian royal prayers, but a friendly reminder of who the real sovereign of time *and* space is and therefore who the guarantor of salvation is. This salvation — so the last temporal reference — is impending: the phrase "quickly" (ἐν τάχει) occurs several times throughout the book and is complementary to the idea of everlasting. In terms of a chronotope, this may also be interpreted as an eschatological idea.[44]

So, we can also count the Book of Baruch as an example of the idea that speculations about its chronotope open our eyes for the idea that the new combination of conventional expressions can lead to new ideas about the fate of God's people in an eschatological perspective.

3 Third Test Case: Wisdom of Solomon

The 19 chapters of the Wisdom of Solomon are probably the youngest texts which found its way into the canon of Jewish authoritative writings in Greek. It was first

---

43 God is θεός αἰώνιος bzw. ὁ αἰώνιος in 4:10 and 4:14; 4:22 (bis); 4:24 ; 4:35; 5:2, as well as the Holy One ὁ ἅγιος in 4:37; 5:5, denoting that his temporal as well as his spatial dimension exceed human experience.

44 Also see the combination ἐν τάχει in 4:24 and 25; the "everlasting joy" in 4:29; 3:29; 4:35 is correlated to the "long time" of suffering.

written in Greek,[45] sometime around the last decades before, or the first decades of the Common Era. In a paper dealing with the feature of chronotopes, you may not find another book less appropriate for analysing, as its vast *relecture* of the salvific history of God and his people meticulously is avoiding any hint towards temporal or spatial information of its origin. The rhetorical device of *antonomasia*, which paraphrases every name of the protagonists mentioned by their characteristics, shows great skills in and familiarity with Greek-Hellenistic literature and makes it likewise only intelligible for an audience familiar with the biblical tradition. Like in the book of Qoheleth, its relation to King Solomon, the wisest of all kings, it can only be deciphered between the lines: the book starts with a first-person speaker addressing the fellow rulers of the world to seek righteousness. This first-person speaker then reports in chapters 7–9 his quest for wisdom which reminds us of Solomon's prayer for wisdom and a "hearing heart" in 1Kgs 3.

We can roughly divide the Book into three parts: chapters 1–6 are an exhortation to seek righteousness in order to gain life, which is exemplified by the fate of a paradigmatic righteous one (δίκαιος) who is tortured by the ungodly/wicked (ἀσεβεῖς), but who is then rewarded after his death to live in constant presence with God. In chapters 7–9 "Solomon" reports how he gained wisdom: he studied hard to gain knowledge to prepare himself for true wisdom as a gift from God. Chapters 10–19 are a very skillful *relecture* of the ancestor stories as well as the Exodus and wilderness narratives. The angle of this presentation is that God is always just and has always helped the righteous, from Adam to the people of Israel, and prosecutes the unjust with benignity, using the same objects for the punishment which the unjust tortured Israel with beforehand. The book is part of the Hellenistic *Protreptikos*-literature whose purpose is to convince the male youth of a mindset which leads to a successful and fulfilling life in society.

It comes as no wonder, that absolute dating is completely absent. The book — like wisdom literature in general — wants to create a timeless or better: time-transcending atmosphere. Thus, it is *eo ipso* a chronotope in itself: by entering — so to say — this chronotope through reading, memorizing, or hearing, the presence is transcended, this creates a *dystopia* of its own kind.

Nonetheless, references to the combination of time and space can be traced, above all, in the first chapters. To start with some philological observations: As terms related to time, we find καιρός 6 times, χρόνος 7 times, and ἄιων 10 times. So nearly every chapter of the book somehow relates to "time."

45 We do not only have no Hebrew text of wisdom but a lot of puns of rhetoric features throughout the book are simply only work in Greek, thus hinting of Greek as Wisdom's original language.

In his thorough analysis of the terms χρόνος and καιρός, Friedrich Reiterer (2022, 242–256) comes to the conclusion that both terms are used in their common semantic range, denoting a finite span of time or a distinct point in time without any philosophical or eschatological implications.

However, this is quite different with ἄιων, especially if applied to the chronotope paradigm. On the one hand, ἄιων is understood as a means of time, a time span without clear end, thus similar to עולם in Hebrew. One example would be 14:13: in a polemic against idolatry the verse states that idols are inane because they did not exist from the beginning (ἀπ'ἀρχῆς). Everyone familiar with the beginning of Genesis in the Septuagint instantaneously is reminded of the phrase ἐν ἀρχῆς: God created the heavens and the earth "in the beginning".

The argument stresses that this "beginning" is qualified, as there are idols only after there have been humans to craft them. Therefore, it is only logical that idols have a distinct "beginning" and will therefore also have a distinct "end," or as 14:13 suggests, it will not exist εἰς τὸν αἰῶνα, "forever" as NETS translates. Yet, this "forever" is finite, as it relates to human craftsmanship. This is not a philosophical idea of "eternity" but as there was a beginning, there must also be a restriction of time, and idols are as "mortal" as humans because without a craftsman there are no crafted idols.

On the other hand, ἄιων can also have a spatial quality, for this usage, 13:9 is a good example: "for if they had the power to know so much that they could investigate the world (τὸν αἰῶνα), how is it that they did not more quickly find the Sovereign Lord of these things" (trans. NETS)

The text stems from a passage discussing the philosophical idea of proving the existence of God. The rhetoric in question accuses people as being unable to find God. He should be easy and quick to find, but most people fail because they are ignorant. Using philosophical terms which were highly *en vogue* and part of the philosophical discussions during late Hellenistic times (Kepper 1998, 170–179; Niebuhr 2015, 246–256), the text states that the human being is inherently, by his nature (φύσει), incapable of finding God, the master of the whole universe (παντοκράτωρ). There is no positive answer to this rhetorical question given here, but the logical answer within Jewish thought would be: by reading the Torah. We can follow this path throughout the Bible. Right from its first chapter in canonical order, Gen 1, God is described as the creator of the world. Yet the accused people do not simply refer to the Torah but investigate the whole world (ἄιων) and still cannot find him because he is the transcendent master and creator of this world. Here, ἄιων has no temporal connotation, denoting that — so to say — historians are accused of being ignorant. Rather natural science, as it is connected to philosophical speculation in antiquity, is an insufficient endeavor, thus applying spatial connotation to the word ἄιων.

Interestingly, these two temporal and spatial connotations of ἄιων are thoroughly combined to create a very new and special chronotope: the main theme of the first chapters are two speeches of the ungodly/wicked (ἀσεβεῖς), who tortured the righteous one to death (chapter 2) because they detested his way of living according to the ancestral laws. After his death (chapter 5), the ungodly/wicked realize that they were deadly wrong — in the literal sense — to think that with physical death, the life of the human being is completely over and vanished. Instead, a long *diatribe* against this view states that there will still be juridical consequences after the physical death of the people involved. These consequences "will" happen in the future, but no exact date nor any distinct place is mentioned (4:20): "And they will come with dread at the reckoning of their sins, and their lawless deeds will convict them to their face" (transl. NETS).

This *ou-topic* judgment of the ungodly/wicked overthrows all conventional expectation: the righteous who have been sentenced to death by them (3:20) will judge over the ungodly/wicked (3:8): "They will judge nations and rule over peoples, and the Lord will be king over them forever" (trans. NETS).

Again, the translation of the term ἄιων as *forever* in the NETS translation is restricting the significance of the term only to its temporal meaning and is, therefore, deficient. To put it simply, if the Lord will rule as a king, there must be a kingdom. So, the term ἄιων here refers to the temporal *as well as* spatial connotation of the term: it denotes and defines a new time-world or world-time with a total new world-order. Maybe this could also be some kind of carnival in the sense of Bakhtin. This new time-world will come in the future: correspondingly, verbs in the future tense and temporal adverbs like τότε or μετὰ τοῦτο accumulate in these chapters.[46] Where exactly this new time-world is, is not stated. We do not have a clear vertical orientation as seen in Baruch, instead the metaphors "in the hand of God" an "in peace" are used (3:1). We can only assume that these "places" are to be thought of in heaven.

4 Conclusion

Is it possible to summarise these various findings? Surely, test cases cannot be extrapolated, and, obviously, not every book offers reliable results of the same theological importance. However, what has been shown is that every book offers a fresh look on old problems when being analysed in terms of its chronotope.

---

46 See, for example, 5:1.

For the book of Ezechiel, its Old Greek version (P. 967) seems to support the probably older idea that the exiles represent the real "Israel" who hopes for restoration. By dating the oracles of doom and the fall of Jerusalem all in the same year, and connecting it to the Merkavah vision in chapter 1 as well as the beginning of the Temple vision in chapter 40, the author stresses this event to be the turning point of Israel's fate. The addressees are encouraged to expect this restoration in due future. MT, on the other hand, probably represents a younger approach by matching the datings verbally to datings that appear in the Torah: the Merkavah dating is traced back to the beginning of Deuteronomy; the word for the eleventh year of Zedekiah is used to date the fall of Jerusalem; the beginning of the Temple vision is marked as one of the special days that show salvific meaning like special days in the diluvial and ancestral times. It seems that this intertextual nexus was practiced by scribes at a later stage of the transmission of the book.

The same phenomenon has already been shown by Michael Segal for the book of Daniel: Daniel's chronological conception of the Persian period and the overall aim of dating and chronological information is triggered by exegetical interest, not historical accuracy. Segal coined this kind of inventing historic references as being "symbolic exegesis" (Segal 2011, 284 n.2) which can clearly be seen when no philological reasons for the interpretation of the date given can be found. He more importantly stresses that, later on, the rabbinic chronography of the Persian period as seen in *Seder Olam* claims that "only years mentioned explicitly in the Bible actually took place in history" (Segal 2011, 298), by tracing the beginning of this chronological approach back to the younger writings of the Hebrew scriptures. His striking argument for this hypothesis is the lack of extrabiblical information: the *Sopherim* simply had no, or only limited, access to other sources than the biblical texts themselves. We could claim this for Ezechiel in its Masoretic form, too.

The book of Baruch shows a quite similar approach. Although no absolute dating is used, the phrasing of the wish for Nebuchadnezzar is telling. At first sight, conventional phrases are used, but are freshly combined and lead to a new interpretation: the new phrase "days of heaven upon the earth" when interpreted as a chronotope shows the exegetical skill to reread the first creation account. As God created night and day on day one (Gen 1:5), he also divided water from water to create heaven (Gen 1:7–8) on day two, and earth beneath heaven (Gen 1:9–10) on day three. By changing the perspective to vertical, Nebuchadnezzar is reminded of God as the real master of his creation.

Even if the book of Wisdom as the third test case shows a quite different approach, it is also heuristically fruitful to examine its chronotope. By expanding the meaning of the primarily temporal word for long-lasting/everlasting time to spatial connotations and placing it in a nexus of eschatological speculations of man's fate after death, the question of space in the afterlife is negotiated. Although not systematically solved, the place for the righteous in the "hand of God" is alluded to and situated in God's heavenly kingdom spatially, as it will be everlasting temporally.

Temporal as well as spatial issues proved to be of high interest to those writing or transmitting the authoritative writings of the Second Temple Period. Scholars nowadays have convenient access to all different kinds of spatial or temporal data, or even different types of data for converting vernacular relative to chronological details into an absolute chronology. It is very unlikely that this is plausible for the *Sopherim* of Persian, Hellenistic, or Roman times. However, and this seems to be kind of a gateway for the adoption of literary devices as chronotopes, it is of high interest what kind of specific concept of time and space the texts favour. Timing and spacing turned out to be at least of some special interest to the authors and scribes. Time is qualified, and datings have a salvific or non-salvific quality. Thus, it may be fair to say that chronology is not only a "branch of historiography" (Gertzen 2022, 9, citing Cryer 1995) but definitely also of theology.

Bibliography

Adams, Sean A. 2014. *Baruch and the Epistle of Jeremiah: A Commentary Based on the Texts in Codex Vaticanus*. Septuagint Commentary Series. Leiden: Brill. https://doi.org/10.1163/9789004278493.

Ausloos, Hans, and Bénédicte Lemmelijn, eds. 2020. *Handbuch zur Septuaginta / Handbook of the Septuagint*. Vol 5, *Die Theologie der Septuaginta / The Theology of the Septuagint*. Gütersloh: Gütersloher Verlagshaus. https://doi.org/10.14315/9783641310943.

Becker, Joachim. 1982. "Erwägungen zur ezechielischen Frage." In *Künder des Wortes: Beiträge zur Theologie der Propheten*, edited by Lothar Ruppert, Peter Weimar, and Erich Zenger, 137–149. Würzburg: Echter.

Bewer, Julius A. 1934. "The Text of Ezek. 1:1–3." *AJSL* 50:96–101. https://doi.org/10.1086/370421.

Ego, Beate. 1998. "'Der Herr blickt herab von der Höhe seines Heiligtums': Gottes himmlisches Thronen in alttestamentlichen Texten aus exilischen-nachexilischen Zeit." *ZAW* 110:556–569. https://doi.org/10.1515/zatw.1998.110.4.556.

Engel, Helmut. 1998. *Das Buch der Weisheit*. NSK.AT 16. Stuttgart: Katholisches Bibelwerk.

Greenberg, Moshe. 2001. *Ezechiel 1–20*. HThKAT. Freiburg i. Br.: Herder.

Greenspoon, Leonard J., and William A. Ross. "Septuagint," *Oxford Bibliographies*, https://www.oxfordbibliographies.com/display/document/obo-9780195393361/obo-9780195393361-0097.xml (24.12.2024).

Kepper, Martina, and Annette Weissenrieder. 2024. "Architexture and Medialized Presence: Jerusalem and Its Temples in Acts 21:27–30 and Ephesians 2:14." In *Vivid Rhetoric and Visual Persuasion: Ekphrasis in Early Christian Literature*, edited by Meghan Henning, and Nils Neumann, 181–224. Grand Rapids, MI: Eerdmans.

Kepper, Martina. 2022. "'All's well that ends well': Protological Speculations and Eschatological Teachings in Hellenistic-Roman Texts." In *Notions of Time in Deuterocanonical and Cognate*

Literature, edited by Stefan Beyerle, and Matthew Goff, 67–91. Berlin: De Gruyter. https://doi.org/10.1515/9783110705454.

Kneucker, Johan Jacob. 1879. *Das Buch Baruch: Geschichte und Kritik, Übersetzung und Erklärung auf Grund des wiederhergestellten hebräischen Urtextes.* Leipzig: Brockhaus.

Kraus, Wolfgang, and Martin Karrer, eds. 2009. *Septuaginta Deutsch: Das griechische Alte Testament in deutscher Übersetzung*. Stuttgart: Deutsche Bibelgesellschaft.

Konkel, Michael. 1998. "Das Datum der zweiten Tempelvision Ezechiels (Ez 40,1)." *BN* 92:55–70. https://doi.org/10.71715/bn.v92i.97613.

Kutsch, Ernst. 1985. *Die chronologischen Daten des Ezechielbuches*. OBO 62. Göttingen: Vandenhoeck & Ruprecht.

La Bible d'Alexandrie, Paris: Editions du Cerf, 1986 ff.

Leuenberger, Martin. 2024. "Die mobile Kabodkonzeption des Ezechielbuches als Transformation klassischer Zionstheologie." In *"Wer ist weise, dass er dies versteht?" (Hos 14,10): Studien zu Ezechiel, Hosea und den Psalmen: Festschrift für Franz Xaver Sedlmeier zum 70. Geburtstag*, HBS 104, edited by Carolin Neuber, and Nicole Katrin Rüttgers, 106–119. Freiburg i. Br.: Herder.

Lilly, Ingrid E. 2012. *Two Books of Ezekiel. Papyrus 967 and the Masoretic Text as Variant Literary Editions*. VT.S 150. Leiden: Brill. https://doi.org/10.1163/9789004222458.

Mackie, Timothy P. 2015. *Expanding Ezekiel: The Hermeneutics of Scribal Addition in the Ancient Text Witnesses of the Book of Ezekiel.* Göttingen: Vandenhoeck & Ruprecht.

Mazzinghi, Luca. 2019. *Wisdom*. International Exegetical Commentary on the Old Testament. Stuttgart: Kohlhammer.

New English Translation of the Septuagint, https://ccat.sas.upenn.edu/nets/edition (24.12.2024).

Otto, Eckart. 2012. *Deuteronomium 1–11*. HThKAT. Freiburg i. Br.: Herder.

Pohlmann, Karl-Friedrich. 1992. *Ezechielstudien: Zur Redaktionsgeschichte des Buches und zur Frage nach den ältesten Texten.* BZAW 202. Berlin: De Gruyter.

Pohlmann, Karl-Friedrich. 2008. *Ezechiel: Der Stand der theologischen Diskussion.* Darmstadt: Wissenschaftliche Buchgesellschaft.

Reiterer, Friedrich V. 2022. "Kairos, Chronos und Aion im Buch der Weisheit." In *Notions of Time in Deuterocanonical and Cognate Literature*, edited by Stefan Beyerle, and Matthew Goff, 235–283. Berlin: De Gruyter. https://doi.org/10.1515/9783110705454.

Rösel, Christoph. 2012. *JHWHs Sieg über Gog aus Magog: Ez 38–39 im Masoretischen Text und in der Septuaginta.* WMANT 132. Neukirchen-Vluyn: Neukirchener Theologie.

Rüterswörden, Udo. 2013. Deuteronomium, BKAT. Göttingen: Vandenhoeck & Ruprecht.

Segal, Michael. 2011. "The Chronological Conception of the Persian Period in Daniel 9." *JAJ* 2:283–303. https://doi.org/10.13109/jaju.2011.2.3.283.

Segev, Yair, and Peter Zilberg. "The Composition of the Book of Ezekiel in Light of Babylonian Sources." *Zeitschrift für die alttestamentliche Wissenschaft*, vol. 137, no. 2, 2025, 279–289. https://doi.org/10.1515/zaw-2025-2007.

Schnocks, Johannes. "Ezechiel," *Wissenschaftliches Bibellexikon*, 2009, https://bibelwissenschaft.de/stichwort/18497 (24.12.2024)

Schöpflin, Karin. 2002. *Theologie als Biographie im Ezechielbuch: Ein Beitrag zur Konzeption alttestamentlicher Prophetie.* FAT 36. Tübingen: Mohr Siebeck. https://doi.org/10.1628/978-3-16-157817-5.

Schwagmeier, Peter. 2004. *Untersuchungen zu Textgeschichte und Entstehung des Ezechielbuches in masoretischer und griechischer Überlieferung*. PhD diss., Universität Zürich.

Steck, Odil Hannes. 1993. *Das apokryphe Baruchbuch: Studien zu Rezeption und Konzentration "kanonischer" Überlieferung*. FRLANT 160. Göttingen: Vandenhoeck & Ruprecht. https://doi.org/10.13109/9783666538421.

Tooman, William A., and Penelope Barter, eds. 2017. *Ezekiel: Current Debates and Future Directions*. FAT 112. Tübingen: Mohr Siebeck. https://doi.org/10.1628/978-3-16-154714-0.

Vogt, Ernestus. 1958. "Der Nehar Kebar: Ez 1." *Biblica* 39.2:211–216.

Weippert, Manfred. 2010. *Historisches Textbuch zum Alten Testament*. GAT 10. Göttingen: Vandenhoeck & Ruprecht.

Daniel K. Falk

Time of Preparing the Way in the Desert: Prayer and Wilderness in the Dead Sea Scrolls

Abstract: This article examines wilderness as a chronotope and its relation to prayer in two texts from the Dead Sea Scrolls: the Rule of the Community and the collection of daily prayers known as the Words of the Luminaries. In both cases, the wilderness motif has both spatial and temporal dimensions, but the temporal is dominant, with the focus on a liminal period and the behavior appropriate to it. Bakhtin's exposition of two ancient novel types helps highlight differences in the use of the wilderness chronotope between these two texts: a liminal time of trial in which human destinies are confirmed versus a transformational journey.

1 Introduction

Jesus is depicted in the Gospels as characteristically retreating to deserted places to pray (e.g., Mark 6:46; Luke 5:16; Matt 14:23) and instructing his disciples also to seek solitude for prayer (Matt 6:6). These traditions about Jesus undoubtedly influenced the prayer practice of the Desert Monastics, but was Jesus's practice typical or unusual in the context of early Jewish piety? The Dead Sea Scrolls and the site of Qumran appear to attest a retreat to the wilderness on the part of some Jews for ideological/theological motivations, and the scrolls also attest highly developed practices of communal prayer. A significant amount of research has explored the meaning of the desert in the ideology of the *Yaḥad* movement, especially in relation to Sinai traditions and prophetic oracles (especially Isaiah 40:3), but there has been little exploration of the wilderness in relation to prayer. This paper will examine prayer in relation to wilderness in the Dead Sea Scrolls focusing on two texts: the Community Rule and the Words of the Luminaries, the one sectarian and the other probably non-sectarian in origin.

Some preliminary matters are in order. First, it must be acknowledged that the data are thin, equivocal, and circumstantial. The circumstantial evidence for a connection, on the face of it, has some appeal. The largest corpus of early Jewish prayers—and the only evidence of daily corporate Jewish worship in the Second Temple period—was found in wilderness caves by the settlement at Qumran, along with documents that describe a comprehensive liturgy of prayers and a theological

https://doi.org/10.1515/9783112240366-008

rationale for the community that cites the way of the wilderness of Isaiah 40:3. But the question is not merely whether the Essene community at Qumran practiced prayer there, but whether there was particular meaning attached to going into the wilderness to pray.[1] As Shemaryahu Talmon (1966, 55–63) noted, wilderness language is less prominent in the sectarian scrolls than one would expect and evidence for a "wilderness ideal" is lacking in the scrolls; rather, wilderness retains a negative connotation in many contexts, and for the covenanters the desert (whether literal or metaphorical) is a transitional stage of purification and preparation, not the goal (63).

Second, there are varying connotations of wilderness in both the Hebrew scriptures and in the Dead Sea Scrolls. Talmon (1966, 40–49, 55–63) groups these under two main groups: spatial-geophysical and temporal-historical. There is the debated issue of literal versus metaphorical wilderness, and there are different motivations attached to wilderness sojourn whether literal or metaphorical (cf. Brooke 1994, 127–132; Collins 2025, 100–103). Moreover, even with regard to the sectarian scrolls we have to account for various communities, most of whom did not live in wilderness but in towns, as well as diachronic development of community practice, ideology, and self-identity (Metso 1997, 143–155; Jokiranta 2013, 107–109).

This conference provided a welcome occasion to reflect on Bakhtin's concept of the chronotope, which proved fruitful for considering the interrelatedness of time and place in the motif of wilderness in the Dead Sea Scrolls, especially as a liminal quality. Admittedly, there is little correspondence between the literature to be considered below—a rule text and a prayer text—and the artistic novels analyzed by Bakhtin. Yet beneath the surface of the texts from Qumran are implicit story arcs that are brought into sharper relief by the concept of the chronotope. Perspectives from ritual studies also inform this study, especially the concept of liminality in rites of passage as developed by Arnold van Gennep and expounded by Victor Turner (1969, 94–130) which Robert Cohn (1981, 8–9) applied to "wilderness as liminality." As with rituals generally, prayer does more than it says, and time and place are meaningful. Liv Lied (2005) and Alison Schofield (2012) have drawn on spatial theory in studying the significance of wilderness in the Dead Sea Scrolls, especially Edward Soja's concept of Thirdspace as "a fully lived space . . . simultaneously real-and-imagined" (Soja 1996, 11) or space as experienced and socially constructed rather than merely geographical space or conceptualized space. Schofield

1 As shorthand for the purpose of this paper I will simply refer to the separatist movement attested in the scrolls as Essenes, even though the relationship between the site of Qumran, various communities attested in the scrolls, and the Essenes mentioned in classical sources is complicated (e.g., Schofield 2009, 66–67; Collins 2010, 209–210). The question of whether Qumran qualifies as wilderness or not is a moot point: it is a wilderness if deemed a wilderness by those concerned.

(2012) also draws on the concept of wilderness as heterotopia to emphasize how space can be contested. Additionally, Carol Newsom's (2004, 6–12) application of rhetorical studies, speech-act theory, and Bakhtin's dialogism helps us think about what prayer does. Hindy Najman (2010) has emphasized the connection between suffering, purification, revelation and prayer, and David Janzen (2020) and Tim Langille (2014) draw on trauma studies for examining reviews of history in the Deuteronomistic literature and the Dead Sea Scrolls respectively as post-memory processing of trauma.

2 The Community Rule

Two key references to wilderness in the Dead Sea Scrolls for this study both occur in a part of the Community Rule often identified as belonging to its core, most fully preserved in the manuscript from Qumran Cave One: 1QS 8:1–9:25. Even before the publication of the Cave 4 manuscripts, scholars recognized that the Community Rule is a composite document. In a detailed redactional analysis, Jerome Murphy-O'Connor (1969) identified four stages of literary development and associated these with successive phases in the history of the *Yaḥad*.[2] According to his analysis, both of the wilderness passages belong to a "manifesto" from the earliest phase of the Essene movement (1QS 8:1–16a; 9:3–10:8a) and provide a theological rationale for establishing a settlement in the desert near Qumran (Murphy-O'Connor 1969, 529–532). Thus, according to this interpretation, the evocation of Isa 40:3 in these two passages concerns the wilderness as a literal place, and specifically, the vicinity near Qumran.

Subsequent research has rendered Murphy-O'Connor's developmental model unfeasible: (1) the Cave 4 manuscripts attest different versions with complex relationships that cannot be explained by linear developments (Metso 1997, 143–149) but more plausibly by dispersed communities (Schofield 2009, 125–130); (2) these passages are not about the founding of the movement but assume its existence (Collins and Nati 2024, 112); and (3) the movement was diverse in various locales, only one of which (as far as we know) was in a location that could be described as wilderness (Collins 2010, 67–68, 208).

The weight of scholarly opinion on these passages has in recent years shifted away from viewing them as referring to wilderness as a literal place and location

2 For a recent brief summary of views about the development of the Community Rule, see Collins and Nati 2024, 5–7. For detailed treatments, see Metso 1997, 107–149, Alexander and Vermes 1998, 9–12, and Schofield 2009, 70–78, 125–130.

for a migration and towards wilderness as primarily metaphorical. In considering the two passages, it is important to allow—along with most recent scholarship—that the references to wilderness may have different signification in different literary and historical contexts. Here are the two passages.[3]

1QS 8:12b–15a

ובהיות אלה ליחד בישראל 13 בתכונים האלה יבדלו מתוך מושב הנשי העול ללכת למדבר לפנות שם את דרכ הואהא
כאשר כתוב במדבר פנו דרך •••• ישרו בערבה מסלה לאלוהינו 15 היאה מדרש התורה א̊[ש]ר̊ צוה
ביד מושה לעשות ככול הנגלה עת בעת 16 וכאשר גלו הנביאים ברוח קודשו 14

When these become a community in Israel, (13) in accordance with these norms, they shall **withdraw** from the company of the people of deceit to go to the wilderness to prepare **there** the way of Him, (14) as it is written: "In the wilderness prepare the way of ••••, make straight in the desert a highway for our God." (15) **That** is the study of the Torah w[hic]h He commanded through Moses to act according to all that has been revealed from time to time (16) and according to that which the prophets have revealed by His holy spirit.

1QS 9:18b–21a

להנחותם בדעה וכן להשכילם ברזי פלא ואמת בתוך 19 אנשי היחד להלכ תמים איש את רעהו בכול הנגלה
להם ה̊היאה עת פנות הדרך 20 למדבר ולהשכילם כול הנמצא לעשות בעת הזואת והבדל מכול איש ולוא הסר
דרכו 21 מכול עול

He shall guide them with knowledge and thus instruct them in the wonderful and true mysteries in the midst (19) of the people of the community so that they may conduct themselves perfectly each with his neighbor according to all that has been revealed to them. This is the time to prepare the way (20) to the wilderness. He shall instruct them (with) all that has been found to do at this time, and they shall keep away from everyone who has not averted his path (21) from all injustice.

There are three different versions of the material found in 1QS 8–9 (Tab. 1). The longest version is extant only in 1QS, beginning with instructions for an elite subgroup, followed by rules of conduct, a penal code, and concluding with statutes for the Instructor (*Maskil*). A version from Cave Four (4Q259 = 4QS[e]) preserves a shorter and somewhat different version, lacking the material corresponding to 1QS 8:15b–9:11. It is probable that this represents an earlier version although copied later than 1QS.[4] Both of these versions include the quotation of Isa 40:3 (1QS 8:12b–

3 Translations are my own, but indebted to previous translations. The superscript words indicate supralinear corrections added in the manuscript by a second scribe.

4 On the basis of paleography, F. M. Cross (1994) dated 1QS to 100–75 BCE and 4QS[e] to 50–25 BCE. But on the basis of textual analysis, 4QS[e] appears to be a shorter, more direct version, lacking some secondary expansions. See Metso 1997, 68–74, 143–149; Schofield 2009, 69–130.

15a; 4QS^{e} 1 iii 3b–6a) and the subsequent allusion to Isa 40:3 (1QS 9:19b–21a; 4QS^{e} 1 iii 19–21). Another version found in Cave Four (4Q258 = 4QS^{d}) preserves all the sections found in 1QS but with a slightly shorter text in places, for example, probably lacking the explicit citation of Isa 40:3.[5]

Tab. 1: 1QS 8–9 and parallels.

	1QS	4QS^{b} (4Q256)	4QS^{d} (4Q258)	4QS^{e} (4Q259)
The council of the community	8:1–16a		6:1–8a	2:9b–3:6a
Deliberate failure to obey	8:16b–19		6:8b–10	—
Rules of conduct and discipline	8:20–9:2		6:12; 7:1–3	—
The community and the cultic realm	9:3–6		7:4–7	—
The authority of the sons of Aaron	9:7		7:7b	—
Conduct of the people of holiness	9:8–11		7:7c–9	—
Statutes for the *Maskil*	9:12–25	18:1–7	7:15–8:9	3:6b–4:8

Only the longer version of this passage—attested in 1QS and incompletely in 4QS^{d}—also includes references to prayer (1QS 9:3–5a). 4QS^{e} lacks the section corresponding to 1QS 9:3–5a with atonement by prayer, and it also did not include the hymn on times of prayer that begins in 1QS 9:26 (cf. 4QS^{b} cols. 19–23; 4QS^{d} cols. 8–13). Thus, the earliest exposition of the way of the wilderness seemingly did not include mention of prayer, and the interpolation represented in 1QS 9:3–6 reinterprets the wilderness in terms of prayer, as discussed further below.[6]

In favor of the view that these passages refer to a literal journey to the desert, scholars have pointed at the language “separate from,” “go to the wilderness,” and especially the specification of “there” (שם) as the place to prepare (e.g., Brooke 1994, 123). On the other hand, we might ask if there is really a “there” there. Arguments against reading this passage as a literal wilderness retreat include the following. First, 1QS 8:3 specifies that the purpose of the community is “to keep faithfulness *in the land* . . . and to atone for sin with works of justice and suffering affliction.” It is difficult to read this as exile *from* the land. Second, the evidence for a spatial separation is thin. The injunctions against mixing property (1QS 9:8) and not to argue with the men of darkness (1QS 9:15b–18a) would seem to assume proximity. Third, in these passages, wilderness seems to be more about time than place. Time language

5 Nothing is extant of this material in 4QS^{b} except scraps corresponding to 1QS 9:17–22; where it is extant, it seems to present a similar version to 4QS^{d}.

6 On the different versions and these sections as secondary additions, see Metso 1997, 69–74, 143–149; Schofield 2009, 69–86, 105–108.

is more prominent than place language: "At *that time* they will separate" (1QS 9:5b); and especially in the exposition in 1QS 9:19b–21a, "That is *the time* of preparing the way to the wilderness."[7] Fourth, what is meant by "that time" in this latter passage is also ambiguous: the phrase has no definitive antecedent. At any rate, it is hopeless to reconstruct a historical sequence of community founding, separation, and atonement for the land (cf. 1QS 8:8–10). Fifth, the motif of wilderness in relation to the founding of the community is elsewhere used quite differently. According to the Damascus Document (CD 1:11–17), at the time of the Teacher of Righteousness it was *traitors* who departed in a trackless wasteland. Sixth, the spatial quality of the desert is ambiguous: in 1QS 8:12b–15a, the covenanters go to the desert to prepare the way of the Lord; in 1QS 9:19b–21a, they prepare the way *to* the desert.

Moreover, as Devorah Dimant has argued (2014, 461), the pesher on Isaiah 40:3 in 1QS 8:15 // 4QS[e] 3:6 "relates the whole verse—the withdrawal to the wilderness and the preparing of the way—to the study of the Torah"; "In this context, the 'desert' cannot be a physical reality but a figurative simile. It probably stands for the isolation of the community and its dissociation from the methods and approaches practiced by other contemporary Jewish groups for interpreting the Torah."[8] Building on Dimant's argument, John Kampen (2025, 136) notes that in light of the rarity of wilderness language in contrast to the much more numerous references to "the way," there is no basis for thinking that the citation of Isa 40:3 constitutes "hard evidence for the desert as a central local for some point in the sectarian history."[9] Rather the emphasis in sectarian texts is on establishment of "His way," as he notes is well captured by Michael Knibb's translation of 1QS 8:15–16: "This (way) is the study of the law which he commanded through Moses, that they should act in accordance with all that has been revealed from time to time and in accordance with what his prophets revealed by his holy spirit" (1987, 128–129; Kampen 2025, 139). As Kampen argues, the focus is on praxis, advocating a way of life not a place to live (140).

These passages, then, do not depend on a move to Qumran to be meaningful. No doubt it would have special evocation for Essenes living at Qumran in the Judean

7 Also 1QS 8:4, 12b; 9:14, 18; cf. CD 1:13, and 4Q177 12–13 i 8, "to scatter [them] in a parched and desolate land. This is a time of affliction. . ."

8 For "that is," Dimant (2014, 461) reads הואה masc. rather than fem. היאה, and argues that it refers to the whole quotation from Isa 40:3. Cf. 4Q258 6:7: the text is broken but is clearly a shorter version than in 1QS and 4Q259, probably lacking the explicit quotation. In this case, it is probably "[the way]" that is interpreted as "[the study of Tor]ah."

9 Kampen 2025, 136. Kampen notes that מדבר occurs only 3 times in the Community Rule and none in the Damascus Document; דרך appears 42 times in the Community Rule, 22 times in the Damascus Document, and 26 times in the Hodayot.

desert, but it could equally well have been appropriated by town-dwelling Essenes. This is effectively what I take to be George Brooke's position (1994, 127–128; 2025, 348–349), that wilderness can be both literal and metaphorical, although his earlier study has been cited mostly with regard to the position that the wilderness in the scrolls refers to a literal retreat.

On this question, a Thirdspace approach helps cut through the knotty problem of literal versus metaphorical. In a Thirdspace perspective, one can experience the desert without being geographically in the desert. One can also be geographically in the desert but experience the garden; one can be stuck on earth but walk among angels in heaven. We will return to this point further below, but first we consider the context of this section in the Community Rule with regard to the activity of prayer.

Atonement language appears in three places in 1QS 8–9. In 1QS 8:1–4a (//4QS[e] 1 ii 7–11), atonement is effected by works of justice and suffering affliction:

> In the council of the association are twelve men and three priests . . . to perform truth, righteousness, justice, love of mercy, and humble behavior with one another . . . and to atone for sin by works of justice and suffering affliction. (1QS 8:3b–4a)

1QS 8:4b–10a (//4QS[e] 1 ii 11–16) states that the council of the community (*Yaḥad*) functions as a Temple in Israel to atone for the land but is ambiguous about the means:

> When these exist in Israel, the council of the community will be established in truth for an eternal planting, a holy house for Israel and a most holy foundation for Aaron . . . to offer a pleasing aroma . . . They shall be favored to atone for the land . . .

The passage is ambiguous as to whether the "pleasing aroma" they offer (1QS 8:9–10) is to be understood literally (animal sacrifice) or metaphorically (some other activity of the community). This is followed by the passage about separation and the allusion to Isa 40:3 (1QS 8:10b–12a,12b–19). In column 9, there is a loose parallel to the sequence, and in broad terms it may be regarded as another version. In 1QS 9:3–5a is a reference to atonement analogous to those in column 8, but this time, specifying prayer as a means of atonement along with perfection of way.

1QS 9:3–5a

> ⟦ ⟧ בהיות אלה בישראל ככול התכונים האלה ליסוד רוח קודש לאמת עולם לכפר על אשמת פשע ומעל חטאת
> ולרצון לארץ מבשר עולות ומחלבי זבח ותרומת שפתים למשפט כניחוח צדק ותמים דרך כנדבת מנחת רצון

> When these are in Israel according to all these rules as a foundation of holy spirit for eternal truth, (4) they shall atone for guilt of transgression and sinful treachery, and obtain favor for

> the land without flesh of burnt offerings and without fat of sacrifice,[10] but the offering (5) of lips for judgment will be as a righteous fragrance and perfection of way as a pleasing freewill offering.

The presentation of prayer as a regular offering to God also appears in the song of the *Maskil* (a liturgical master) at the end of 1QS (9:26–11:22; also partly preserved in 4QS[b, d, f, j]) which celebrates prayer at divinely appointed times: "the offering of lips" (9:26; 10:6, 14) and "the portion of my lips" (10:8).

As noted above, the two sections containing reference to prayer as sacrifice (1QS 8:16–9:11 [9:3–6] and 9:26–11:22 [9:26–10:17]) are lacking in 4QS[e], suggesting that the presentation of prayer as sacrifice is a secondary expansion in 1QS and 4QS[d].[11] That is, it is not part of the earliest "way of the wilderness" scheme. Although not explicitly stated, the addition of these sections reinterprets the way of the wilderness to include prayer. Whereas in 1QS 8:3 atonement is effected by works of judgment and suffering affliction, in both 1QS 9:26 and 10:15–17 affliction is specified as an occasion for praise of God: "[In affl]iction he will bless his maker . . ." (1QS 9:26); "At the beginning of dread and terror and in the place of distress (צרה) with desolation, I will bless him . . . When distress (צרה) is unleashed I will praise him . . ." (1QS 10:15–17). The connection between speech and judgment in 1QS 9 and 10 could refer to spoken judgments but I suggest it refers to penitential prayer: confessing guilt and the rightness of God's judgment: ". . . the offerings of lips for judgment (למשפט) will be as a righteous fragrance . . ." (1QS 9:5); "I will sing with knowledge, and all my song (will be) for the glory of God, and the strings of my harp (will be) for the measure of his holiness, and the flute of my lips I will raise in line with his judgment (משפטו)"(1QS 10:9); "By his judgment (משפטו) I will reprove myself according to my sin, and my transgressions are before my eyes as an engraved statute. To God I say, 'My Righteousness' . . ." (1QS 10:11).

Thus, in the version of 1QS (also 4QS[b] and 4QS[d]), the way of the wilderness corresponds to the core activities of the community as expressed in 1QS 6—communal study of scripture and prayer:

> In these (regulations) (2) they will conduct themselves wherever they dwell . . . They shall eat together, (3) pray together, and deliberate together. In every place where

10 The phrase מבשר עולות ומחלבי זבח has been understood in two opposing ways: "without the flesh of burnt offerings . . . but the offerings of lips" (Collins and Nati 2024, 114–115) or "by means of . . . and the offerings of lips . . ." (Hempel 2020, 242). On the topic, see Collins and Nati 2024, 118–120. The matter is not critical to the present argument; all that is important here is that speech and perfection of way are explicitly presented as metaphorical sacrifices by means of which the community effects atonement for the land.

11 See Metso 1997, 118–119; Hempel 2020, 241.

there are ten men of the council of the *Yaḥad*, they shall not lack (4) a priest . . . (6) . . . In every place where there are ten men, they shall not lack an interpreter of Torah, day and night (7) continually one relieving another. The Many shall watch together a third of every night of the year: reading in Scripture, studying judgment, (8) and praying together. (1QS 6:1b–8)

Notably, however, these activities are not tied to any one place, but "wherever they dwell" and "in every place" where they are (1QS 6:2–3).

Nothing is indicated of place for prayer in the Community Rule, but there is an intriguing comment in the song of the *Maskil* about communal prayer in some sort of formation.

ואברכנו תרומת מוצא שפתי ממערכת אנשים ובטרם ארים ידי להדשן בעדני תנובת תבל
ברשית פחד ואימה ובמכון צרה עם בוקה אברכנו

> I will bless him (with) the offering of the utterance of my lips from the ranked array of men (ממערכת אנשים), (15) and before I raise my hand to enjoy the pleasures of earth's produce. At the beginning of dread and terror and in the place of distress (במכון צרה) with desolation, (16) I will bless him. (1QS 10:14b–16a)

The term מערכה occurs mostly in the War Scroll, and almost exclusively for battle lines; in the War Scroll this is imagined on the model of the Israelite camp in the wilderness, in units of thousands, hundreds, fifties and tens (1QM 4:1–5). It is possible, then, that communal prayer could be conducted in formation, imitating an idealized army of Israel in the wilderness. The War Scroll describes such ritualized processions of prayer before and after war (e.g. 1QM 13:1–15:3; 18:3b–19:13), and it is possible that the War Scroll was used for ritualized enactment in the present in some form (Falk 2015b, 293–294). It is also possible that the reference to "the place of distress with desolation" in 1QS 10:15 is a wilderness allusion. Even if so, however, the emphasis is on time rather than place: the song as a whole concerns occasions for prayer and lists various appointed times as well as meals and times of distress.

Alternatively, מערכה could also refer to people arranged for a meal, as in 1QSa 2:21–22.[12] This would fit the immediately following reference to food and correspond even more closely to the paradigm of 1QS 6:2–8 with communal meals, study, and prayer (see Collins and Nati 2024, 128). In any case, although there is some evidence of wilderness imagery in prayer, this does not require prayer located geographically in wilderness.

Finally, we need also to consider the covenant ceremony as described in 1QS 1:16–2:18. This is perhaps the most important ritual for the movement, seemingly

---

12 Cf. ערך in Exod 40:4,23; Isa 21:5; 65:11; Ps 23:5.

carried out annually on the Festival of Pentecost. It was an occasion of high drama, with processions of the whole community according to rank, and solemn prayers, blessings and curses. We might easily imagine the ceremony taking place on the plateau to the east of Qumran, and it cannot be denied that such a ritual enacted at Qumran would evoke powerful images of Israel in the desert. But there is not a single hint as to location. Even more importantly, there is no reason to believe that this ritual would be carried out only at Qumran. It is not plausible to imagine that all Essenes made pilgrimage to Qumran every year to be ranked. It is more likely that this ritual would be carried out—as in the language of 1QS 6:1–2—wherever they dwell (cf. CD 14:3–6). Thus, we need to be cautious with imagining the liturgy performed in the desert (e.g., Schofield 2008, 52). This would only pertain to the setting of Qumran. For the most part, we should probably imagine that the covenant ceremony, as well as the other liturgies, was recited in the various towns where Essenes lived.

Even so, however, they could with full conviction speak of themselves as in the wilderness. The chronotope of wilderness here is about time more than place. That is, the way of the wilderness is not primarily about "where," but a "when": the liminal era of the dominion of Belial, a wilderness kind of time. Or more specifically, as Kampen (2025, 140) has argued, the behavior appropriate to the era (e.g., 1QS 8:4, 15; 9:12–14, 19–22; 10:25–26; CD 12:20–21; 1QM 15:4–5). Another way to put this is that we are dealing with a liminal time portrayed as a road, one of the important chronotopes explored by Bakhtin (1981, 98). Although Bakhtin's typology of ancient novels does not map onto the type of material we are considering in the scrolls, his analysis of the different ways that time and space are configured is helpful in highlighting different qualities of the wilderness chronotope in our texts. What Bakhtin calls the "adventure novel of ordeal" is structured around what happens between two fixed poles (meeting and consummation): The action takes place during an "extratemporal hiatus" in which nothing essentially changes (89–90). The world and characters are static (110), and the true nature of the heroes is tested and confirmed rather than transformed (105). The plot is controlled by the intervention of non-human forces beyond the agency of the heroes (94–95). The chronotope of the road is closely tied to the motif of meeting (98), but belongs to the hiatus between times.

Given the deterministic views in the sectarian scrolls, this could be an apt description of their underlying narrative arc. Not only is the character of all eras of history strictly predetermined, but also the essential nature and fate of all humans (1QS 3:13–23; 4:14–26; 9:12–14a; 11:9–18; 1QH[a] 5:24b–30; 7:25–27; 9:9–36; CD 2:2–13). The way of the "wilderness" belongs to the present "age of wrath," a hiatus during which the sons of light are to "walk" in the way appropriate for that time (1QS 9:12–14a). This is not preparation in the sense of transformation, since the destiny of all is impossible to change (1QS 3:15–16). Rather it is a period of trial, with human affairs dominated by the struggle between two spirits (1QS 3:18–23; 4:14–19a, 23); at the consummation of God's plan the true nature and destiny of all humans will be confirmed (1QS 4:18–21a). Thus, as in Bakhtin's "adventure time," there is no essential development on the wilderness road.

3 Words of the Luminaries

The work known as Words of the Luminaries (4Q504, 4Q506) is also promising with regard to our question, but similarly ambiguous. This is a collection of prayers for days of the week: petitions for physical and/or spiritual assistance on weekdays, a different one for each day; and a hymn of praise on Sabbath. As Esther Chazon (1992a, 448–450) has shown, the prayers call to God's remembrance the biblical story from creation to the post-exilic period over the course of the week. I suggest, however, that it is not entirely a successive telling. The weekday prayers are dominated by motifs from Sinai/Horeb and the wilderness wanderings. Whereas creation to Moses is covered briefly, most of the weekday prayers are fixated on Sinai and the wilderness, with the covenant at Horeb on Wednesday in the middle of the week.[13]

Thus, Sunday's prayer begins with the creation of humans, reminding God that "[Adam] our [fa]ther you formed in the likeness of [your] glory [. . .]," but it very quickly gets to the wilderness before Sinai, with allusions to Exod 19:4 and Deut 32:11.[14]

---

13 I have argued elsewhere that this is a carefully crafted liturgical sequence (Falk 2015a, 269–277). Carol Newsom (2014, 45) notices a similar lingering on the wilderness period in the historical review in Psalm 106: "In contrast to the configuration of promise and journey in Ps 105, here the structure is highly repetitious, as every incident recalled is shaped to illustrate the theme of rebellion. Indeed, one might say that only one thing happens over and over. The time period framed is also different, beginning with the rebellion at the Sea of Reeds and concluding with the speaker's present in exile and diaspora. The author's emplotment, however, allows him to distort natural temporality. Some twenty-seven verses, including all of the episodes described with specific detail, concern the exodus and wilderness period, while the subsequent centuries-long period from the entry into the land until the exile is narrated in ten very general verses. It would seem that the strong paradigm of the wilderness rebellion exhausts the very possibility of history, since seemingly nothing new can happen, yet the rhetorical purpose of the psalm includes the construction of a hopeful future."

14 On the allusions, see also Schofield 2008, 43–44.

> [. . . Re]member, please, that all of us are your people, and you bore us up wonder[fully on the wings] of eagles and you have brought us to yourself. And as an eagle rouses its brood, hovers [above its young], spreads its wings, and takes and lifts them on [its pinions . . .] we [l]ive apart and are not counted among the nations [. . .] you are in our midst in a column of fire and cloud [. . .] your [holi]ness goes before us and our glory is in [our] mid[st . . .] (4Q504 6 6–11)

Little survives of Monday's prayer, but Tuesday's prayer reminds God of the promises to the patriarchs before moving back to the Exodus and the people standing before Sinai.

> . . . [to Abraham, Isaac, and Jacob. And you chose] their descendants after them for [. . .] a holy [people] standing before y[ou . . . Re]member, O Lord, that [. . .] us [. . .] let us celebrate the festival of [our] freedom [. . .] (4Q504 5 ii + 3 i 14–18)

Wednesday's prayer, in the middle of the week, focuses on the covenant at Horeb.

> [. . . face] to face you appeared in our midst [. . .] and w[e] heard your holy words [in order to test us and in order that the fear of] you [might be] in our presence, so that we might not s[in . . .] your great [ho]ly [name . . . the] earth [. . .] and so that we may believe [. . .] forever. And you made with us a covenant at Ho[reb . . .] concerning all th[ese] l[a]ws and commandments [. . .] and the good,[pure] and holy things [. . .] which [you commanded through] Moses and . . . [. . .] face to face [yo]u spoke with hi[m and you made [your] glor[y pass before his face] . . . (4Q504 3 ii 10–21)

It reminds God of the rebellion of Israel in the wilderness, but also God's forgiveness and revelation in the wilderness.

> [. . . sins wh]ich you forgave [to our ancestors . . . in the wild]erness where they spurned [your command. And] you [g]ave to them a heart[to know] and they tested you and they found you [and you gave to them eyes to see and ears to hear, but th]ey did n[ot] trust [you . . .] (4Q504 7+18 15–18)

Thursday's prayer reminds God of his anger against the people in the wilderness to the point of wanting to destroy them, but his mercy due to Moses' intercession.

> You were so angry with them as to destroy them, but you had pity on them because of your love for them and for the sake of your covenant—for [M]oses had atoned for their sins—and so that your great strength and the abundance of yo[ur] mercy might be known to distant generations. (4Q504 1–2 ii recto 9–12)

This is the basis for the petition for God to have mercy on the contemporary community.

> May your anger and your wrath turn away from your people Israel on account of all [their] si[ns], but may you remember your wonders which you did before the eyes of the nations, for we bear your name. (4Q504 1–2 ii recto 12–13)

Thursday's prayer refers back to the birth of Israel in the wilderness.

> Only on your name have we [ca]lled. You created us for your glory, and you made us your children in the sight of all the nations, for you called [I]srael "My son, My firstborn," and you disciplined us as a man disciplines his son. (4Q504 1–2 iii recto 5–8)

But it continues to the monarchy, the Temple, and the exile as the fulfilment of the curses of the Mosaic covenant.

> You raised us throughout the years of our generations, [correcting us by means of] severe illness, famine, thirst, plague, and the sword [of vengeance avenging] your covenant. Because you have chosen us for yourself [to be a people from all] the earth, therefore you poured out on us your wrath [and] your [jeal]ousy with all the heat of your anger. You made stick to us [the curse] of your [pl]agues of which Moses and your servants the prophets wrote, th[at] you [would s]end evil a[ga]inst us in days to come. (4Q504 1–2 iii recto 8–15)

Friday's prayer focuses on the post-exilic situation but alludes to the exodus and compares the exile to regression to wilderness.

> [. . . they abandoned] the spring of living waters [. . .] and they served a foreign god in their land. Then their land became desolate (שממה) because of their enemies. For your wrath was [po]ured out, and the burning of your anger with the fire of your jealousy, to make it a wasteland (להחריבה) so that there was no going or coming. In spite of all this you did not reject the descendants of Jacob and you did not detest Israel so as to finish them off, to break your covenant with them. . . . you remembered your covenant, (you) who brought us out in the sight of the nations, and you did not abandon us among the nations. You were gracious toward your people Israel in all [the] lands to which you banished them, to cause them to turn their heart(s) to return to you and to obey your voice [according] to all you commanded through Moses your servant. [Fo]r you poured out your Holy Spirit on us [to br]ing your blessings to us, so that (we) might seek you in our distress [and so that (we) might wh]isper (prayers) under the pressure of your correction (בצקון מוסרכה לפ֯קו֯דכה בצר לנו [ולל]חש). (4Q504 1–2 v recto 2–18)

Equally important, the praying community identifies with Israel of old in a striking manner: the diction throughout the prayers alternates between "they" speech and "we" speech, but apparently not randomly. From what survives, it seems that descriptions of willful rejection against God are phrased in the third person: the present community keeps some distance from the "they" who abandoned God. They do confess solidarity with Israel of old in repentance, but it is particularly in the language of relationship with God that they use "we" language. That is, the praying community places itself in the wilderness with Israel, primarily with regard to the positive aspects: revelation, covenant, repentance and forgiveness, sonship, receiving holy spirit (Falk 2015a, 274–275): "face to face you appeared in *our* midst"; "*we* heard your holy words in order to test *us*"; "you made a covenant with *us* at Horeb"; "*we* bear your name"; "you made *us* your children."

Parenthetically, we may note that these features correspond to a process in the post-memory processing of trauma, as Tim Langille (2014, 73) describes in an article on memory and identity in the Damascus Document and the Habakkuk pesher: "The result of restoration is twofold: not only do social groups try to remove themselves mnemonically and discursively from perceived impurities; they also create a bond or common culture with those with whom they identify."

In the context of this identification of the praying community with wilderness and exile, the distress is to lead to penitential prayer, if it is correct to understand לְלַחֵשׁ here as whispered prayer: "... so that (we) might seek you in our distress [and so that (we) might wh]isper (prayers) under the pressure of your correction (לפֹּקוֹדכה בצר לנו [וללֿ]חש בצקוןמוסרכה)" (4Q504 1–2 v recto 16–17). It is especially in the bold claims of faithfulness that the significance of this distinction is clear: "we have called only on your name"; "You [thre]w away fr[o]m us all ou[r] transgressions, and you [p]urified us from our sin for your sake"; "And now, as today when our heart is humbled, we have atoned for our sins and the sins of our ancestors—in our unfaithfulness and in which we behaved stubbornly. We have not rejected your tests or your blows."

The praying community claims to have fulfilled atonement for both their own sins and the sins of the ancestors. In the liturgy, they re-enter the wilderness to undo Israel's rebellion. As Alison Schofield has noted (2008, 44), we could certainly imagine that this liturgy would take on special meaning for a community actually reciting it at Qumran in the wilderness and claiming fulfilment of the core mandate of the community, but it is very unlikely that these prayers were composed at Qumran or for a community that had physically separated themselves from others. As Esther Chazon (1992b) has argued, the early date of 4Q504—dated to the middle of the 2nd c. BCE on the basis of paleography—and the all-Israel stance without any sectarian self-consciousness seem to point rather to a pre-sectarian origin. There is no hint of a separatist outlook here other than Israel in contrast to the nations. There is also no basis for connecting the liturgical wilderness with geographical wilderness. A Thirdspace perspective is again helpful: one can ritually enter the wilderness without leaving inhabited areas. This is not about the present wilderness, but the wilderness of Mosaic times, and the wilderness of exile, and it requires ritually being *there* and *then*. Once again, we could certainly imagine that this liturgy would take on special meaning for a community actually reciting it at Qumran in the wilderness—although it would be ritually effective wherever it was performed.

The wilderness chronotope in Words of the Luminaries may also be compared to Bakhtin's chronotope of the road, but this time, Bakhtin's exposition of what he calls the "adventure novel of everyday life" helps highlight differences from our investigation in the Community Rule. "The most characteristic thing about this novel is the way it fuses the course of an individual's life (at its major turning points) with his actual spatial course or road—that is, with his wanderings" (Bakhtin 1981, 120). Character development along the "path of life" progresses through a "sequence of guilt > retribution > redemption > blessedness" (121). That is, I find in the wilderness chronotope in Words of the Luminaries more of a motif of transformational journey.

4 Conclusions

We have considered the use of wilderness in relation to prayer in two texts from the Dead Sea Scrolls. In the sectarian Community Rule, Isa 40:3 is evoked to portray core functions of the community as preparing the way of the wilderness: works of justice and suffering affliction, and penitential prayer. That is, the community's ritual is portrayed as enacting a new Exodus. Importantly, the way of the wilderness in these texts is more about time than a place, and specifically about a way of life appropriate to the time. Notably, prayer is an important part of this appropriate behavior during wilderness time, although it seems to be an addition to the way of the wilderness motif, perhaps reflecting an increased importance of prayer.

To borrow J. Z. Smith's famous pun (1987), though, communal prayer does have to *take place*. Bodies are somewhere and in relation to each other. Whatever that arrangement would look like to others, and wherever one might observe it if one could, the sectarian texts characteristically adopt language of the wilderness camp for the community at prayer. Did they actually arrange themselves in military lines in worship? Was there an actual procession during the annual covenant ceremony? Maybe, but maybe not. Either way, though, this would not necessitate an emplacement in a literal wilderness. The varying connotations of wilderness between alienation and danger on the one hand and preparation and provision on the other are rich context for the ritualized structuring of the liturgical community on the model of Israel in the desert.

The collection of daily prayers in Words of the Luminaries provides an illuminating example of the wilderness motif temporally actualized in liturgy. In a historical review serialized over the course of the weekday prayers, the community liturgically lingers in the wilderness period. Here the wilderness chronotope is evoked in the course of regularized prayer at fixed times. Again, there is both a spatial and temporal dynamic, but I argue that the temporal is dominant in the nature of a journey: re-journeying through the wilderness rebellion. But we noted a fascinating aspect: a distancing from rebellious Israel (they/them) and identification with purified Israel (we/us). Once again, Bakhtin's literary chronotope of liminal time as a road is apt, but I also suggest that Bakhtin's characterization of two different ancient novel types helps illuminate different emphases in the wilderness chronotope: the degree to which the hiatus is transformative.

Bibliography

Alexander, Philip S., and Geza Vermes, eds. 1998. *Qumran Cave 4: XIX: Serekh Ha-Yaḥad and Two Related Texts*. DJD 26. Oxford: Clarendon Press.

Bakhtin, Mikhail M. 1981. "Forms of Time and of the Chronotope in the Novel: Notes Toward a Historical Poetics." In *The Dialogic Imagination: Four Essays*, 84–258. Austin: University of Texas Press.

Brooke, George J. 1994. "Isaiah 40:3 and the Wilderness Community." In *New Qumran Texts and Studies: Proceedings of the First Meeting of the International Organization for Qumran Studies, Paris, 1992*, edited by George J. Brooke and Florentino García Martínez, 117–132. StDJ 15. Leiden: Brill. https://doi.org/10.1163/9789004350175_015.

Brooke, George J. 2025. "Locating the Wilderness in the Dead Sea Scrolls and the New Testament: A Study in Mutual Illumination." In *The Dead Sea Scrolls at Seventy: "Clear a Path in the Wilderness!"*, edited by Esther G. Chazon, Ruth A. Clements, Armin Lange, Adolfo D. Roitman, Lawrence H. Schiffman, and Pnina Shor, 333–353. StDJ 147. Leiden: Brill. https://doi.org/10.1163/9789004698079_019.

Chazon, Esther G. 1992a. "4QDibHam: Liturgy or Literature?" *RdQ* 15 (58):447–455.

Chazon, Esther G. 1992b. "Is Divrei Ha-Me'orot a Sectarian Prayer?" In *The Dead Sea Scrolls: Forty Years of Research*, edited by Devorah Dimant and Uriel Rappaport, 3–17. *StDJ* 10. Leiden: Brill.

Cohn, Robert L. 1981. "Liminality in the Wilderness." In *The Shape of Sacred Space: Four Biblical Studies*, 7–20. Chico, CA: Scholars Press.

Collins, John J. 2010. *Beyond the Qumran Community: The Sectarian Movement of the Dead Sea Scrolls*. Grand Rapids, Mich.: Eerdmans.

Collins, John J. 2025. "The Significance of the Wilderness for the Yaḥad of the Scrolls." In *The Dead Sea Scrolls at Seventy: "Clear a Path in the Wilderness!"*, edited by Esther G. Chazon, Ruth A. Clements, Armin Lange, Adolfo D. Roitman, Lawrence H. Schiffman, and Pnina Shor, 87–105. StDJ 147. Leiden: Brill. https://doi.org/10.1163/9789004698079_006.

Collins, John J., and James Nati. 2024. *The Rule of the Association and Related Texts*. Oxford: Oxford University Press. https://doi.org/10.1093/oso/9780198845744.001.0001.

Cross, Frank Moore. 1994. "Paleographical Dates of the Manuscripts." In *The Dead Sea Scrolls: Hebrew, Aramaic, and Greek Texts with English Translations. Vol. 1. Rule of the Community and Related Documents*, edited by James H. Charlesworth, 57. The Princeton Theological Seminary Dead Sea Scrolls Project 1. Tübingen: Mohr Siebeck.

Davies, W. D., and Dale C. Allison. 1988. *A Critical and Exegetical Commentary on the Gospel According to Saint Matthew*. Vol. 1. Edinburgh: T&T Clark.

Dimant, Devorah. 2014. "Not Exile in the Desert but Exile in Spirit: The Pesher of Isa 40:3 in the Rule of the Community and the History of the Scrolls Community." In *History, Ideology and Bible Interpretation in the Dead Sea Scrolls: Collected Studies*, 455–464. FAT 90. Tübingen: Mohr Siebeck.

Falk, Daniel K. 2015a. "Liturgical Progression and the Experience of Transformation in Prayers From Qumran." *DSD* 22:267–284. https://doi.org/10.1163/15685179-12341362.

Falk, Daniel K. 2015b. "Prayer, Liturgy, and War." In *The War Scroll, Violence, War and Peace in the Dead Sea Scrolls and Related Literature. Essays in Honour of Martin G. Abegg on the Occasion of His 65th Birthday*, edited by Kipp Davis, Kyung S. Baek, Peter W. Flint, and Dorothy M. Peters, 275–294. StDJ 115. Leiden: Brill. https://doi.org/10.1163/9789004301634_016.

Hempel, Charlotte. 2020. *The Community Rules from Qumran: A Commentary*. Tübingen: Mohr Siebeck. https://doi.org/10.1628/978-3-16-157027-8.

Janzen, David. 2020. "The Deuteronomistic History as Literature of Trauma." In *The Oxford Handbook of the Historical Books of the Hebrew Bible*, edited by Brad E. Kelle, and Brent A. Strawn, 421–433. Oxford: Oxford University Press. https://doi.org/10.1093/oxfordhb/9780190261160.013.21.

Jokiranta, Jutta. 2013. *Social Identity and Sectarianism in the Qumran Movement*. StDJ 105. Leiden: Brill. https://doi.org/10.1163/9789004238640.

Kampen, John. 2025. "Does the Use of Isaiah 40:3 Necessarily Point to the Wilderness?" In *The Dead Sea Scrolls at Seventy: "Clear a Path in the Wilderness!"*, edited by Esther G. Chazon, Ruth A. Clements, Armin Lange, Adolfo D. Roitman, Lawrence H. Schiffman, and Pnina Shor, 130–142. StDJ 147. Leiden: Brill. https://doi.org/10.1163/9789004698079_008.

Knibb, Michael A. 1987. *The Qumran Community*. Cambridge Commentaries on Writings of the Jewish and Christian World 200 BC to AD 200 2. Cambridge: Cambridge University Press.

Langille, Tim. 2014. "Old Memories, New Identities: Traumatic Memory, Exile, and Identity Formation in the Damascus Document and Pesher Habakkuk." In *Memory and Identity in Ancient Judaism and Early Christianity: A Conversation with Barry Schwartz*, edited by Tom Thatcher, 57–88. Atlanta: SBL Press. https://doi.org/10.2307/j.ctt1287n36.7.

Lied, Liv Ingeborg. 2005. "Another Look at the Land of Damascus: The Spaces of the Damascus Document in the Light of Edward W. Soja's Thirdspace Approach." In *New Directions in Qumran Studies: Proceedings of the Bristol Colloquium on the Dead Sea Scrolls, 8–10th September 2003*, edited by Jonathan G. Campbell, William J. Lyons, and Lloyd K. Pietersen, 101–125. Library of Second Temple Studies 52. London: T&T Clark International.

Metso, Sarianna. 1997. *The Textual Development of the Qumran Community Rule*. StDJ 21. Leiden: Brill. https://doi.org/10.1163/9789004350236.

Murphy-O'Connor, Jerome. 1969. "La genèse littéraire de la Règle de la Communauté." *RB* 76(4):528–549.

Najman, Hindy. 2010. "Towards a Study of the Uses of the Concept of Wilderness in Ancient Judaism." In *Past Renewals: Interpretative Authority, Renewed Revelation, and the Quest for Perfection in Jewish Antiquity*, 143–159. JSJSup 53. Leiden: Brill. https://doi.org/10.1163/ej.9789004180468.i-270.30.

Newsom, Carol A. 2004. *The Self as Symbolic Space: Constructing Identity and Community at Qumran*. StDJ 52. Leiden: Brill. https://doi.org/10.1163/9789047405153.

Newsom, Carol A. 2014. "Selective Recall and Ghost Memories: Two Aspects of Cultural Memory in the Hebrew Bible." In *Memory and Identity in Ancient Judaism and Early Christianity: A Conversation with Barry Schwartz*, edited by Tom Thatcher, 41–56. Atlanta: SBL Press. https://doi.org/10.2307/j.ctt1287n36.6.

Schofield, Alison. 2008. "The Wilderness Motif in the Dead Sea Scrolls." In *Israel in the Wilderness: Interpretations of the Biblical Narratives in Jewish and Christian Traditions*, edited by Kenneth Pomykala, 37–53. Themes in Biblical Narrative 10. Leiden: Brill. https://doi.org/10.1163/ej.9789004164246.I-247.13.

Schofield, Alison. 2009. *From Qumran to the* Yaḥad*: A New Paradigm of Textual Development for the Community Rule*. StDJ 77. Leiden: Brill. https://doi.org/10.1163/ej.9789004170070.i-326.

Schofield, Alison. 2012. "Re-Placing Priestly Space: The Wilderness as Heterotopia in the Dead Sea Scrolls." In *A Teacher for All Generations: Essays in Honor of James C. Vanderkam*, edited by Eric

Farrel Mason, Samuel I. Thomas, Alison Schofield, Eugene Ulrich, Kelley Coblentz Bautch, Angela Kim Harkins, and Daniel A. Machiela, 469–490. JSJSup 153. Leiden: Brill. https://doi.org/10.1163/9789004224087_026.

Smith, Jonathan Z. 1987. *To Take Place: Toward Theory in Ritual*. Chicago: University of Chicago Press.

Soja, Edward W. 1996. *Thirdspace: Journeys to Los Angeles and Other Real-and-imagined Places*. London: Blackwell Publishers.

Talmon, Shemaryahu. 1966. "The 'Desert Motif' in the Bible and in Qumran Literature." In *Biblical Motifs, Origins and Transformations*, edited by Alexander Altmann, 31–63. Cambridge, MA: Harvard University Press.

Turner, Victor Witter. 1969. *The Ritual Process: Structure and Anti-Structure*. Chicago: Aldine.

Sarah Wisialowski

Apocalyptic Visions and Historical Revisions: Time in the Book of Daniel

Abstract: This article examines how concepts of apocalypticism and historical revision in the book of Daniel shape its understanding of time and revelation, arguing that the prayer of Daniel 9 is not just an address to the divine but a performative act of revelation that allows Daniel to actively reinterpret history. By re-engaging with Jeremiah's prophecy of seventy years, Daniel's prayer demonstrates a malleability of temporality, weaving together past, present, and future to provide hope and direction in a time of trauma. The article shows how prayer serves as a conduit for revelation, moving beyond rigid genre boundaries, and enabling Daniel to restructure his understanding of history and his community's place within it. Ultimately, this article concludes that while apocalyptic elements are a part of the text, the book of Daniel presents a multifaceted and intertwined understanding of time, revelation, and history that cannot be reduced to a single genre.

1 Introduction

How do apocalypticism and understanding modes of history present a different way of reading temporality in the Hellenistic-Jewish period? The book of Daniel is a text that seeks hidden knowledge, seeking what has previously been unknown. Daniel has long been understood as an exemplary text for conversations around time, apocalypse, and revelation due to its engagement with divine beings, along with revelatory moments and calculations of time. This is particularly apparent in the latter half of the book of Daniel (Dan 7–12), which has been termed the apocalypses of Daniel (Segal 2011; 2016; 2018).

While the focus of this article is to consider the paradigmatic confession prayer of Dan 9, to avoid a decontextualized reading of the prayer in a microcosm, the other apocalypses within the text will be briefly addressed. Additionally, the structure found in the latter half of Daniel will be examined, where Daniel's prayer in Dan 9 transitions into his visions and the time calculations presented in Dan 9–12. Dan 9 shows how Dan 10–12 is already read early in its narrative life. This does not imply that the later chapters of Daniel form a single work; instead, they demonstrate a cohesive reading practice. Hindy Najman (2025, 5) argues that "reading practices thus perform and exemplify the inheritance of earlier textual traditions through explication and interpretation of those texts by the dynamic enlivenment of those traditions in the context of history and culture, and by the communities and writers who are first readers." Like any part of a text, prayers are affected by and affect other texts. Thus, while Dan 10–12 may be compositionally earlier than Dan 9 (Segal 2011, 2018; Newman 2017), the prayer becomes the basis by which the revelatory is read, thereby showing the importance of prayer throughout the narrative. Through a close reading of these texts, we can see how the interplay of apocalyptic visions and historical revisions in the book of Daniel informs our understanding of time and revelation.

In the early twentieth century, Mikhail Bakhtin developed the language of the chronotope to speak about how time and space are represented in language and discourse (1981, 84). He writes, "The chronotope in a work always contains within it an evaluating aspect that can be isolated from the whole artistic chronotope only in abstract analysis" (Bakhtin 1981, 243). That is to say, every representation of time and space within a work of literature carries particular meanings and judgments. When examining literary works, such as the book of Daniel, we can isolate these aspects, such as the construction of spaces and places in the text or understanding of time. However, this can only be done through abstract analysis, and the interconnectedness of time and space in the narrative is essential to understanding the work as a whole. For this article, I am concerned with focusing on the chronos, that is, the temporal aspects of the book of Daniel, yet these aspects cannot be isolated from the surrounding context of Bakhtin's whole chronotope.

Throughout this paper, the apocalyptic visions in the book of Daniel are engaged with particular attention to the concept of apocalypse in Hellenistic-Jewish material. Speaking of these texts as concerned with otherworldly concepts is not innovative. However, we can open the text's historical revisions by focusing on how history is both discussed and experienced. Finally, the article considers how prayer enacts time within the narrative, a dynamic that emerges through closely reading its apocalyptic elements and its portrayal of history.

2 Characteristics of Apocalyptic Literature

'Apocalypse' or 'apocalyptic' are catchwords when discussing esoteric literature from the Hellenistic-Jewish period through the early Christian period. Scholars have turned to the book of Revelation in the New Testament, a title compatible with the Greek term ἀποκάλυψις (revelation or disclosing), yet this is bound up on the definition of apocalypse put forward in *Semeia* 14 by John Collins (1979, 9), which defines apocalypse as,

> A genre of revelatory literature with a narrative framework, in which a revelation is mediated by an otherworldly being to a human recipient disclosing a transcendent reality that is both temporal, insofar as it envisages eschatological salvation, and spatial insofar as it involves another supernatural world.

Through this definition, the term has come to be used to refer to all texts that "share a cluster of traits" (Collins 2016, 13–14) and has been superimposed on the book of Daniel. This conception of apocalypse is broad and can be used to describe many of the elements found within the book of Daniel, such as the presence of angelic beings (e.g., Dan 9:21; 10:5,18; 12:6–7) and the revelation of divine knowledge (e.g., Dan 12:4,10–13). However, the definition can be broadened to be more capacious, focusing not on the apocalyptic genre but on the experience of the revelatory, to leave room for the distinctive features of the book of Daniel, which engage in other generic categories, such as sapiential literature, prayer texts, and history. Instead, it is better to speak of the apocalyptic traditions within a text without constraining it to generic boundaries. Following Matthew J. Goff, it is best to understand Jewish apocalypticism as "a sort of intellectual shorthand" (2018, 18). Instead of adhering to a strict notion of what is or is not apocalyptic, looking for the characteristic threads that may run throughout the text is best. Elements of Daniel that have been termed apocalyptic can then help to read the paradigmatic prayer through its relationship to temporality rather than being reduced to an apocalyptic text.

What defines an apocalyptic vision, and how do these visions function within the broader context of biblical literature? It is essential to be careful in using the language of apocalypse and apocalypticism because it can lead to neglect of other characteristics of a text (Najman 2012, 316). It cannot be denied that apocalyptic characteristics appear in the text, and I do not intend to abandon Collins' understanding of apocalypticism. Still, I intend to add further nuance to how it is used in analyzing ancient Jewish literature.

2.1 Apocalyptic Traditions and the Book of Daniel

The book of Daniel, alongside later Jewish texts such as 4Ezra, has been characterized as apocalyptic due to a preoccupation with visions, end times, and cosmic events. Yet, further textual markers would also place them into other generic categories. In the remainder of this article, while I will speak about the apocalyptic characteristic or through the language of apocalyptic thinking (Crawford and Wassén 2018), I do not mean to relegate these texts solely to the apocalyptic platform.

The aspects of Daniel that are often considered apocalyptic cannot be overlooked. The apocalypses in the book are traditionally defined as Dan 7 (the vision of the four beasts), Dan 8 (the episode of the ram and the goat), Dan 9 (the confession prayer), and Dan 10–12 (the vision of the kings of the north and the south and the calculation of the קֵץ הַיָּמִין).

The vision of Dan 7 presents a sequence of four kingdoms and then a different eternal kingdom. The four kingdoms are presented as hybrid beasts (cf. Dan 7:4–7). Sometimes compared to the Animal Apocalypse in 1Enoch, Dan 7 presents the exhortative function of visionary experiences building on other biblical material to present an idea of history (Rillera 2019, 775). Dan 7 uses the vision to present a recourse to action.

The following vision in Dan 8 similarly metaphorically analyzes the present history and how time might end. It depicts a two-horned ram that is destroyed by a one-horned goat. Like Dan 7, it alludes to Antiochus IV Epiphanes' rise and ends with an interpretation about the end of time. Both chapters have deep concerns about calculating time — calculating an end to oppression. While this is relevant for chronological calculations, it also fundamentally affects how history is experienced — Dan 8's notion of temporality attempts to reconceive Daniel's own present.

The historical crisis of the Seleucid era transforms the book of Daniel's focus from prophetic promises to a mode of re-reading history. The epilogue of Daniel, chapters 10–12, is the most well-known example of eschatology and apocalypse within the book of Daniel.[1] This passage is presented as a combined epilogue unit to the book of Daniel and forms the final vision that Daniel receives as he looks towards the future in its conclusion. Within the epilogue, each chapter explores a particular vision which, when placed together, can be read as a single, complete vision that acts within mythical and liminal realms and presents a solution to exile. Like the previous two visions within Daniel, Dan 10–12 is imbued with apocalyptic tradition. The figure, Daniel, experiences revelatory acts (most notably his vision of the war between the king of the north and the king of the south). He meets and engages with otherworldly mediators (such as angels like Gabriel, who come to explain his visions), and he receives previously unknown knowledge (like the calculation of the קֵץ הַיָּמִין at the end of Dan 12). These chapters present a liminal,

1 Eschatology and apocalypse are distinct but related terms, often combined in scholarship as apocalyptic eschatology. Eschatology generally refers to the end of times, deriving from the Greek ἔσχατος, meaning "last." Meanwhile, apocalypse is derived from the Greek ἀποκάλυψις, meaning "revelation" or "disclosure." This article focuses on characteristics and traits rather than rigid categories, however in Second Temple scholarship, apocalypse is the term used to define a genre of literature that shares specific traits, including otherworldly mediators, transcendent realities, and a supernatural world, and which addresses future concerns, particularly those related to the end times. The combined term, apocalyptic eschatology, specifically refers to this revelatory literature that arose in times of crisis (such as the persecution under King Antiochus IV Epiphanes) to re-evaluate concepts of temporality, the future, and the past.

or perhaps transcendent world, in which Daniel bridges the past and the future, standing in a place of no time.[2] However, despite these types of apocalyptic tendencies, this is not enough to reduce the book of Daniel to an apocalyptic genre or category. Instead, the text's intersection of history (past), divine revelation (present understanding), and eschatological anticipation (future) is mandated by the historical crisis (the rule of Antiochus IV Epiphanes), transforming the prophetic promises into a communal reading practice that reinterprets temporal reality.

2.2 Prayer in Apocalyptic Contexts

The book of Daniel is a text of upheaval and learning how to deal with experiences of trauma, such as exile and loss of place. Daniel sits at a crossroads in that it is set in the Babylonian exile of the sixth century BCE but likely was composed in the second century BCE during a different period of disruption. As such, Daniel plays with impressionable notions of time, creating a timelessness in the text that is tied to its sense of place.

While the papers in the volume discuss Bakhtin's chronotope from various angles, as mentioned in the introduction, the primary focus is on the temporal role, particularly as the time of prayer is essential to how and when a prayer is performed. For instance, Dan 9:21 states that Daniel prays this prayer of Dan 9 at the time of the evening sacrifice,

> [21] וְעוֹד אֲנִי מְדַבֵּר בַּתְּפִלָּה וְהָאִישׁ גַּבְרִיאֵל אֲשֶׁר רָאִיתִי בֶחָזוֹן בַּתְּחִלָּה מֻעָף בִּיעָף נֹגֵעַ אֵלַי כְּעֵת מִנְחַת־עָרֶב׃

> [21] And while I was still speaking in prayer, the man Gabriel, who I had seen in the vision in the beginning, approached me in flight, at the time of the evening sacrifice.[3]

Time is impacted by prayer and ritual. When Daniel prays and performs the evening sacrifice, he creates a window into history. Prayer, liturgy, and time come together to create a moment when ritual is created. The מִנְחַת־עָרֶב (evening sacrifice) is vital in its reference to the time of the prayer but also because of its reference to a space

---

2 I am suggesting that prayer creates a space where history can be reconceptualized or re-imagined. History is not solely historiography and "true" history, but it is also the formation of communal identity. Therefore, through prayer, the people who pray, in this case, the Jewish community who rebuild the temple, participate in the creation of a new identity. As I will continue to argue, they are participating in a type of divine action by doing this. Prayer opens a liminal space between human and divine, as it is the crux of the relationship between God and the people and their communication.

3 All translations are my own.

or place. Daniel is in exile, in the courts of Babylon, far from the Temple.[4] This does not stop Daniel from participating in the מִנְחַת־עָרֶב. Instead, he creates his own place of worship beyond the Temple, participating in what Arjen Bakker has recently called the "translation of sacrifice," in which the performance of rituals related to sacrifice "generate[s] new forms of worship that do not necessarily involve animal sacrifice, but nonetheless absorb essential features of the sacrificial system which they transform and project onto domains outside the Temple" (Bakker 2024, 462). This suggests that the evening sacrifice is prayer for Daniel. Prayer did not replace sacrifice but instead remained a part of the performance of sacrifice (Bakker 2024).

2.2.1 Understanding Prayer

Dan 9 is, first and foremost, a prayer. However, it is necessary to ask what a prayer is. Judith H. Newman (1999, 6–7) defined prayer as

> Prayer is address to God that is initiated by humans; it is not conversational in nature; and it includes address to God in the second person, although it can include a third-person description of God.

For Newman, the importance of the address being human-initiated and often single-sided is crucial for understanding what constitutes prayer. I agree with Newman's definition in its capaciousness. Yet, prayer must also have an element of performance in addition to Newman's requirements. This could manifest in expressions of physicality — such as the communal gathering of people in Neh 9, the lifting of hands in prayer in Lam 3:41, or Daniel's physical change in appearance in Dan 10:8 — or it could arise through the historical aspects of prayer — such as appealing to the history of the people in Neh 9:31. Thus, the act of praying according to these designations, not the content of the prayer, is what makes prayer a prayer.

Dan 9 easily fits into these categories: Daniel initiates his prayer to God (Dan 9:3), although Daniel asks for things from God, this is not a conversation (Dan 9:17–19), God is addressed in the second person (Dan 9:5–8,11,13,15–19), and Daniel performs the prayer through ritual performance (Dan 9:3).

This prayer exemplifies the intertwining of human agency and divine disclosure in the context of apocalyptic thinking. In this way, the prayer inherently blurs boundaries. It encompasses multiple genres: sapiential, prophetic, prayer, and apocalyptic. Specifically, the structure of Daniel's prayer, and its subsequent divine response, which centers on a reinterpretation of the seventy years of exile, directly

4 Despite being in exile, Daniel can still access the divine.

links Daniel's supplication to the calculation of prophecy time. The prayer in Dan 9 speaks to the book of Daniel's relationship with temporality. For Daniel, to pray is to experience time, and to calculate time is to pray.[5]

2.2.2 Elements of Performance in Prayer

To return to the discussion of genre, reading Dan 9 into a strict generic category is far too rigid. However, Bakker offers a helpful corrective in his reading of the Dead Sea Scrolls as he writes: "We can use literary genres as a heuristic tool to compare forms and trace literary developments. But we cannot impose rigid boundaries because, with each new example, we need to reconsider the entire generic category" (Bakker 2023, 11). The same can be applied to Dan 9. It is impossible to classify this text as either prayer or revelation or apocalyptic, which appears to encompass many categories, but rather, we must consider how these texts participate in multiple modes simultaneously.

Daniel, as the human agent behind the prayer, is the one who enacts or initiates his prayer. After perceiving or understanding (בין) from the book or books of Jeremiah the number of years until the end of the desolation, Daniel enacts his prayer (Dan 9:2–3),

> 2 בִּשְׁנַת אַחַת לְמָלְכוֹ אֲנִי דָּנִיֵּאל בִּינֹתִי בַּסְּפָרִים מִסְפַּר הַשָּׁנִים אֲשֶׁר הָיָה דְבַר־יְהֹוָה אֶל־יִרְמְיָה הַנָּבִיא לְמַלֹּאות לְחָרְבוֹת יְרוּשָׁלִַם שִׁבְעִים שָׁנָה׃ 3 וָאֶתְּנָה אֶת־פָּנַי אֶל־אֲדֹנָי הָאֱלֹהִים לְבַקֵּשׁ תְּפִלָּה וְתַחֲנוּנִים בְּצוֹם וְשַׂק וָאֵפֶר׃
>
> 2 In the first year of his reign, I, Daniel, perceived in the books the number of years that, according to the word of the Lord to Jeremiah the prophet, must be fulfilled before the end of the desolations of Jerusalem, namely, seventy years. 3 Then I turned my face to the Lord God, seeking him by prayer and pleas for mercy with fasting and sackcloth and ashes.

Daniel acts as the instigator of the prayer with his own agency. The text shows that divine disclosure, specifically the revelation found in Jeremiah's recontextualized prophecy, precedes Daniel's prayer and motivates his supplication. Although the revelation occurs first, it is also part of the performance of the prayer unit itself. The prayer, therefore, is what recontextualizes the past revelation (Jeremiah's prophecy) and makes it a present revelation, establishing itself as a mode for continuing revelation. This suggests that prayer is not merely a response to revelation; rather prayer functions as the necessary human mechanism by which the sup-

5 The active participation in time calculation (a human attempt to understand divine temporality) can be viewed as a type of prayer practice. By attempting to understand God's temporal plan, Daniel steps beyond ordinary time and into the transcendent reality revealed by the vision, essentially turning the act of intellectual calculation into a continued, participatory act of prayer.

plicant (Daniel) participates in the divine disclosure, making the revelation itself dependent on the human act of prayer to be fully manifest and effective in the praying community's present reality.

The critique of rigid genre classification adds further dimensions to understanding or problematizing apocalypticism when thinking about the role of the time in the narrative. By relying on an apocalyptic category for reading Daniel or other texts (e.g., 4Ezra or Neh 9 for the history genre), the boundaries remain rigid, and prayer and revelation are distinguished as opposites. Thus, it has been argued that prayer moves directionally from human to divine, while revelation moves from divine to human. This becomes problematized when reading prayer and revelation together. They need not be in opposition, but each can work to strengthen the other.

2.2.3 Prayer and Multiplicity of Genre

Turning to another biblical text can help illuminate this relationship. Neh 8–10 embodies the connections between revelation and prayer.[6] This unit understands the relationship between prayer, time, and history by engaging these ideas within discrete textual units. Independently, the (re)giving of the law in Neh 8, the confession prayer of Neh 9, and the reaffirmation of the covenant in Neh 10 can stand alone. However, when we read the chapters as a narrative together, each moment can become efficacious and wield performative power. The elements of history renewal and the perception of history broaden in Neh 8–10.

The book of Nehemiah's engagement with the revelatory, that is, the law and the covenant, is underscored and strengthened by the performance of prayer that is central to the text. Thus, Daniel's prayer in Dan 9 also acts transformationally by complicating how we view apocalypticism. Like the narrative history that is portrayed in Neh 8–10, Dan's prayer allows Daniel to act in a God-like manner in how the text engages with its history and its future. To use Hindy Najman's language (2014, passim), Daniel uses the past to recover the future. We should be clear that this language of recovering a future or changing time does not refer to an actual change in the past. Instead, the way figures such as Daniel use prayer to conceive of the past and to reinterpret events in light of future circumstances within the framework of the changing socio-historical contexts.

6 Like the latter half of the book of Daniel, Nehemiah is entrenched in the liturgical practices of the Second Temple period, problematizing static notions of prayer in its generative use of history throughout its prayers.

For this reason, we can speak of texts such as Dan 9 as engaging with the revelatory while also avoiding a rigid generic reading as revelation. The revelatory should not be reserved for the otherworldly adventures of Ezra in 4Ezra or for the visions in one's head, as in the earlier episodes of Daniel (cf. Dan 7:1). As a result, it also encompasses the mundane and the quotidian, such as the (re)giving of the law and affirmation of covenant in Neh 8 and 10. By reading Daniel with texts not generally placed alongside one another due to generic divides, new readings of Daniel emerge from one limited solely to the paradigms of an apocalyptic or revelatory text to an active reading practice of the book of Daniel as a text that aims to do something new with its engagement with temporality.

3 Ritualizing Memory and Time in Dan 9

Philosophical readings are one way to address this type of reading practice. Friedrich Nietzsche (1997, 62) explores a concept he calls *active forgetting*, saying: "It is altogether impossible to *live* at all without forgetting." Ciano Aydin (2017, 125), a philosopher who discusses how ritual and ritualization of history contribute to how cultures experience trauma, provides an alternative perspective on this same issue and speaks instead about "selective remembering." An individual or a community can rebuild or reshape their story based on how they choose to remember or reuse history. Dan 9 exemplifies this, as Jeremiah's prophecy does not come true. However, this does not remove the authority of the prophecy for Daniel or later for 4Ezra. Instead, it allows Daniel to choose to reuse and reimagine the prophecy. The people are in the midst of suffering, but Daniel can still pray to change the narrative history.

3.1 The Role of Prayer in Historical Reinterpretation

In order for Daniel's reinterpretations to take hold, he must gain help from the divine through the performance of prayer. Within the prayer, Daniel actively voices the collective guilt of the people in Dan 9:11,

11 וְכָל־יִשְׂרָאֵ֗ל עָֽבְרוּ֙ אֶת־תּ֣וֹרָתֶ֔ךָ וְס֕וֹר לְבִלְתִּ֖י שְׁמ֣וֹעַ בְּקֹלֶ֑ךָ וַתִּתַּ֨ךְ עָלֵ֜ינוּ הָאָלָ֣ה וְהַשְּׁבֻעָ֗ה אֲשֶׁ֤ר כְּתוּבָה֙ בְּתוֹרַת֙ מֹשֶׁ֣ה
עֶֽבֶד־הָאֱלֹהִ֔ים כִּ֥י חָטָ֖אנוּ לֽוֹ׃

11 All of Israel have transgressed your teaching, turning away, not hearing your voice, and the curse and the oath, which are written in the Law of Moses, the servant of God, have befallen us, for we have sinned against him.

In this formulaic discussion of the past history of the people, Jeremiah's unfulfilled prophecy, and the collective memory of Israelite disobedience, Daniel ritualizes the remembering of history in his prayer. In his discussion of the ritualization of history, Aydin (2017, 134) writes: "By repeating it in its proper setting, the traumatic event is remembered and given the required significance. By appropriating it and making it an automatic part of cultural identity, it is banished and forgotten. It is remembered and forgotten at the same time. It is actively forgotten." Daniel's prayer exemplifies this as it continues to use and be used in performance. In the writing and scripturalisation of texts such as Daniel, the threads of connection through history remain embedded. The book of Daniel participates in writing a *new history* while simultaneously inserting itself in the long narrative of history that already exists.

3.2 Textual Continuity and New Meanings

The production of new texts or the creation of new meanings should not be seen as overriding the history of the past. Instead, it is an insertion of the present into the past. Daniel's prayer does not aim to create a new prophecy or rewrite the history, yet it inevitably does so. With each new iteration of events, temporal layers are added. Gary Knoppers (2021, 93) has explored this through the concept of *mimesis*, suggesting the deliberate reuse and revitalization of traditions throughout antiquity, particularly noting that in the Second Temple period, "the interest in the past was especially acute." For Knoppers, *mimesis* is not defined as mere imitation but as the deliberate, creative reuse and revitalization of traditions and texts. This inquiry into the past is a surprisingly active endeavor. The act of writing and historical inquiry allowed history to be reimagined, or even changed, producing new literature rather than serving just as interpretations of past literature.

3.2.1 Temporal Awareness in Daniel's Prayer

The history explored in Daniel is structured around the experience of time. Daniel does not exist in a microcosm of his own temporality but in how Daniel's time relates both to the past and the future. To the giving of the law and Jeremiah's prophecy, as well as the overcoming of trauma and the return from exile. In Dan 9, there is an awareness of time. His time is layered in relation to the history within which Daniel situates himself. The history he perceives changes his experience of his own time and his sense of what may happen in the future. This concept is platformed in his prayer, providing the method for the continuous rhythm of time.

The past provides architecture for the present. It is essential for shaping an individual's, in this case, Daniel's, orientation toward the present because of the constant influence it exerts on the present and future expectations. The temporality experienced in Daniel's prayer provides patterns and blueprints for future actions (Najman 2025, 132–139).

Dan 9 uses prayer as a form of revelation to affect the present and the future. It seamlessly distorts the variations of past, present, and future, and in doing so, his prayer and the subsequent revelation seem to mitigate, or at the very least contextualize, the trauma experienced by diaspora Jews. Therefore, the apocalyptic elements present in Daniel do help shape Daniel's reading of time, but it is not the only aspect that does so.

4 Interplay of History and Revelation in the Book of Daniel

How does history interact with revelation, and how does this interaction impact the understanding of the book of Daniel's treatment of time and history? Throughout this article, I explore the conceptual nature of Hellenistic-Jewish time and temporality rather than any chronological time. The goal is not to plot out on a calendar when these events would have occurred or the veracity of Daniel's calculations (Grabbe 1997; Segal 2011; 2018; 2020).

Due to the lack of an abstract term for 'time' some scholars have questioned whether the ancient Jewish writers possessed a concept of time comparable to philosophical notions of temporality. This perspective is exemplified by figures like Gerhard von Rad (1961, 113), who asserted that the ancient Hebrews lacked the abstract philosophical concept of absolute, independent time. Von Rad argued that ancient Hebrews did not conceive of time in the same universal manner as is often associated with Greek or later Western thought, and G. A. F. Knight (1959, 314), who argued, "the Hebrews conceived of time quite differently from us. To the Hebrews, time was identical with its substance." Even more recently, Sacha Stern (2007, 3) has maintained this view, arguing that "the absence of a concept of time in ancient Judaism is manifest... in the absence of a word for time (as a whole) in ancient Hebrew and Jewish Aramaic sources."

In this article, I aim to make the shift from chronological inquiry (*i.e.*, when did X event happen) to conceptual analysis (*i.e.*, how was time understood and experienced). While scholars such as Arnaldo Momigliano (1966) and Lynn Kaye (2018) have explored this idea of abstract thinking, there is still a need for scholarship to fully embrace this shift to recognizing the conceptual presence of temporality, even if not the same as the Greco-Roman world. Daniel's engagement with temporality is fundamentally connected to its actions as prayer through history, meaning that the act of prayer serves as the mechanism by which the praying community actively reinterprets past tradition to shape its understanding of the future.

4.1 History as a Process of Understanding

History can then be seen as an aspect of time and a way of appropriating the past to make sense of the present and the community within a present time. In this way, history is the act of processing time. It can relate to a past history as a historical retrospective, or it can relate to a future history that has not yet been realized. Speaking about the narrative form of wisdom literature, Hans Z. Decker (forthcoming) writes that the text can embody a nostalgic past while "enculturing the viewing and transforming the present and the future." In telling history through prayer, we could say the past is repurposed as the present.

In other words, we return to timelessness. Embodying this practice, Daniel engages with and is engaged by a long history of early Jewish interpretation. The act of reading, and thus praying, is something generative, or what Hindy Najman (2025) calls "scriptural vitality." Hindy Najman and Irene Peirano Garrison (2019, 331) have recently argued that reading "is fundamentally interpretive." This interpretive act does not exclude the performative nature of prayer, as a conceptual thinking and physical gestures are intertwined in the prayer experience to create an active mode of encountering the divine.[7] This phenomenon examines how a text evolves and may change our understanding of history. Daniel's perspectives of the past, particularly concerning the book or books of Jeremiah, are shaped by changing societal dynamics. This highlights the intricate interplay between personal perception, societal change, and historical interpretation. The differences between the past and present start to blur, showing how prayer enables Daniel and the text's readers to reshape their understanding of time. This new understanding or perception of time is also a new history. Thinking back to Knoppers (2021, 88) and his use of mimesis, there is a "selective reuse, reworking, supplementation, and recontextualization of older material such that the borrowed material is recreated as the borrower's 'own property' (*private iuris*) in a new work."

7 Performance can be understood as the convergence of compositional practices and liturgical enactment, thus encompassing performative gestures, rituals, etc., and also including the act of reading. Taking place in both the written and oral contexts, performance creates a dynamic interaction between the text's first writers and first readers, allowing a text to be reinterpreted and revitalized in light of current circumstances and communal needs.

4.2 Daniel's Engagement with Scriptural Texts

To read Daniel is to know and understand other scriptural texts. Daniel refers to Jeremiah, an earlier text, and is referred to by 4Ezra, a later text that builds upon ideas present in Daniel. Yet, Daniel stands out in how it does something new with its use of scripture. Dan 9:2 references the סְפָרִים of Jeremiah, which acknowledges the specific period of the שִׁבְעִים שָׁנָה (Dan 9:2) before the desolation of Jerusalem comes to an end. The reflection upon the סְפָרִים of Jeremiah likely refers to Jer 25:11 and 29:10.

Both of these passages from Jeremiah address the desolation of the land; however, each addresses a different aspect of the interpretation. Jer 25:11–12 speaks of the שִׁבְעִים שָׁנָה under Babylonian dominion, after which, the Lord will restore Israel from their destruction,

> [11] וְהָיְתָה כָּל־הָאָרֶץ הַזֹּאת לְחָרְבָּה לְשַׁמָּה וְעָבְדוּ הַגּוֹיִם הָאֵלֶּה אֶת־מֶלֶךְ בָּבֶל שִׁבְעִים שָׁנָה׃ [12] וְהָיָה כִמְלֹאות שִׁבְעִים
> שָׁנָה אֶפְקֹד עַל־מֶלֶךְ־בָּבֶל וְעַל־הַגּוֹי הַהוּא נְאֻם־יְהוָה אֶת־עֲוֺנָם וְעַל־אֶרֶץ כַּשְׂדִּים וְשַׂמְתִּי אֹתוֹ לְשִׁמְמוֹת עוֹלָם׃

> [11] The whole land shall become a ruin and a waste, and these nations shall serve the king of Babylon seventy years. [12] Then after seventy years are completed, I will punish the king of Babylon and that nation, the land of the Chaldeans, for their iniquity, declares the Lord, making the land an everlasting waste.

This prophecy foretells the land's ruin and the people's servitude to Babylon, with the Lord only punishing Babylon after seventy years of devastation. Jer 25 does not refer to the people's restoration but solely to the ensuing punishment of Babylon. Jer 29 takes these ideas and shifts the attention to the people of Israel,

> [10] כִּי־כֹה אָמַר יְהוָה כִּי לְפִי מְלֹאת לְבָבֶל שִׁבְעִים שָׁנָה אֶפְקֹד אֶתְכֶם וַהֲקִמֹתִי עֲלֵיכֶם אֶת־דְּבָרִי הַטּוֹב לְהָשִׁיב אֶתְכֶם
> אֶל־הַמָּקוֹם הַזֶּה׃

> [10] For thus says the Lord: When seventy years are completed for Babylon, I will visit you, and I will fulfill to you my promise and bring you back to this place.

Here, the focus shifts from punishment to recompense. Dan 9 reads Jeremiah's prophecy of restoration within its prayer context — as he is concerned about returning from exile and the desolation to be reaped upon the oppressors. Yet, the seventy years from Jeremiah are problematic for Daniel because they proved to not be true historically. Scholars have concentrated on understanding this and the ensuing re-calculation of the events in Daniel. For example, Segal (2011, 302) understands the seventy weeks of years in Daniel as an expanded prophetic period based upon the seventy years of Jeremiah but does not reinterpret them.

4.2.1 The Challenge of the Seventy Years Prophecy

Regardless of how this prophecy is recalculated, Daniel reads and re-reads Jeremiah and uses his seventy years to conceptualize the notion of weeks of years, striving to reimagine a prophecy from the past. Daniel reinterprets, or perhaps more accurately, reuses, Jeremiah's prophecy. In this way, time is used by the prophet as a means to understand and perhaps overcome a history through performance.

Echoing Elizabeth Stell's (2022, 411) argument, "the prophetic is imagined and reimagined through textual, oral, and bodily performance." Dan 9 re-performs Jeremiah's prophecies to transform them into a new prophecy. This rests upon the way Daniel understands history. There is a transformation in the role of the prophetic, as well as in history. While re-use occurs, something new is created as Jeremiah's prophecy is not just placed into Daniel's context, but is actively fused with Daniel's present circumstances to generate a new prophetic chronotope, one that is layered and encompasses both the past and the anticipated future.

4.3 Danielic Influence in 4Ezra's Narrative

The same argument can be made for the texts that use Daniel, such as 4Ezra. Like the book of Daniel, 4Ezra also straddles multiple periods. Although it was written circa 100 CE, the text claims to have been written shortly following the destruction of the First Temple (Stone 1990; Collins 2016), and as Najman (2014, 26) aptly states, 4Ezra "portrays its time as one of confusion and loss." The text explores questions of theodicy and restoration and has been studied due to its many apocalyptic visions (Hogan 2008, 42). The text explicitly draws from the book of Daniel as Ezra "is given a *vision* that supplements the *vision* of Daniel" (Najman 2014, 90 [emphasis in original]). 4Ezra uses Daniel to reimagine a future trajectory of history.

This is most explicitly seen in the paralleling of Daniel's and Ezra's prayer practice. In Dan 9:3–5, Daniel seeks God and understanding through prayer:

[3] וָאֶתְּנָה אֶת־פָּנַי אֶל־אֲדֹנָי הָאֱלֹהִים לְבַקֵּשׁ תְּפִלָּה וְתַחֲנוּנִים בְּצוֹם וְשַׂק וָאֵפֶר׃ [4] וָאֶתְפַּלְלָה לַיהוָה אֱלֹהַי וָאֶתְוַדֶּה
וָאֹמְרָה אָנָּא אֲדֹנָי הָאֵל הַגָּדוֹל וְהַנּוֹרָא שֹׁמֵר הַבְּרִית וְהַחֶסֶד לְאֹהֲבָיו וּלְשֹׁמְרֵי מִצְוֺתָיו׃ [5] חָטָאנוּ וְעָוִינוּ
וְהִרְשַׁעְנוּ וּמָרָדְנוּ וְסוֹר מִמִּצְוֺתֶךָ וּמִמִּשְׁפָּטֶיךָ׃

[3] Then I turned my face to the Lord God, seeking him by prayer and pleas for mercy with fasting and sackcloth and ashes. [4] I prayed to the Lord my God, and I made confession, saying, 'O Lord, the great and awesome God, who keeps covenant and steadfast love with those who love him and keep his commandments, [5] we have sinned and done wrong and acted wickedly and rebelled, turning aside from your commandments and rules.

These verses contain a string of confession verbs, such as חָטָאנוּ and וְעָוִינוּ (9:5) that set the context for the following prayer. Likewise, in Ezra's visions, Ezra repeatedly asks for understanding, employing prayer as the means to gain an understanding of the future. As the seven visions of Ezra, the scribe unfolds throughout 4Ezra, Ezra interacts with angels to understand what has happened and what will happen to Israel. Ezra's first vision is punctuated by prayer in 4Ezra 4:22,

[22] ܘܥܢܝܬ ܘܐܡܪܬ ܒܥܐ ܐܢܐ ܡܢܟ ܡܪܝ، ܠܡܢܐ ܡܪܝ، ܐܬܝܗܒ ܠܝ ܡܕܥܐ ܠܡܬܒܝܢܘ

[22] And I asked and said, I seek from you Lord, why Lord was a mind to know given to me?

Like in Dan 9:3–5, Ezra seeks understanding through prayer. While the word prayer does not appear here, the word ܒܥܐ (to seek, desire, beseech) is used. The language of asking or requesting often relates to prayer and liturgy (Newman 1999, 63). As Daniel prays to understand his past and future, this thinking also appears in 4Ezra as Ezra recognizes the ability of prayers to connect him to the divine (Bakker 2022).

Following this verse in Ezra 4:22, Ezra remains confused, as he continues to ask for clarification in 4Ezra 4:33,

[33] ܘܥܢܝܬ ܘܐܡܪܬ ܥܕܡܐ ܠܐܡܬܝ، ܘܐܝܡܬܝ، ܗܠܝܢ. ܡܛܠ ܕܙܥܘܪ̈ܝܢ ܐܢܝܢ ܘܒܝܫܝܢ ܫܢܝܢ ܀

[33] And I answered and said, how long and when are these things because few and bad are our years.

Ezra is fundamentally concerned with calculating time, which comes through prayer. Just as Daniel's prayer in Dan 9 is answered by a re-calculation of the seventy years prophecy, Ezra's prayer is answered by a discussion of the measuring of time in 4Ezra 4:36–37,

[36] ܘܥܢܐ ܪܡܝܐܝܠ ܡܠܐܟܐ ܘܐܡܪ ܠܗܘܢ ܥܕܡܐ ܕܢܬܡܠܐ ܡܢܝܢܐ ܕܐܝܠܝܢ ܕܕܡܝܢ ܠܟܘܢ. ܡܛܠ ܕܡܬܩܠ ܬܩܠܗ ܩܕܝܫܐ ܠܥܠܡܐ
[37] ܘܡܡܫܚ ܡܫܚ ܐܢܘܢ، ܠܙܒܢܐ ܘܡܡܢܐ ܡܢܐ ܐܢܘܢ، ܠܥܕܢܐ ܘܠܐ ܢܙܝܥ ܘܠܐ ܢܥܝܪ ܥܕܡܐ ܕܢܬܡܠܐ ܡܢܝܢܐ ܕܐܬܐܡܪ

[36] And Remiel the angel answered and said to them, "Until the number of those who resemble you is fulfilled. Because the holy one measuring, measured the world," [37] And measuring he measured the times and numbering he numbered the seasons and he will not cease and will not rouse until the number which is said/appointed is fulfilled.

He is not able to comprehend this time yet. Ezra will only understand through continued participation in this prayer performance.

4.4 Historical Revisionism — Intertwining Past and Future

Both instances of Daniel's use of Jeremiah and Daniel's use within 4Ezra speak to a type of historical revision. The future and the past are entangled. This prayer from

Daniel is focused on calculating time, which becomes a form of prayer for Daniel. As he prays his daily prayers and performs this confession prayer to make sense of the oppression and persecution that the Jews faced both in history and in his time, Daniel begins to gain previously restricted knowledge.

Temporality can be a powerful tool for overcoming adversity and facing trauma while living in the diaspora. Daniel, who was able to repurpose Jeremiah's prophecy and then be re-purposed in turn by 4Ezra, provides a compelling example of how the flexibility of temporality can shape one's worldview and offer hope for the future. By projecting himself toward a future history that has not yet been realized, Daniel found purpose in reinterpreting the prophecy and direction under challenging circumstances, demonstrating the transformative power of a forward-looking perspective.

Daniel's treatment of the history in Jeremiah is not set in stone. While he engages with historical memory and perhaps a collective understanding of history, Daniel's use of that history creates a new future. The same can be said in 4Ezra. 4Ezra is set in a moment of distress and loss, and to try to understand that moment, it rewrites or *reboots* the past (Najman 2014). The past and the future reconfigured through the particulars of the present. This reconfiguration occurs because the crisis of the present compels the community to use older prophecies (past) to anticipate divine action (future). This results in a present time and a present history. This is a history that is not historical, that is, a static record of cultural events, but cultural. It is a living narrative actively shaped by the community's reading practice and eschatological hope. And this cultural history, which is constantly renewed through the act of reinterpretation and prayer, is precisely what yields the efficacy of the texts.

5 Temporal Interplay in Daniel's Prayer

Having established that elements of apocalypticism contribute to our understanding of the text's relationship to temporality, it's important to note that this does not mean we must adopt apocalyptic readings of the text. Instead, we can explore a variety of interpretive frameworks while considering the multifaceted nature of its temporal dimensions. Prayer is actively involved in receiving revelation, acting as a cultural history. Therefore, revelation is the cornerstone of how time plays a role in the book of Daniel, particularly within the prayer of Dan 9.

5.1 Textualization and Authority in the Formation of Prayer

In Dan 9, Daniel prays for change through confession and exploring history. This performance of prayer is connected to time-telling. The formation of prayer in Dan 9 is informed by complex understandings of sin, prayer, and community that are deeply rooted in the biblical material, for example, in Lev 26, in which individual and communal laments are outlined (Newsom 2014, 293), or within Jos 7, in which prayer and penitence are embodied to be efficacious. Daniel's prayer acts as a bridge between his contemporary context and the prayers and prophecies of old, becoming a part of a textualized process.

The act of textualization is the "generation of textual objects that structure social interactions around their use and transmission" (Bell 1988, 390). Textualization establishes a new form of authority. The transmission of ritual manuals and explanations from knowledgeable figures dominates the transmission of scriptures and grants liturgical authority.

Converting something from its oral form into a written, textualized form is significant for our biblical texts. Most of the texts that we understand to be liturgical in Jewish and Christian contexts are understood as such due to their scripturalization (Newman 2018, 1). Yet, these texts are formed by a traditionary process "that encompasses both textual formation and textual interpretation, as well as a variety of text-involving practices, individual and communal" (Najman 2012, 7–8). This can be applied to Dan 9, which has undergone textualization through a tradition that understands and continues to use the text.

Daniel performs this confession prayer to make sense of the oppression and the persecution that the Jews faced from the Hellenistic rulers in the second century BCE. Therefore, in Daniel's prayer in Dan 9 to God on behalf of the Jews, Daniel attempts to fulfill the prophecy found in Jeremiah. By recontextualizing an older prophecy that did not unfold as expected, originating from a prophet from the distant past, Daniel initiates an intricate blending of the past, present, and even the future. Dan 9 does this in the performance of prayer. By turning to a prophecy that did not materialize as expected from a prophet well in the past, Dan 9 begins to weave together the past, present, and future through prayer. In doing so, Daniel shows the malleability of temporality in his world.

5.2 Liminality and Divine Interaction in Prayer

Daniel's prayer and revelatory experiences allow him to enter a liminal space — a space of prayer between the earthly and the divine. The liminality exists beyond human experience alone, encompassing an angelic presence within the act of prayer. Angels are often depicted as exemplary divine beings in Hellenistic texts, and humans can often worship alongside them (Penner 2013, 41). Through prayer, individuals dismantle the constraints of time and enter into a divine realm. It also reconstructs history, as can be seen as Daniel recounts the cycle of God's righteousness and the people's disobedience throughout his prayer.

To put it differently, by engaging with Jeremiah's prophecy, the text of Daniel not only engages with notions of prophecy and prayer but, fundamentally, with time. This comes through the performance of revelation as Daniel shows how a moment in the present or future might interpret or reinterpret the past, not just the prophecy of the past but the actual perception of and relation to the past.

5.2.1 The Reconstruction of History Through Prayer and Revelation

Therefore, we can better understand how figures such as Daniel perceive and reinterpret past events in light of future circumstances in the context of changing historical structures. This phenomenon involves a retrospective analysis influenced by anticipated developments, potentially altering the understanding of history by examining how Daniel's perspective on the past, particularly concerning the book of Jeremiah, is shaped by changing societal dynamics, highlighting the intricate interplay between personal perception, social change, and historical interpretation. In doing so, the distinctions between the past and the present begin to collapse, and we see how prayer allows Daniel and the readers of the text to reconceptualize how they understand history. Despite using familiar ideas, Daniel creates a new history.

6 Conclusions

Time, revelation, and historical revision are intertwined throughout the book of Daniel, shaping our reading of the text and the importance of time within the text. However, Daniel still presents a multifaceted understanding of time; different conceptions and realities of time can work together. That is to say, the past, the present, and the future are closely entangled in their cultural and cognitive use. Daniel sits between two texts — as it engages Jeremiah and is engaged by 4Ezra — throughout which prayer can occur continuously.

Dan 9's framework includes precise readings of scriptural materials to conceptualize history, which are then reused to reimagine an ideal past through 4Ezra. There is little doubt that the latter half of Daniel is concerned with temporality, past, present, and future, as it attempts to negotiate an uncertain moment in history.

Still, it cannot be reduced to a solely apocalyptic text. It is also about prophecy, prayer, and merging different genres. In reading Dan 9, not through New Testament apocalypticism but through these multifaceted reading practices, it is both a revelatory and prayer text.

I have offered a way to read Hellenistic-Jewish texts that does not rewrite how we view apocalypse but provides a more capacious reading practice. While apocalypticism is necessary to understand temporality in the text, it cannot be overemphasized as a genre, but rather that the apocalyptic elements enable prayer to serve as a form of revelation. This is about how prayer influences the perception of history and acts as a conduit for revelation, thus expanding the way in which time works in the book of Daniel.

Bibliography

Aydin, Ciano. 2017. "How to Forget the Unforgettable? On Collective Trauma, Cultural Identity, and Mnemotechnologies." *Identity* 17.3:125–137. https://doi.org/10.1080/15283488.2017.1340160.

Bakhtin, Mikhail. 1981. *The Dialogic Imagination: 4 Essays*. Edited by Michael Holquist and Caryl Emerson. Austin, TX: University of Texas Press.

Bakker, Arjen. 2024. "Early Configurations of Jewish Prayer: Translating Sacrifice in the Second Temple Period." *JSJ* 55:459–489. https://doi.org/10.1163/15700631-bja10091

Bakker, Arjen. 2022. "The Performance of Blessing as Imitation of Divine Beings: Acknowledging the Creator in the Hymns of the Maśkîl and Related Texts." *DSD* 29:325–341. https://doi.org/10.1163/15685179-02903002.

Bakker, Arjen. 2023. *The Secret of Time: Reconfiguring Wisdom in the Dead Sea Scrolls*. Leiden: Brill. https://doi.org/10.1163/9789004537798

Bell, Catherine. 1988. "Ritualization of Texts and Textualization of Ritual in the Codification of Taoist Liturgy" *History of Religions*, 27, 366–392

Collins, John J. 1979. "Towards the Morphology of a Genre: Introduction." *Semeia* 14:1–20.

Collins, John J. 2016. *The Apocalyptic Imagination: An Introduction to Jewish Apocalyptic Literature*. 3rd ed. Grand Rapids, MI: Eerdmans.

Crawford, Sidnie White, and Cecilia Wassén, eds. 2018. *Apocalyptic Thinking in Early Judaism: Engaging with John Collins' The Apocalyptic Imagination*. JSJ.S 182. Leiden: Brill. https://doi.org/10.1163/9789004358386.

Decker, Hans Z. Forthcoming. *Biblical Wisdom and the Hermeneutics of Nostalgia*. Oxford: Oxford University Press.

Goff, Matthew J. 2018. "The Apocalypse and the Sage: Assessing the Contribution of John J. Collins to the Study of Apocalypticism." In *Apocalyptic Thinking in Early Judaism: Engaging with John Collins' The Apocalyptic Imagination*. JSJ.S 182, edited by Sidnie White Crawford, and Cecilia Wassén, 8–22. Leiden: Brill. https://doi.org/10.1163/9789004358386_003.

Grabbe, Lester L. 1997. "The Seventy-Weeks Prophecy (Daniel 9:24–27) in Early Jewish Interpretation." In *The Quest for Context and Meaning: Studies in Biblical Intertextuality in Honor of James A.*

Sanders, edited by Craig A. Evans, and Shemaryahu Talmon, 595–611. Leiden: Brill. https://doi.org/10.1163/9789004497672_037.

Hogan, Karina Martin. 2008. *Theologies in Conflict in 4 Ezra: Wisdom, Debate, and Apocalyptic Solution*. JSJ.S 130. Leiden: Brill. https://doi.org/10.1163/ej.9789004129696.i-272.

Kaye, Lynn. 2018. *Time in the Babylonian Talmud: Natural and Imaginative Times in Jewish Law and Narrative*. Cambridge: Cambridge University Press. https://doi.org/10.1017/9781108525619.

Knight, George A. F. 1959. *A Christian Theology of the Old Testament.* London: SCM Press.

Knoppers, Gary N. 2021. *Prophets, Priests, and Promises: Essays on the Deuteronomistic History, Chronicles, and Ezra-Nehemiah,* edited by Christl M. Maier, and H. G. M. Williamson. Leiden: Brill. https://doi.org/10.1163/9789004444898

Momigliano, Arnaldo. 1966. "Time in Ancient Historiography." *HistTh* 6.6:1–23. https://doi.org/10.2307/2504249.

Najman, Hindy, and Irene Peirano Garrison. 2019. "Pseudepigraphy as an Interpretive Construct." In *The Old Testament Pseudepigrapha: Fifty Years of the Pseudepigrapha Section at the SBL,* edited by Matthias Henze, and Liv Ingeborg Lied, Early Judaism and Its Literature 50, 331–356. Atlanta, GA: Society of Biblical Literature. https://doi.org/10.2307/j.ctvr33b6k.20.

Najman, Hindy. 2012a. "Configuring the Text in Biblical Studies." In *A Teacher for All Generations Essays in Honor of James C. Vanderkam,* edited by Eric F. Mason, Samuel I. Thomas, Alison Schofield, and Eugene Ulrich, vol. 1, 1–22. Leiden: Brill. https://doi.org/10.1163/9789004224087_002.

Najman, Hindy. 2012b. "The Idea of Biblical Genre: From Discourse to Constellation." In *Prayer and Poetry in the Dead Sea Scrolls and Related Literature: Essays in Honor of Eileen Schuller on the Occasion of Her 65th Birthday,* edited by Jeremy Penner, Ken M. Penner, and Cecilia Wassén, 307–321. Leiden: Brill. https://doi.org/10.1163/9789004215016_018.

Najman, Hindy. 2014. *Losing the Temple and Recovering the Future: An Analysis of 4 Ezra*. Cambridge: Cambridge University Press. https://doi.org/10.1017/CBO9781139051651.

Najman, Hindy. 2025. *Scriptural Vitality: Rethinking Philology and Hermeneutics*. Oxford: Oxford University Press. https://doi.org/10.1093/9780191898037.001.0001.

Newman, Judith H. 1999. *Praying by the Book: The Scripturalization of Prayer in Second Temple Judaism*. Atlanta, GA: Scholars Press.

Newman, Judith H. 2017. "Confessing in Exile: The Reception and Composition of Jeremiah in (Daniel and) Baruch." In *Jeremiah's Scriptures: Production, Reception, Interaction, and Transformation,* edited by Konrad Schmid and Hindy Najman, 229–252. Leiden: Brill. https://doi.org/10.1163/9789004320253_020.

Newman, Judith H. 2018. *Before the Bible: The Liturgical Body and the Formation of Scriptures in Early Judaism*. New York, NY: Oxford University Press. https://doi.org/10.1093/oso/9780190212216.001.0001.

Newsom, Carol A. 2014. *Daniel: A Commentary.* The Old Testament Library. Louisville, KY: Westminster John Knox.

Nietzsche, Friedrich. 1997. *Untimely Meditations*. Edited by Daniel Breazeale. Translated by R. J. Hollingdale. 2nd ed. Cambridge: Cambridge University Press. https://doi.org/10.1017/CBO9780511812101

Penner, Jeremy. 2013. "With the Coming Light, At the Appointed Time: Daily Prayer and Its Importance at Qumran." *JAJ* 4:27–47. https://doi.org/10.30965/21967954-00401003.

Rad, Gerhard von. 1958. *Theologie des Alten Testaments*. 2. Munich: C. Kaiser.

Rillera, Andrew Remington. 2019. "A Call to Resistance: The Exhortative Function of Daniel 7." *JBL* 138.4:757–776.

Segal, Michael. 2011. "The Chronological Conception of the Persian Period in Daniel 9." *JAJ* 2:283–303. https://doi.org/10.30965/21967954-00203001.

Segal, Michael. 2016. *Dreams, Riddles, and Visions: Textual, Contextual, and Intertextual Approaches to the Book of Daniel*. Berlin: De Gruyter. https://doi.org/10.1515/9783110330991.

Segal, Michael. 2018. "Calculating the End: Inner-Danielic Chronological Developments." *VT* 68:272–296. https://doi.org/10.1163/15685330-12341313.

Segal, Michael. 2020. "The Four Kingdoms and Other Chronological Conceptions in the Book of Daniel." In *Four Kingdom Motifs before and beyond the Book of Daniel.* Themes in Biblical Narrative 26, edited by Andrew B. Perrin, and Loren T. Stuckenbruck, 13–38. Leiden: Brill. https://doi.org/10.1163/9789004443280_003.

Stell, Elizabeth. 2022. "Beyond Oral and Written Prophecy: Prophetic Performance and Performativity." *DSD* 29:410–437. https://doi.org/10.1163/15685179-02903007.

Stern, Sacha. 2007. *Time and Process in Ancient Judaism*. Oxford: The Littman Library of Jewish Civilization.

Stone, Michael E. 1990. *Fourth Ezra: A Commentary on the Book of Fourth Ezra*. Edited by Frank Moore Cross. Hermeneia—A Critical and Historical Commentary on the Bible. Minneapolis, MN: Fortress.

Jonathan Ben-Dov

A Sundial from the Southern Wall Excavations, Jerusalem: The Historical–Cultural Context

Abstract: This small sundial was found in the Benjamin Mazar Excavations to the south of the Double Gate of the Temple Mount. It is on display at the Hecht Museum, University of Haifa. An early image of the Menorah is carved on the back of the object. It is one of approximately 15 sundials of various sizes found in early Roman Judea: around the Temple, in the Upper City and in the Lower City. The find was recently surveyed by Rony Reich and by Hillel Geva. The present article discusses the following aspects in order to shed light on the wider historical context of this sundial:

1. The invention of sundials and their dispersion through the Hellenistic period
2. A special connection between sundials and the temple context among priests
3. The meaning of the crude and imprecise set of marks on the sundial and its small size
4. The meaning of the Menorah iconography as part of astral imagery in the early Roman period.

A small-sized sundial was discovered in Benjamin Mazar's excavations south of the Temple Mount in Jerusalem (Locus 12030; Fig. 1a–b). It was found south of the Double Gate of the Temple Mount, in proximity to several water cisterns used by pilgrims who visited the Herodian temple (Mazar 1972, 82; Magen 2002, 115). An engraving of the *menorah*, the temple lampstand, appears on the back of the dial. The object is now exhibited in the Hecht Museum at the University of Haifa. Mazar (1972) briefly noted this item in his survey. Since then, the dial has been briefly mentioned in several publications and in a semi-academic article (Levy 1998), but a full study was never dedicated to it. The unique spatial and temporal context of this dial in Herodian Jerusalem, its unique scientific use and the special iconography, all raise the need for a dedicated study of this special object. Together with other sundials from Roman Jeru-

Note: My thanks to Perry Harel of the Hecht Museum for her assistance in examining the item and for providing me with the photographs. Guy Stiebel, Orit Peleg-Barkat, and Eran Aryeh provided additional advice. Special thanks to Ronny Reich, who first introduced me to the time-measuring devices from his excavations in Jerusalem. A Hebrew version of this article was published in *Innovations in the Study of Jerusalem and its Environs* 10 (2025), 67–80.

salem, the dial attests to a new kind of temporality that arose in late Second Temple Jerusalem, which, in turn, corresponds to the prevalence of time and temporality in Roman culture of the early empire. In the present article I discuss the scientific and intellectual background of the sundial in the history of ancient astronomy and time measurement, and present insights regarding its design and technical context.

The dial (4.5 × 4.5 × 6.5 cm; its wider face at the front) is made of limestone, which is well-suited for carving and shaping. Most of its surface is covered in soot, evidence of fire (Fig. 1a–b). Fine engravings are visible on the two sides of the dial and on the upper step of its base.[1] Some of these engravings turned black due to the burning, and so did the hour lines at the top of the dial.

Fig. 1a–b: The sundial from the Southern Wall excavations, Jerusalem: front (right) and left face (left); note the soot marks. Courtesy of the Hecht Museum, University of Haifa; photo by Shai Levy.

The front of the dial is set upon a stepped base, a feature known from other Greco-Roman sundials (Schaldach 2021, 166). The top features a groove in which a metal pin (*gnomon*) was placed to cast its shadow during the day. The hour-lines radiate from the gnomon's slot in the concave surface of the dial; the engraving is coarse and does not provide a precise mathematical structure for measuring hours

1 While the patina on the upper stair is equally spread, its middle part was disturbed by additional incisions. These incisions are too vague to be marks of writing. I thank Shai Halevi, the expert photographer of the Israel Antiquities Authority, for producing RTI images of the item to help clarify this point.

at Jerusalem's latitude, contrary to Levy's claim (1998, 20). An equinox line runs across the concave surface in an equally inaccurate manner.[2]

The back of the dial shows a unique engraving of a seven-branched *menorah*—one of the earliest known representations of the Temple lampstand (Fig. 2). The Menorah is carved upside down, that is, when the sundial stands on its base, the top of the menorah faces downwards. There are two small sockets at the sides of the Menorah, used either for fastening the object in its place (Levy 1998) or for the inlay of additional fittings (Mazar 1972, 82). The base of the Menorah is represented with three legs, as seen on other contemporaneous examples (Hachlili 2018, 85).

Fig. 2: Close-up of the menorah engraving on the back of the sundial. Courtesy of the Hecht Museum, University of Haifa; photo by Shai Levy.

This object is one of thirteen sundials discovered in Second Temple Jerusalem: around the Temple Mount, in the Upper City, and in the City of David (Geva 2022, 377–389).[3] While this corpus merits detailed discussion, the present paper offers the first focused examination of a single item. It aims at clarifying the historical background of the use of sundials and of time-measurement in general, and in

2 The equinoctial line is a term from the field of dialing, describing the line or mark upon which the shadow of the gnomon (the upright rod) falls exactly during the equinoxes, hence occurring twice a year: on the vernal (spring) equinox and the autumnal (fall) equinox.

3 In the Qumran excavations, a round stone disc was discovered bearing numerous carvings that resemble scale markings of a circle, proposed to be interpreted as a sundial (Glessmer and Albani 1999). It appears as such in the Shrine of the Book exhibition at the Israel Museum (Roitman 1997). However, the item does not resemble other sundials from Jerusalem dating to the late Second Temple period, and its interpretation as a sundial does not account for all the details carved on it. Therefore, in my opinion, it is not a sundial at all (J. Ben-Dov 2011).

Early Roman Jerusalem in particular, and at illuminating the relationship of the dial to the Temple and to the priesthood. I will also suggest explanations for the small dimensions of the dial and for its menorah decoration. Altogether, this item attests to a unique temporality anchored in the sacred space of the Temple.

This paper will not discuss the immediate archaeological context of the find, nor the detailed iconography of the menorah. Furthermore, it will not include a geometrical analysis of the hour and equinox lines, since in this specimen they are rough and imprecise.

1 Sundials and Seasonal Hours: Background

The following brief survey traces the development of sundials, including their various types, up to the appearance of these instruments in the first century CE, or perhaps already in the first century BCE, in Jerusalem.[4]

The distribution of sundials in the archaeological record is closely connected with the process by which ancient societies began to adopt the concept of hours as a time unit, for administrative and religious purposes. Time could, of course, also be managed without such a division, as many people refer to mere general times of day such as "evening", "morning" or "midday". Day and night were sometimes subdivided into watches, as in the Bible (Judg 7:19) and in Cuneiform texts (Streck 2021). In the developed Mesopotamian science of the first millennium BCE, the unit of *bēru* served both as a measure of distance and as a "double hour", i.e., 1/12 of the full day-night cycle (Steele 2019). It was an absolute unit, measured by water-clocks rather than sundials (Fermor and Steele 2000).[5]

Time designations in units of twelve hours per day first appeared in classical Greece, though still in scientific rather than popular contexts, and the instruments used for such measurement were not yet common in material culture (Remijsen 2021). This process developed gradually in the Hellenistic and Roman world during the centuries BCE and CE. The Jerusalem sundials of the Roman period are therefore part of a wider historical development and must be understood within that framework.

4 For the Hellenistic-Roman sundials, see Evans 1998; Hannah 2009, 91–115; Jones 2017; Schaldach 2021. For a comprehensive overview of the history of short time measurement, see Ratzon 2019, which also includes a review of Jewish sources relevant to the topic.

5 The astronomical text MUL.APIN includes a chapter on measuring the length of the shadow cast by a stick placed in the ground over the course of the seasons. However, this chapter did not deal with the division of the day or the measurement of hours, but rather with schematic determinations of the shadow's length during the solstices and equinoxes (Steele 2013).

Unlike Greece and Mesopotamia, various forms of sundials were already known in Egypt by the mid-second millennium BCE, where the division of day and night each into twelve hours was first introduced (Symons 2019). Initially, the night was divided into twelve portions using star clocks of various kinds. The day was divided using sundials (Symons and Khurana 2016). The Egyptian twenty-four hours system was seasonal, i.e., each hour was one-twelfth of the daylight or the night period, thus varying in length according to the season. Interestingly, this Egyptian custom did not spread outside Egypt for many centuries, even a millennium, after its introduction.

By the mid-first millennium BCE, Egyptian sundials gained significant circulation when adopted in Greece, while incorporating the innovations characteristic of Greek culture. Greek sources mention sundials as early as the sixth and fifth centuries BCE, but it seems that at that time these devices (with their various names) were utilized mainly to indicate the equinoxes and solstices (Hannah 2009, 71). The first sundials appeared in Greece in the fourth century BCE, and were, surprisingly, equinoctial, i.e., instruments that were designed and placed to measure fixed, equal-length hours throughout the year, much like our modern hours (Schaldach 2017; Remijsen 2021; Schaldach 2021, 125–131). During that same period, the concept of the "hour" solidified in Greek vocabulary as the word *ὥρα*, which had previously meant a vague portion of time, acquired its later sense of a twelfth of the day (Hannah 2009, 73).

Sundials gained popularity during the Hellenistic period, as various technical prototypes were formed (Evans 1998, 129–141). Most Hellenistic dials were concave, unlike their Egyptian predecessors, the most popular model being of a conical design, first to be documented in the third century BCE (Hannah 2009, 91). Few sundials have been found in the Seleucid Empire, among them the half-spherical dial from Ai Khanoum in modern Afghanistan, dating to the third to second century BCE (Rohr 1980). Ptolemaic Egypt, in contrast, yielded a greater number of sundials, probably due to confluence of Greek scientific knowledge and the early tradition of hour-reckoning. In Egypt, there is also widespread documentation for the use of hours for administrative purposes, an area in which Egypt spearheaded its cultural environment (Remijsen 2007).

With the sharp increase in the popularity of sundials in the Roman world, they became fashionable items, used in a wide range of public and private contexts (Schaldach 2021, 161–163). Simultaneously, the use of seasonal hours expanded. These processes reflect the growing significance of time and temporality in the Roman world, from the time of Julius Caesar and Augustus, and even more so in the first centuries CE (Wallace-Hadrill 2005; Feeney 2008). Growing importance of temporal matters included the major calendar reform and the emergence of the seven-day, planetary week. Cities enacted increased public display of *fasti* (holiday lists) and *παραπήγματα*, i.e., public tablets that included lists of astronomical phenomena, weather forecasts and agricultural instructions arranged by the yearly order. All of the above were contained within the Imperial ideology, whose pinnacle was realized through two major constructive projects in the city of Rome: the Horologium Augusti (or Solarium Augusti), a monumental sundial located in the *campus martius* (Haselberger 2014; Schaldach 2021, 226–229), and the nearby Pantheon, which some scholars interpret as a sort of a sundial. Its oculus projects a circle of light onto its ceiling and walls, shifts throughout the seasons and marks the cardinal points of the year (Hannah and Magli 2011). Astrology gained rising importance too as temporality became a salient part of imperial ideology.

The hours of the day became ubiquitous in administrative documents, contracts, in documentation of irrigation rights, in medicine, literature, and indeed, in all spheres of life (Wolkenhauer 2011; Jackson Miller 2018). Noblemen and common people integrated the hours into their daily routine, a fact manifested in contemporary poetry and drama. The time for the main meal (*cena*) and other meals was anchored to the hours of the day. A mosaic from Daphne in Roman Antioch, dating to the fourth century CE, depicts a sundial standing on a pillar in a public place, with a man looking at it and being disappointed that he missed the ninth-hour meal (Schaldach 2021, 195, 640, Item D.36). Sundials were found in public places and functioned as luxury items in villas and other private locations, such as the dozens of sundials discovered in the city of Pompeii (Schaldach 2021, 250–253). One such item was discovered in Judea, in a villa from the Early Roman period at Khirbet Murak (Hilkia Palace) in the Hebron Hills (Damati 1983). Portable sundials were also found in various locations throughout the Empire, which included instructions for calibrating the device according to different latitudes and longitudes. These clocks illustrate how the Roman Empire sought not only to control a vast geographical area, but also to unify it under a consistent conception of time, order, and authority — or, in Talbert's words: "The Empire in your hand" (Talbert 2017). However, in common public use, dials were not always rigorously calibrated to their location, and at times served as a means of displaying status, wealth, and sophistication rather than as a precise instrument for measuring time. For instance, Pliny the Elder recounts (*Nat. Hist.* 7.213) the story of a sundial designed for the latitude of Catania in Sicily and placed in the Forum of Rome for more than a hundred years, its lack of accuracy troubling no one.[6]

The iconographic decoration of Roman sundials often included mythological figures that had connection to time measuring or cosmological ideas, like Atlas or

6 For another example see Jones 2017, 153.

Heracles. Dials also carried dedication inscriptions to various gods, while figures of gods decorated only a few of them (Schaldach 2021, 127–172).

Jewish-Hellenistic authors writing in Egypt mentioned seasonal hours in their works as early as the second century BCE (Let. Aris. 303), and thereafter (3Macc 5:14).[7] From the First century CE, seasonal hours appear in time indications by Jewish authors from the land of Israel.[8] This fact is important for understanding the background of the emergence of sundials in Jerusalem in the late days of the Second Temple. This trend is evident in the writings of Josephus, for example, in his description of the daily routine of the Essenes (*J.W.* 2.129; *Ag. Ap.* 2.105), and in the New Testament (Matt 20:6; Acts 3:1). Rabbinic literature from the second and third centuries CE, such as the Mishnah and Tosefta, attests to the consistent use of seasonal hours, alongside a historical memory about the antiquity of this practice in Jerusalem during the Second Temple period (m. Ketub. 10:5).

2 Sundials in Temples and Synagogues

It has long been recognized that several synagogues in the Jewish diaspora of the Hellenistic period employed sundials (Levine 2005, 87, 138). This practice accords with the abundant evidence for sundial use in Greek sanctuaries: according to Schaldach (2021, 239), about 60 percent of the Greek sundials archaeologically known originated from temples, usually as votive dedications by worshippers. One

7 The sixth hour, or midday, is mentioned in the Testaments of the Twelve Patriarchs (T. Jos. 8:1). However, since book underwent many editorial processes before reaching its current form it is impossible to determine when this time indication specification was inserted. The mention of twelve 'periods' in the Animal Apocalypse (1Enoch 89:72) does not deal with hours, but rather with undetermined spans of time (Ratzon 2019, 27).

8 An earlier Jewish source is *the Book of Luminaries*, a Jewish astronomy text written in Aramaic, that had been composed in the third century BCE and was later included in the Ethiopic Book of Enoch (chapters 72–82). In the Ethiopic version, in chapter 72, a division of the day into 18 parts is demonstrated, intended to measure the change in the length of day and night according to the seasons. These parts are fixed in their length and do not change with the seasons. Conversely, the Aramaic version of *the Book of Luminaries*, fragments of which were discovered at Qumran, shows a division of the day and night into 14 parts whose length does change with the seasons. Ratzon (2019) argued that these parts should be viewed as seasonal hours, thereby constituting an early Jewish division of the day into 14 'hours'. However, these parts were not measured with instruments, nor were they used to indicate specific points in time, but merely duration. Furthermore, they were not designated by ordinal numbers (such as 'the second/third part), not even for indicating the phases of the moon for which they were defined. It therefore appears to be a schematic calculation of durations rather than proper seasonal hours.

clear example of Jewish use of a sundial comes from the synagogue on the island of Delos (Locus 80 GD), dated to the second century BCE, in which a fragment of a sundial was discovered (Trümper 2004; 2020; Schaldach 2021, 341), one of twenty-two dials whose remains were found on this small island (Schaldach 2021, 253–257). In addition, a Greek inscription (CIJ ii 1531), found adjacent to a synagogue (*προσευχή*) in the Fayum region of Egypt, attests that "Eleazar, son of Nikolaos the officer, on behalf of himself and Eirene his wife (set up) the sundial (*ὡρολόγιον*) and the well". Diaspora synagogues thus used sundials already in the second century BCE – at a time when such instruments were still rare in Judaea itself. Their presence is ubiquitous in Egypt, with its long history of dialing, and on the island of Delos, that was under a significant Egyptian influence (Moyer 2011). Synagogues presumably used the sundials to determine prayer times, but they may also have served as luxury or prestige items, as their exact use remains uncertain.

At this point it is instructive to consider a miniature device discovered in late Ptolemaic Egypt, in the city of Tanis in Egypt. This item dates to the late first century BCE, contemporaneous with the final phase of the Second Temple in Jerusalem (Evans and Maree 2008). Flinders Petrie excavated in Tanis in 1884 a walled temple compound surrounded by priests' or administrators' private houses. A tiny ivory sundial (4 × 6 cm; Fig. 3) was discovered in one of them. This item mimics the larger, monumental sundials. It disintegrated in the fire that consumed the entire compound and was repaired only in 2005 at the British Museum. Though minute, it was carefully designed, with precise hour lines and date lines marking the sun's entry into each zodiacal sign. The minuscule dial had been mounted on a column and fixed in place with nails and cast lead, so that its inclination would correspond exactly to the intended latitude.

Fig. 3: Ivory sundial from Tanis , Egypt (BM EA 68475). https://www.britishmuseum.org/collection/object/Y_EA68475.

This is a rare find of a sundial found in archeological temple context, alongside other cultic items including figurines and magical objects. Evans and Maree concluded that it belonged to a wealthy person, who was part of the administrative or ritual apparatus of the temple. This unique sundial must be understood within the Egyptian context, which sustained an ancient tradition of ritual timing according to the hours of the day, and where priests served as astronomers and astrologers (Clarysse 2010; Quack 2018; Winkler 2021).

It is against this background that the Judean sundials in the late Second Temple era must be interpreted, particularly their presence in Jerusalem, the Temple city. The dials were found around the Temple itself and in priestly dwellings in the Upper City, as well as in the Lower City, which recent research has identified as a wealthy residential area at the time (Zilberstein 2016). According to Geva (2022, 389), the distribution of the loci of extant dials (or fragments thereof) is as follows: 7 in the Upper City; 1 in the Southern Wall excavations, near the Double Gate; 2 in the Herodian Street beneath Robinson's Arch; and 3 in the City of David.

Outside Jerusalem, Yitzhak Magen discovered a Hellenistic-period sundial in the Temple on Mount Gerizim, inscribed in Greek *ΘΕΟΣ ΥΨΙΣΤΟΣ* ("God Most High"; Magen 2008, Pl. XXI; Meerson 2010).[9] Another was unearthed by Zissu and Ganor (2002) at Horvat ʿEthri in the Judean foothills, within a public building that may have functioned as a synagogue in the late Second Temple period or shortly thereafter.[10] It thus appears that by the end of the Second Temple period, sundials had become integrated into the Temple gear and amongst priests in both Jerusalem and Samaria, as well as in some synagogues. Practices of diaspora Jews and priests outside Judea were thus integrated into the Judaean priestly establishment. Moreover, the presence of sundials in early Roman Jerusalem points to an adoption of contemporary Roman fashion at the heart of the Jerusalem establishment. This cultural receptivity stands out when compared with the resistance in Judaea to other Roman temporal mechanisms, primarily the Julian calendar (Stern 2012, 331–349).

---

9 A later and more advanced sundial, dating to the Roman era, was also discovered on Mount Gerizim (Bull 1975).

10 A sundial from the Hellenistic period, found in secondary use, was also discovered at the fortress in Ḥorvat ʿAleq in the southern Carmel region (Tepper and Peleg-Barkat 2019, 97).

3 The Sundial Found South of the Double Gate

The sundial discovered south of the Double Gate is unique for three features: its minute dimensions, its inaccuracy in marking the hour and date lines, and its decoration of a menorah.

The miniature scale of this item corresponds with other small specimens found in Jerusalem: three small items from the Upper City (Geva 2022, 389, Pl. 24.3) and one from the Lower City (Area J) excavations of Reich and Shukron (2021, 626–628). Comparable miniature dials have been found at Akradina in Sicily — less than 10 cm high, sometimes even about 5 cm (Hannah 2009, 171, n. 92).

The Double-Gate sundial shows coarse, uneven incisions and crooked lines, inferior in accuracy to the medium-sized dials found in the City of David and in the Upper City, which excel in precise incisions and orderly geometric proportions. The hour lines of the dial found near the Double Gate were deep and apparently highlighted with a dark substance that had been inlaid into the grooves even prior to the fire soot, unlike the shallow, unpainted grooves of the smaller Upper City exemplars. The concave shape in the small items from the Upper City is inaccurate as well, and their performance is even poorer than that of the Double Gate dial. Furthermore, the items from the Upper City were carved in small lumps of stone that seem to have been originally part of an interior of a larger object — probably a byproduct or rubble from the stone industry of Jerusalem, as is evident from the lathe marks upon them (Magen 2002, 115; Geva 2022, 381). Thus, it is reasonable to hypothesize that the pieces from the Upper City, especially items 5 and 6, which were found inside a water cistern — and perhaps discarded during production — were practice pieces rather than functional instruments. This is not the case, however, for the sundial from the Southern Wall excavations, whose basic carving is intact, even though the marking of the lines is inaccurate.

This imprecision stands in contrast to the ivory sundial from Tanis mentioned above. Despite its petty dimensions, it exhibits perfect accuracy and was fixed in its place in the accurate angle. Its makers were not only skilled sculptors and engravers, but also scientifically literate in the astronomical and geometrical knowledge required for designing sundials. In comparison to the larger dials that were presumably put on top of the Temple Mount in Jerusalem, usually meeting Roman standards, the dial from the Double Gate was carved with less attention to details, and it is safe to assume that it had served not as a true time-measuring device but as a status symbol and as a declaration of cultural capital (Reich and Shukron 2021, 627). Whoever possessed that dial was showcasing their engagement in time measuring and the ownership of that item, thereby demonstrating status and wealth. Its very presence conveyed prestige on the owner — a symbol of a cosmopolitan individual, engaged in technology and precise in his actions down to the hour. Since the sundial was found adjacent to the Temple, it may have belonged to priests who timed ritual actions according to hours.

To date, no definite evidence has been found for monumental sundials in Jerusalem's public sphere. Yet large, precise dials probably stood upon the Temple Mount itself, similar to the dial found in the Herodian Street beneath Robinson's Arch (Mazar 1972, 169), which may have been cast down from the corner of the Mount.

A unique feature of the Double Gate sundial is the engraving of the Menorah on its back; a motif whose interpretation remains uncertain (Magen 2002, 115). During the Second Temple period, the Menorah was not yet a common Jewish emblem as it would become in the later Roman period. A few depictions are known from the Second Temple period (Levine 2000; 2005; Hachlili 2018, 21–24),[11] the most striking being the recently revealed stone from the synagogue at Magdala (see e.g., Hachlili 2017; Fine 2017; Doering 2020; Talgam, Gorni, and Najar 2024). Regardless of the broader iconographic debates, all scholars agree that the menorah motif alludes to a Temple or priestly context. The question, then, is why the craftsman chose to engrave a menorah on a sundial, and how this carving contributed to the item's purpose?

The findspot lies near the southern gate used by pilgrims ascending to the Temple, but it is difficult to know whether the sundial arrived there during the destruction of 70 CE or had been placed there originally. Given its small size, it was likely a portable, privately owned dial, rather than a public installation. Menorah decorations are known from the vicinity of the Temple Mount, but their appearance on a sundial adds a new dimension to the engraving. In the early Roman period, that is, in the late Second Temple period, aligning with the rise of astrology in Rome, an interpretation of the Menorah as an astral or planetary symbol was becoming prominent.

Thus Philo writes (*Vit. Mos.* 2.102–103; trans. S. Fine. Cf. *QE.* 2.73–81):

> The candlestick he (Moses) placed at the south (of the Tabernacle) figuring thereby the movements of the luminaries above; for the sun and the moon and the others run their courses in the south far away from the north. And therefore six branches, three on each side, issue from the central candlestick, bringing up the number to seven, and on all these are set seven lamps

11 An updated list of such finds was collected by Doering (2020, 132): a carving on a wall in the Upper City of Jerusalem; carvings of menorahs in the Jason's Tomb in Jerusalem; a coin of Mattathias Antigonus; drawings on a wall in the 'Al-Alaliyat' Caves (Michmash); graffiti in Khirbet Beit Lei in the Shephelah (Judean Foothills); a stone carving found by Ronny Reich near the Temple Mount (Reich 2014); an illustration carved on a ring from the excavations of the Southern Wall, arguably a menorah or a plant pattern (E. Mazar 2020, 186); and several menorahs carved on ossuaries.

> and candle bearers, symbols of what the men of science call planets. For the sun, like the candlestick, has the fourth place in the middle of the six and gives light to the three above and the three below it, so tuning to harmony an instrument of music truly divine.

Josephus offers a similar interpretation (*J.W.* 5. 216–218):

> In the first section, forty cubits long, stood three of the most marvelous and known things: the Menorah, the table, and the altar of incense. The seven lamps — that is the number [of the arms] that branched from the Menorah — represented the seven planets; the twelve loaves of bread upon the table symbolized the Zodiac and the months of the year; the altar had symbolized — with its thirteen incense ingredients of the sea and earth, the desolate and the inhabited, that had filled it completely — that all things come from God and belong to him.

Josephus offers a similar explanation in *Antiquities* (3.146) when describing the Tabernacle Menorah, as part of a long list of contemporary cosmological explanations for the Temple and its vessels (Angel 2019). Yossef Patrich recently suggested that the Herodian Temple was intentionally oriented to the azimuth of sunrise at the time of morning prayer throughout the seasons of the year (Patrich, Dvor, and Albag 2021). While it remains to be seen whether this was the original intention of the temple builders, it is clear that in the first century CE an astral interpretation of the Menorah and the Temple's vessels existed. At that time, the engraving of the menorah on the sundial endowed it with symbolic meaning as representing the seven planets. Steven Fine (2020) argued that this was how the Romans perceived the Menorah when it arrived as war spoil in Rome. He claims it was conceived as analogous to a Roman statuette, dating to 150–220 CE, of the goddess *Tutela* surrounded by seven heads of gods representing the days of the week and the planets. It is plausible that some of the priests entertained this view already in the time of the Second Temple. Thus, one might suggest that the Jewish artisan who produced the Double Gate sundial may have sought to give his work a decorative aspect of astral divinity, in line with Roman contemporary fashion. Faithful to his aniconic Jewish principles, he replaced pagan deities with the Jewish contemporary astral symbol par excellence — the menorah.

The two depressions on the sides of the engraving may have played a role in this context. If they once held inlays, one might imagine small inserts representing the sun and moon or other planets, akin to the astrologically engraved gemstones known from the Roman world (Jones 2017, 143–161).[12] More plausibly, however, these depressions had initially served for fixing the dial to its place, the menorah being carved only later after it was detached from its original spot. According to

---

12 Carved gems owned by Roman legionaries were discovered in Jerusalem (M. Ben-Dov 1982, 195).

this possibility, the recesses were not incorporated into the iconographic ensemble of the Menorah from the outset, but they may have served this purpose later.

4 Conclusion

A considerable number of sundials have been discovered in early Roman Jerusalem: around the Temple, in the Upper City, and in the City of David. They have recently been fully published and catalogued in the definitive work of Ronny Reich and Hillel Geva (Reich and Shukron 2021, 626–662; Geva 2022, 377–389). With this corpus complete, historians and scholars of material culture can now begin to interpret this special find. The investigation of the sundials from mathematical-physical aspects is a compelling task, but alongside it, one must also provide an interpretation of the iconography against the background of its place and meaning in the Greco-Roman world.

From the fourth century BCE, sundials gradually came into use throughout the Hellenistic-Roman world, when the Greek civilization had adopted the Egyptian sundials and the concept of seasonal hours, refining it with Greek scientific competence. As sundials spread, the practice of reckoning time by hours became embedded in daily life, in contexts that were once estimated or not quantifiable. This process accelerated under early Roman rule, when multiple attestations of temporality — days, festivals, astronomical occurrences, the calendar, astrology — took part in public expressions of imperial ideology. At the same time, sundials appeared also in public spaces and became coveted ornaments in rural villas and in other contexts of prestige. These attitudes toward time also reached Jerusalem of the late Second Temple period, alongside other cultural influences of Roman culture.

In the Hellenistic world, sundials played a crucial role in temple complexes, providing exact timing for certain rituals. The temporal aspect of temple services was particularly strong in Egypt and in regions under Egyptian influence such as Delos. There, a thousand-year tradition of solar time measurement produced a vast distribution of sundials. A small yet exquisitely made sundial from a temple in Tanis dates to a time contemporary with the late Second Temple period and provides good illustration of the background for the Jewish item. Synagogues in the diaspora also incorporated sundials, perhaps for scheduling prayers, but maybe also as markers of prestige and visibility.

The cultural value of the Jerusalem sundials in the Roman era becomes clearer against this background. The dial found in the Southern Wall excavations is of particular importance because of the Menorah decorative engraving on its back, as opposed to the other Jerusalem dials, which were decorated only with geometric or vegetational engravings. I contend that this decoration should be understood in light of the Menorah's description as an astrological device, known from the writings of Philo of Alexandria and Josephus. The growing public expression of time and temporality in the Roman world and the widespread use of sundials in the early Roman period find their continuity in the minute sundial from the Southern Wall excavations, though in a typical Jewish mode.

Bibliography

Angel, Joseph L. 2019. "The Second Temple of Jerusalem: Center of the Jewish Universe." In *Jewish Religious Architecture: From Biblical Israel to Modern Judaism*, edited by Steven Fine, 51–71. Leiden: Brill. https://doi.org/10.1163/9789004370098_005.

Ben-Dov, Jonathan. 2011. "The Qumran Dial: Artifact, Text, and Context." In *Qumran und die Archäologie: Texte und Kontexte*, WUNT 278, edited by Jörg Frey, Carsten Claußen, and Nadine Kessler, 211–237. Tübingen: Mohr Siebeck.

Ben-Dov, Meir. 1982. *The Temple Mount Excavations: In the Shadow of the Walls and in the Light of Discoveries* [in Hebrew]. Jerusalem: Keter. [engl.: New York: Harper & Row 1985].

Bull, Robert J. 1975. "A Tripartite Sundial from Tell er Râs on Mt. Gerizim." *BASOR* 219: 29–37. https://doi.org/10.2307/1356439.

Clarysse, Willy. 2010. "Egyptian Temples and Priests: Graeco-Roman." In *A Companion to Ancient Egypt*, edited by Alan B. Loyd, 274–290. Malden, MA: Blackwell. https://doi.org/10.1002/9781444320053.ch15.

Damati, Emanuel. 1982. "The Palace of Ḥilkiya." [In Hebrew.] *Qadmoniot* 15/4:117–121.

Doering, Lutz. 2020. "The Synagogue at Magdala: Between Localized Practice and Reference to the Temple." In *Synagogues in the Hellenistic and Roman Periods: Archaeological Finds, New Methods, New Theories*, Lutz Doering, and Andrew R. Krause, 127–153. Göttingen: Vandenhoeck & Ruprecht.

Evans, James. 1998. *The History and Practice of Ancient Astronomy.* New York: Oxford University Press.

Evans, James, and Marcel Maree. 2008. "A Miniature Ivory Sundial with Equinox Indicator from Ptolemaic Tanis, Egypt." *Journal for the History of Astronomy* 39:1–17. https://doi.org/10.1177/002182860803900101.

Feeney, Denis C. 2008. *Caesar's Calendar: Ancient Time and the Beginnings of History.* Berkeley, CA: University of California Press.

Fermor John, and Steele John. 2000. "The Design of Babylonian Waterclocks: Astronomical and Experimental Evidence." *Centaurus* 42/3:210–222.

Fine, Steven. 2017. "From Synagogue Furnishing to Media Event: The Magdala Ashlar." *ArsJud* 13:27–38. https://doi.org/10.3828/AJ.2017.3.

Fine, Steven. "Menorah, Its 'Branches' and Their Cosmic Significance," *The Torah*, 2020, https://www.thetorah.com/article/menorah-its-branches-and-their-cosmic-significance (17.02.2026).

Geva, Hillel. 2022. *Architecture and Stratigraphy: The Palatial Mansion.* Vol. VIII, *Jewish Quarter Excavations in the Old City of Jerusalem Conducted by Nahman Avigad, 1969–1982.* Jerusalem: Israel Exploration Society.

Gleßmer, Uwe, and Matthias Albani. 1999. "An Astronomical Measuring Instrument from Qumran." In *Provo International Conference on the Dead Sea Scrolls: Technological Innovations, New Texts, and*

Reformulated Issues, STDJ 30, edited by Donald Parry, and Eugene Ulrich, 407–442. Leiden: Brill. https://doi.org/10.1163/9789004350311_035.

Hachlili, Rachel. 2017. "The Migdal Stone and Its Ornamentation." *RB* 124:245–272. https://doi.org/10.2143/RBI.124.2.3239931.

Hachlili, Rachel. 2018. *The Menorah: Evolving into the Most Important Jewish Symbol.* Leiden: Brill.

Hannah, Rrobert. 2009. *Time in Antiquity.* London: Routledge. https://doi.org/10.4324/9780203392478.

Hannah Robert, and Giulio Magli. 2011. "The Role of the Sun in the Pantheon's Design and Meaning." *Numen* 58/4:486–513. https://doi.org/10.1163/156852711X577050.

Haselberger, Lothar, ed. 2014. *The Horologium of Augustus: Debate and Context.* JRArS 99. Portsmouth, RI: JRA.

Jackson Miller, Kassandra. 2018. "From Critical Days to Critical Hours: Galenic Refinements of Hippocratic Models." *TAPA* 148.1:111–138. https://doi.org/10.1353/apa.2018.0005.

Jones, Alexander, ed. 2017. *Time and Cosmos in Greco-Roman Antiquity.* Princeton: Princeton University Press.

Levine, Lee I. 2000. "The History and Meaning of the Menorah in Antiquity." [In Hebrew.] *Kathedra* 7:32–98.

Levine, Lee I. 2005. *The Ancient Synagogue: The First Thousand Years.* 2nd ed. New Haven: Yale University Press.

Levy, Abraham. 1998. "Bad Timing." *BArR* 24/4:18–23.

Magen, Izchak. 2002. *The Stone Vessel Industry in the Second Temple Period: Excavations at Ḥizma and the Jerusalem Temple Mount.* Judea and Samaria Publication 1. Jerusalem: Israel Exploration Society.

Magen, Izchak. 2008. *Mount Gerizim Excavations II: A Temple City.* Jerusalem: Israel Exploration Society.

Mazar. Benjamin. 1972. "Excavations near the Temple Mount." [In Hebrew.] *Qadmoniot* 5/3–4:74–90.

Mazar, Eilat. 2020. *Over the Crossroads of Time: Jerusalem's Temple Mount Monumental Staircases as Revealed in Benjamin Mazar's Excavations (1968–1978).* Jerusalem: Israel Exploration Society.

Meerson, Michael. 2010. "One God Supreme: A Case Study of Religious Tolerance and Survival." *Journal of Greco-Roman Christianity and Judaism* 7:32–50.

Moyer, Ian S. 2011. *Egypt and the Limits of Hellenism*. New York: Cambridge University Press. https://doi.org/10.1017/CBO9780511894992.

Patrich, Yossef, Devor, Jonathan, and Albag, Roy. 2021. "'Awake, Why Do You Sleep, O Lord?' (Ps. 44:24): On the Temple's Orientation, Dedication, and the Sunrise." [In Hebrew.] *Te'uda* 32–33:339–372. https://doi.org/10.1484/J.JAAJ.5.133953.

Quack, Joachim F. 2018. "Egypt as an Astronomical-Astrological Centre between Mesopotamia, Greece, and India." In *The Interactions of Ancient Astral Science*, edited by David Brown, 69–123. Bremen: Hempen. https://doi.org/10.11588/propylaeumdok.00005323.

Ratzon, Eshbal. 2019. "Jewish Time: First Stages of Seasonal Hours in Judea." *Studies in History and Philosophy of Science* 75:23–33. https://doi.org/10.1016/j.shpsa.2018.11.003.

Reich, Ronny. 2014. "A Depiction of a Menorah Found near the Temple Mount and the Shape of Its Base." *ZDPV* 130/1:96–101.

Reich, Ronny, and Shukron, Eli. 2021. *Excavations in the City of David, Jerusalem (1995–2010): Areas A, J, F, H, D and L; Final Report.* College Park, PA: Eisenbrauns. https://doi.org/10.5325/j.ctv1w36prd.

Remijsen, Sofie. 2007. "The Postal Service and the Hour as a Unit of Time in Antiquity." *Historia* 56/2:127–140.

Remijsen, Sophie. 2021. "Living by the Clock: The Introduction of Clock Time in the Greek World." *Klio* 103/1:1–29.

Rohr, René R. J. 1980. "A Unique Greek Sundial Recently Discovered in Central Asia." *Journal of the Royal Astronomical Society of Canada* 74:271–277.

Roitman, Adolfo. 1997. *A Day at Qumran: The Dead Sea Sect and Its Scrolls*. Jerusalem: The Israel Museum.

Schaldach, Karlheinz. 2017. "Frühe Arachnen: Über die Anfänge der Zeitmessung in Griechenland." *AA* 1:39–67.

Schaldach, Karlheinz. 2021. *Die Antiken Sonnenuhren Griechenlands: Die Funde in Historischer Sicht*. 2 vols. Berlin: Edition Topoi. https://doi.org/10.17171/3-76-1.

Steele, John. 2013. "Shadow-Length Schemes in Babylonian Astronomy." *SCIAMVS* 14:3–39.

Steele, John. 2019. "Short Time in Mesopotamia." In *Down to the Hour: Short Time in the Ancient Mediterranean and Near East*, edited by Kassandra J. Miller, and Sarah Symons, 90–124. Leiden: Brill. https://doi.org/10.1163/9789004416291_005.

Streck, Michael P. 2021. "The Terminology for Times of the Day in Akkadian." In *At the Dawn of History: Ancient Near Eastern Studies in Honour of J.N. Postgate*, edited by Yagmur Heffron, Adam Stone, and Martin Worthington, 583–610. Winona Lake: Eisenbrauns.

Stern, Sacha. 2012. *Calendars in Antiquity. Empires, States, and Societies*. Oxford: Oxford University Press. https://doi.org/10.1093/acprof:oso/9780199589449.001.0001.

Symons, Sarah, and Himanshi Khurana. 2016. "A Catalogue of Ancient Egyptian Sundials." *Journal for the History of Astronomy* 47/4:375–385. https://doi.org/10.1177/0021828616675962.

Symons, Sarah. 2019. "Sun and Stars: Astronomical Timekeeping in Ancient Egypt." In *Down to the Hour: Short Time in the Ancient Mediterranean and Near East*, edited by Kassandra J. Miller, and Sarah Symons, 14–51. Leiden: Brill. https://doi.org/10.1163/9789004416291_003.

Talbert, Richard J. A. 2017. *Roman Portable Sundials: The Empire in Your Hand*. New York: Oxford University Press. https://doi.org/10.1093/acprof:oso/9780190273484.001.0001.

Talgam, Rina, Dina Avshalom Gorni, and Arfan Najar. 2024. *From the Magdala Stone to the Syriac Bema: Mutual Influences between the Liturgical Space in the Early Synagogue and Church*. JSJ.S 218. Leiden: Brill. https://doi.org/10.1163/9789004707733.

Tepper, Yotam, and Orit Peleg-Barkat. 2019. "The Fortified Complex at Ḥorvat ʿAleq." [In Hebrew.] *Qadmoniot* 52:92–98.

Trümper, Monika. 2004. "The Oldest Original Synagogue Building in the Diaspora: The Delos Synagogue Reconsidered." *Hesperia* 73:513–598.

Trümper, Monika. 2020. "The Synagogue in Delos Revisited." In *Synagogues in the Hellenistic and Roman Periods*, edited by Lutz Doering, and Andrew R. Krause, 81–123. Göttingen: Vandenhoeck & Ruprecht. https://doi.org/10.13109/9783666522154.81.

Wallace-Hadrill, Andrew. 2005. "Mutatas Formas: The Augustan Transformation of Roman Knowledge." In *The Cambridge Companion to the Age of Augustus*, edited by Karl Galinsky, 55–84. New York: Cambridge University Press. https://doi.org/10.1017/CCOL0521807964.004.

Winkler, Andreas. 2021. "Stellar Scientists: The Egyptian Temple Astrologers." *Journal of Ancient Near Eastern History* 8/1–2:91–145.

Wolkenhauer, Anja. 2011. *Sonne und Mond, Kalender und Uhr*. Berlin: De Gruyter.

Zilberstein, Ayala. 2016. "Jerusalem of Below? The Southern Extent of Jerusalem in the Early Roman Period." In *New Studies in the Archaeology of Jerusalem and Its Region* [in Hebrew], vol. 21, edited by Eyal Baruch, and Avraham Faust, 81–107. Jerusalem: The Israel Antiquities Authority.

Zissu, Boas, and Amir Ganor. 2002. "Horvat ʿEthri: A Jewish Village from the Second Temple Period in the Judean Foothills." [In Hebrew.] *Qadmoniot* 35/1:18–27.

Index

The following volumes have been published in this series:

Volume 2
Detel, Wolfgang. *Subjektive und objektive Zeit: Aristoteles und die moderne Zeit-Theorie*. Berlin/Boston: De Gruyter, 2021.

Volume 3
Singer, P. N. *Time for the Ancients: Measurement, Theory, Experience*. Berlin/Boston: De Gruyter, 2022.

Volume 4
Gertzen, Thomas L. *Aber die Zeit fürchtet die Pyramiden: Die Wissenschaften vom Alten Orient und die zeitliche Dimension von Kulturgeschichte*. Berlin/Boston: De Gruyter, 2022.

Volume 6
Zachhuber, Johannes. *Time and Soul: From Aristotle to St. Augustine*. Berlin/Boston: De Gruyter, 2022.

Volume 7
Golitsis, Pantelis. *Damascius' Philosophy of Time*. Berlin/Boston: De Gruyter, 2023.

Volume 8
Defaux, Olivier. *La Table des rois: Contribution à l'histoire textuelle des ›Tables faciles‹ de Ptolémée*. Berlin/Boston: De Gruyter, 2023.

Volume 9
Fischer, Julia (ed.). *Zwiegespräche über die Zeit: Dialoge in der Berlin-Brandenburgischen Akademie der Wissenschaften aus Anlass des sechzigsten Geburtstags von Christoph Markschies*. Berlin/Boston: De Gruyter, 2024.

Volume 10
Walter, Anke (ed.). *The Temporality of Festivals: Approaches to Festive Time in Ancient Babylon, Greece, Rome, and Medieval China*. Berlin/Boston: De Gruyter, 2024.

Volume 11
Ben Sasson, Menahem. *Time and Revelation in the Vision of Daniel from the St. Petersburg Collection*. Berlin/Boston: De Gruyter, 2026.

Volume 12
Sieroka, Norman. *Zeit-Hören: Erfahrungen, Taktungen, Musik*. Berlin/Boston: De Gruyter, 2024.

Volume 13
Birk, Ralph/Coulon, Laurent (eds.). *The Thebaid in Times of Crisis: Revolt and Response in Ptolemaic Egypt*. Berlin/Boston: De Gruyter, 2025.

Volume 14
Pallavidini, Marta. *(A)synchronic (Re)actions: Crises and Their Perception in Hittite History*. Berlin/Boston: De Gruyter, 2025.

Volume 15
Nosch, Marie-Louise Bech. *Time and Textiles in Ancient Greece*. Berlin/Boston: De Gruyter, 2025.

Volume 16
Klinger, Jörg. *Das Erfassen von Zeit im Kontext der Vergangenheit*. Berlin/Boston: De Gruyter, 2026.

Volume 17
Zachhuber, Johannes. *Time and History in Denis Pétau. Philosophy, Science, and Religion in Early Modern France*. Berlin/Boston: De Gruyter, 2026.

Volume 18
Ossendrijver, Mathieu. *Conceptions of Cyclicity in Babylonian and Greco-Roman Scholarship*. Berlin/Boston: De Gruyter, 2025.

Volume 19
Schumacher, Lydia. *From Eternal to Everlasting: God and Time in Franciscan Thought*. Berlin/Boston: De Gruyter, 2026.

Volume 20
Wiedemann, Felix. *The Modern Hammurapi: An Old Babylonian King in Imperial Germany*. Berlin/Boston: De Gruyter, 2026.

Volume 21
Niehoff, Maren R./Markschies, Christoph (eds.). *Aspects of Time in Jewish and Christian Exegesis*. Berlin/Boston: De Gruyter, 2026.

Volume 22
Korobili, Giouli/Miller, Kassandra/van der Eijk, Philip (eds.). *Synchronizing the Body in Ancient Medicine and Philosophy*. Berlin/Boston: De Gruyter, 2026.

Volume 23
Kraft, András. *Time in Byzantine Apocalyptica*. Berlin/Boston: De Gruyter, 2026.

www.ingramcontent.com/pod-product-compliance
Lightning Source LLC
LaVergne TN
LVHW020054110826
845155LV00022B/82

* 9 7 8 3 1 1 2 2 4 0 3 5 9 *